POPULAR JUSTICE

POPULAR JUSTICE

A HISTORY
OF AMERICAN CRIMINAL JUSTICE

Samuel Walker
University of Nebraska at Omaha

New York   Oxford
OXFORD UNIVERSITY PRESS
1980

Copyright © 1980 by Oxford University Press, Inc.

Library of Congress Cataloging in Publication Data

Walker, Samuel, 1942–
  Popular justice.
  Bibliography: p.
  Includes index.
  1. Criminal justice, Administration of—United
States—History. I. Title.
HV8138.W342   364′.973   79-13958
ISBN 0-19-502655-1
ISBN 0-19-502654-3 pbk.

Printed in the United States of America

To
THE NEBRASKA CIVIL LIBERTIES UNION
and
THE AMERICAN CIVIL LIBERTIES UNION

Preface

Nothing is more fundamental to the quality of life than the question of criminal justice. The machinery of criminal justice represents the ultimate power of the state to invade the privacy of the individual, to deprive that person of his or her liberty, and in the extreme event, to take that person's life.

Despite the importance of this machinery, what we now call the "criminal justice system," we know surprisingly little about it. Fifteen years ago, when crime became a volatile political issue, the president of the United States appointed a national commission to study the administration of criminal justice. That commission helped to launch a massive reconsideration of the entire subject, yielding a steadily mounting volume of information. Today, as the criminal justice "research revolution" reaches flood tide, we have a reasonably good understanding of how our criminal justice system works.

What we lack is perspective. Inundated by a wealth of new data, we do not know what it all means. Is the quality of justice better or worse than before? What is the role of the police today, compared with fifty or one hundred years ago? This book is written to provide a brief interpretive overview of the development of the criminal justice system in America. The reader will gain insight into the origins of such institutions as the police and the prison as well as the factors that have shaped their development. The author views the criminal justice system as a political entity, responding to the changing context of social and political controversies in our society.

This account will challenge many popular assumptions. There never was a "golden age" of law, order, and justice in this country. From the earliest colonial days we have endured not only widespread crime and disorder, but also a criminal justice system pervaded by corruption, inefficiency, and injustice. The idea that criminal justice institutions are resistant to change is also a myth. The account here indicates that our agencies are capable of dramatic changes in rather short periods of time. Finally, this book should dispel the popular notion that the system is "collapsing." The historical record clearly indicates that institutions can survive no matter how serious the overcrowding, how gross the injustice, or how intense the public dissatisfaction.

Our system of criminal justice is here to stay. It will not only survive, for better or worse, but will continue to change. I hope this book will provide some insight into how it came to be what it is today and the direction in which it appears to be heading.

ACKNOWLEDGMENTS

Many people have assisted in the writing of this book. David Rothman read the manuscript on three separate occasions. In response to his comments, most of the chapters were extensively revised. It is a much better book because of the time and effort he contributed. He is of course not responsible for whatever errors of omission or commission remain. Gordon Misner also read an early draft and offered considerable encouragement during his semester in residence at the University of Nebraska at Omaha. Douglas Greenberg commented on a paper at an Academy of Criminal Justice Sciences meeting and offered some helpful comments on the treatment of the colonial period. During his semester in residence in Omaha, Kempes Schnell also helped me to rethink some of the broader themes. Finally, Nancy Lane of Oxford University Press has been a superb editor, a sharp critic where needed but always supportive.

My colleagues in the Criminal Justice Department at the University of Nebraska at Omaha, especially Vince Webb, chairperson, also helped to make this book possible by cultivating an atmosphere that respects scholarship in general and the study of the history of criminal justice in particular. And there are several other friends who helped me through the difficult process of writing this book. To them, my appreciation.

S.E.W.

Omaha
October 1979

CONTENTS

POPULAR JUSTICE

INTRODUCTION

THE MEANING OF "POPULAR JUSTICE"

Running someone out of town on a rail, Garry Wills recently observed, is almost as strong an American tradition as defending his constitutional rights. Wills's remark provides a starting point for understanding the history of American criminal justice. American attitudes toward law and justice have always been wildly contradictory. While everyone pays homage to the ideas of the rule of law and the protection of individual rights, Americans have not hesitated to violate the rights of individuals and groups they regard as "undesirable."

This book is a brief history of American criminal justice. It examines the changing patterns of criminal activity, the growth and development of the criminal-justice system, and the major themes in the administration of justice.

The central theme revolves around the concept of "popular justice." The special character of American criminal justice lies in the high degree of direct and indirect popular influence over its administration. Popular influence takes many forms: criminal codes written by democratically elected legislatures; the direct election of many officials such as sheriffs and judges; citizen participation on juries; the control of police departments and other agencies by political machines responsive to their constituents; and, finally, the pervasive influence of public opinion over day-to-day decisions. Compared with that in other countries, the extent of this participation is extremely high.

Popular influence has not always produced the best results, however. This book argues that it accounts for both *the best and the worst* in the history of American criminal justice. Citizen participation is of course consistent with the idea of democracy. Only an unreconstructed monarchist could argue otherwise. Yet, popular influence has contributed to corruption, inefficiency, and injustice. Criminal codes are filled with ill-considered laws. The election of sheriffs, judges, and prosecutors hardly ensures quality. Political control over police departments has been responsible for the worst forms of corruption and inefficiency. And public opinion is notoriously fickle and given to outbursts of passion and prejudice.

Some of the worst injustices in our history, moreover, have occurred when the people took the law into their own hands. The vigilante committee represents the most direct form of popular justice: members of the community using extralegal means to impose their will upon others. Many of the worst abuses of official criminal-justice agencies represent a form of "delegated vigilantism." The public has tended to condone, if not encourage, police brutality directed against the outcasts of society, or the mistreatment of inmates in penal institutions.

A major theme in the history of American criminal justice is the tension between the rule of law and the passions of popular justice. The idea of the rule of law implies fairness, equality, and consistency. But the history of the administration of justice is largely the story of arbitrary and capricious justice, often carried out in the name of community prejudice. The struggle for justice involves reconciling democratic principles, and all their pitfalls, with standards of fairness and equality.

HISTORY AND CRIMINAL JUSTICE

One might well ask, why bother to study the history of criminal justice? How can an understanding of colonial forms of punishment or the early forms of police administration possibly contribute to the solution of our present problems? These are serious questions which merit thoughtful consideration.

The study of history can have enormous contemporary relevance. Recent scholarship on slavery and the black experience, for example, has contributed greatly to our understanding of the contemporary racial problem. Unfortunately, the study of history is too often little more than a sterile recitation of names, dates, and facts. History of this sort is indeed boring and of little interest. But the study of history can be much more. It can, in the words of William Appleman Williams, be "a way of learning." Properly organized and interpreted, the facts of history can illuminate the dynamics of change. It is useful for us to know, for example, how and why our various criminal-justice agencies originated. Who wanted them? For what purposes? To cite only two recent examples, David Rothman's *The Discovery of the Asylum* and Anthony Platt's *The Child Savers* have contributed greatly to the reconsideration of the proper role of the prison and the juvenile court. The study of history can tell us something about how people in different times viewed their own problems and how new ideas became translated into social policy. This can help us to understand our own response to contemporary problems.

Perspective on contemporary problems is invaluable. It is important to recognize that there has never been a "golden age" of law and justice in our history. Crime, disorder, deviance, and injustice have always been serious problems. Life and property have never been secure from attack. Our cities have a long history of riotous disorder. We also have a long and sad history of corruption, inefficiency, and misconduct on the part of criminal-justice agencies. Today's problems are serious, but they are hardly new ones. Nostalgia for some nonexistent golden age only inhibits our attempt to deal with our problems.

The myth of a changeless criminal-justice system also hinders a proper understanding of our present situation. The popular cliché that "the system never changes" is simply not true. This book traces the very substantial changes in our criminal-justice system over the past three hundred and fifty years. Even the changes of the last fifteen years have been quite dramatic.

PAST AND PRESENT

Inevitably, this history of American criminal justice is shaped by present concerns. It views the past in terms of the present, seeking perspective on contemporary issues. The first issue involves an understanding of the criminal-justice system *as a system*. Informed discussions about the administration of justice recognize the interrelationship of the various criminal-justice agencies. The institutional growth and development of the system provide the basic framework for this book. The three sections of the book trace the establishment of the first institutions in the colonial era, the development of the major institutions in the nineteenth century, and the quest for reform in the twentieth century.

A second issue is the informal decision-making process that pervades the administration of justice. The law is not applied in a mechanical and impersonal fashion; discretionary decision-making is a constant theme in the history of American criminal justice. The amount of discretion has neither increased or decreased, but has largely moved from one agency to another.

One consequence of discretionary decision-making, and the third issue of this book, is the arbitrary, capricious, and often discriminatory pattern in the administration of justice. The demand for equal justice today makes us highly conscious of the unequal application of the law. Our heightened consciousness of racial and economic injustice should not lead us to believe that the situation has suddenly worsened. Injustice has been a tragic constant theme in the history of American criminal justice. Indeed, in many respects the quality of justice was far worse fifty, one hundred, or two hundred years ago.

A fourth issue is the influence of politics over the administration of justice. The criminal-justice system is an agency of social control. It defines the boundaries of acceptable conduct and punishes those who transgress them. But the administration of justice mirrors the distribution of political power in society. Those with power have never hesitated to use the criminal-justice system to serve their own interests at the expense of the less powerful: racial and ethnic minorities, political dissidents, and those pursuing alternative cultures and lifestyles.

Each of these issues illustrates the struggle between the rule of law and the demands of "popular justice." Criminal-justice agencies have too often been used to serve partisan political ends rather than the public interest. Discretionary decision-making has permitted both random capriciousness and more systematic patterns of favoritism and discrimination. The struggle for justice today involves undertaking the unfinished business of our criminal-justice history: making the rule of law a reality and not merely a dream.

I

CRIMINAL JUSTICE IN EARLY AMERICA, TO 1815

1

THE COLONIAL EXPERIENCE

FOUNDATIONS

The history of American criminal justice begins with the transplanting of European institutions into the new world. The colonists brought a criminal-justice system to America along with the rest of their cultural baggage. The criminal codes, law-enforcement systems, courts, and methods of punishment resembled those of England, Holland, and France, depending upon the particular colony. The subsequent development of American criminal justice is the story of the modification of that inheritance.

Two forces shaped this modification. First, colonists borrowed selectively, leaving behind elements they did not like. Second, settlers adapted their inherited institutions to the circumstances of the new environment, often out of necessity. The process of settling new territories and the conditions of the frontier exerted a powerful influence. By the time of the American Revolution, a distinct American approach to criminal justice had emerged, an Anglo-Saxon legal heritage modified by new-world circumstances.

Colonists began the process of adaptation by writing criminal codes that differed from English law in several respects. The 1648 *Book of the General Lawes and Libertyes* of the Massachusetts Bay Colony carried a much stronger biblical influence than could be found either in England or the other colonies. The Puritans of Massachusetts Bay injected a strong dose of the Old Testament into the English Common Law heritage. The *Book of the General Lawes and Libertyes* cited biblical authority for each crime and punishment: "If any man or woman be a WITCH . . . they shall be put to death. *Exod.* 22. 18 *Levit.* 20. 27 *Deut.* 18. 10.11."[1]

Colonial criminal codes were also more lenient in their approach to punishment than was English law. The most obvious difference involved the death penalty, which the colonists prescribed much less often. The first Pennsylvania criminal code (1676) contained eleven crimes punishable by death. The other colonies had roughly the same number. This contrasted sharply with the situation in England, where the number of crimes carrying the death penalty increased from fifty in the late 1600s to more than two hundred by the late 1700s. England was an extreme case. According to one observer in 1810, "there is probably no other country in the world in which so many and so great a variety of human actions are punishable with loss of life as in England."[2]

The frontier was an even more important source of change in the long run. In each colony settlers encountered the problem of establishing stable communities in a wilderness. Governmental authority was chronically weak on the frontier, and communities lacked the resources to provide the law-enforcement agencies, courts, and punishment systems they might have wanted. As a result, they frequently devised temporary solutions to immediate problems. The weakness of official authority often led individuals to take the law into their own hands. From this sprang the American tradition of vigilantism.[3]

The colonial era lasted nearly one hundred and fifty years and was a period of both diversity and change. The Dutch and French influence in different colonies gradually disappeared, and other variations between colonies also diminished. By the time of the American Revolution, religious influence had declined noticeably, replaced by a more secular outlook even in Puritan Massachusetts. Quaker influence remained strong in Pennsylvania, but Quaker ideas on punishment proved to be a harbinger of things to come in the rest of the country. Urbanization was another important change. In Boston, New York, Philadelphia, Baltimore, and Charleston, urban growth brought new social problems and imposed new burdens on the criminal-justice system. Law-enforcement agencies in particular became larger and more specialized.

Colonial Criminology

The colonists possessed a coherent philosophy of crime and punishment. While it was not a "science" of criminology in the modern sense, they knew why wrongdoing occurred and what society should do about it. Their approach to crime and punishment reflected their understanding of God, man, and society. Civil society was designed to fulfill the will of God. The clergy wielded authority in society, and the father exercised similar authority within the family. It was a patriarchal and authoritarian system of discipline.

Crime and sin were virtually synonymous in this religion-centered society. An offense against God (e.g., blasphemy) was a crime against society; and a crime against society was an offense against God. This explains why the crime of blasphemy carried the death penalty in most colonies. Criminal codes were designed to enforce public and private morals. The Puritans of Massachusetts Bay Colony saw themselves on an "errand into the wilderness" to build a model community of righteousness that would be a beacon to the world. Offenses against the official morality were not to be taken lightly. The Quakers of Pennsylvania were no less stern in their preoccupation with public morals. These communities were not tolerant, liberal, and pluralist in their outlook. They were rigidly conformist with little forbearance for deviance or dissent.[4]

The colonial system of punishment reflected the equation of crime and sin. The colonists took a pessimistic view of humankind: man was a depraved creature, cursed by original sin. There was no hope of "correcting" or "rehabilitating" the offender. An inscrutable God controlled the fate of the individual. The various forms of punishments were designed to accomplish a few specific ends.

The most serious offenses carried the death penalty. Connecticut imposed the death penalty for a total of fourteen crimes in

1650, including murder, rape, adultery, kidnapping, and blasphemy. A convicted burglar in the colony of East Jersey in 1668 faced the prospect of "being burnt in the hand with the letter T," in addition to making full restitution, for a first offense. For a second offense he might "be branded on the forehead with the letter R. And for the third offense to be put to death as incorrigible." Capital punishment was both a form of retribution and a way of simply removing the chronic recidivist from society.

As the Connecticut statute indicates, branding and mutilation were common forms of punishment. Public whipping was perhaps the most widely used punishment for both felonies and misdemeanors. The Puritans of Massachusetts sought to suppress Quakerism by cropping ears and administering severe whippings. In East Jersey, meanwhile, a third-offense drunkard could also be whipped. While corporal punishment seems barbaric by our standards, it was the norm in the seventeenth and eighteenth centuries. As Graeme Newman suggests in his provocative historical account *The Punishment Response,* few people escaped some form of corporal punishment in colonial society. It was perhaps even more common as a form of discipline within the family.[5]

Public humiliation was an important dimension of colonial punishment. Whippings were administered in the public square. Even executions were public events, often attended by hundreds or thousands of spectators. The stocks were used for minor offenses and sentences were usually short, no longer than an hour or two. In East Jersey disturbers of the peace "shall be put in stocks, until they are sober, or during the pleasure of the officer in chief." Hester Prynne, protagonist of Nathaniel Hawthorne's novel *The Scarlet Letter,* was forced to wear a letter A, cut from red cloth, upon her breast to mark her as an adulteress. Public humiliation served the purpose not of changing the offender but simply of identifying him or her in the eyes of the entire community. In colonial society, unlike our own, punishment was more of an open, public, and collective endeavor.

For property crimes and even offenses against public decency, fines and restitution were common punishments. The first- and second-offense thief in East Jersey had to make full restitution in addition to the other penalties. More serious property offenses in different colonies often called for restitution at double or triple the value of the property stolen. Those found guilty of blasphemy in East Jersey were fined one shilling, "half to the informer, and the other half to the county."

Communities simply banished many offenders, in effect saying they were unfit to remain in their midst. The colonies inherited this form of punishment from England, where the transportation of convicts was widely used in the seventeenth and eighteenth centuries. England sent an estimated thirty thousand felons to the American colonies following a parliamentary act of 1717. Nearly two thirds of the total went to Virginia and Maryland alone. After the American Revolution, the English developed new penal colonies in Australia and New Zealand. American colonial communities continued the practice of banishment.[6] As adulterer in East Jersey "shall be divorced, corporally punished or banished, either or all of them." The law granted the judge broad discretionary power and this opened the door for highly arbitrary sentences.

Punishment and Social Control

The absence of imprisonment as a basic form of punishment is the most striking contrast between the colonial world and our own. The modern prison did not begin to appear until the late eighteenth century and did not fully develop until the early nineteenth century. Nonetheless, forms of imprisonment did exist in colonial society (and had an even longer history in Europe, extending into the Middle Ages). The origins of the prison to a great extent lie in the institutions of social welfare.[7]

Colonial communities treated the poor in much the same way they treated criminals. Individuals without jobs or considered likely to become public charges were often "warned out." That is, county officials ordered them to leave and warned that if they stayed they would not be eligible for relief. Some communities required bonds of new arrivals and citizens could be punished for lodging guests for more than three days. The practice of warning out the poor was essentially the same as banishing the convicted offender. The poor who were allowed to stay were often punished for receiving public welfare. A 1718 law in Pennsylvania required persons on relief to wear "upon the shoulder of the right sleeve . . . in an open and visible manner . . . a large Roman 'P' . . . cut either in red or blue cloth." For failing to wear the badge of poverty, the individual could be denied further relief, whipped, and sent to the house of correction for up to twenty-one days at hard labor.[8]

The county workhouse or house of correction resembled the modern prison in terms of its purpose if not its structure. It was designed to "correct" behavior, to "rehabilitate" the individual, and make him or her a productive member of the community. (Later, the development of the prison involved borrowing these principles from the institutions of social welfare). The colonists could understand and accept the "deserving" poor. But the "undeserving," the person who was willfully idle, was as much a threat to the community as the criminal. A Pennsylvania act "to prevent the mischief arising from the increase of vagabonds and other idle and disorderly persons within this province" called for a one-month term in the workhouse. A separate act, applying only to Philadelphia where the problem of indigency apparently aroused greater concern, called for a sentence of up to three months at hard labor.[9]

The social-welfare and criminal-justice systems, then, combined to maintain control over the poor, the idle, and the lower classes in general. Most of the working class were indentured servants, and the criminal law gave much attention to the problem of maintaining the authority of masters over their servants. The colonial preoccupation with sexual offenses was in part an attempt to prevent illicit sex between men and their female servants. Should the woman bear a child, it would have to be supported at public expense.

The criminal-justice system was an instrument of economic regulation in other respects as well. Colonial society controlled prices and wages. The first person sentenced to the stocks in Boston was Edward Palmer, the carpenter hired to build them!

For the crime of charging an excessive fee, he was given a one-hour sentence. In southern colonies the pillory was used for merchants who gained unreasonable profits through the speculative sale of goods. A device for holding the head up for public view, the pillory was reserved for the "better class" of wrongdoers: common citizens, the disreputable, and women offenders were sentenced to the stocks.[10]

The criminal law also served to maintain patterns of authority within the family. A 1650 Connecticut law specified the death penalty for any sixteen-year-old child who "shall curse or smite their natural father or mother."[11] Respect for parental authority was seen as the necessary and proper training for both religious discipline and citizenship. Responsibility for the behavior of children was almost exclusively the task of the family. Colonial society maintained no separate juvenile-justice institutions.

Finally, the criminal-justice system sustained a racist social order. Records indicate racial inequities in sentences for criminal offenses. A. Leon Higginbotham found that Massachusetts developed a system of penal slavery in the 1630s. For the crime of robbery an offender could be sentenced to either a life of servitude, a fixed term, or until restitution was made. Although all offenders were theoretically eligible, life servitude was reserved particularly for Indians captured in war. Eventually, servitude was a punishment used exclusively for nonwhites. Examining the Massachusetts Black Codes of 1752, Higginbotham found that many kinds of behavior by nonwhites were defined as public nuisances. The implication was clear: "Nonwhites were the cause of all disorder and inconvenience."[12]

THE INSTITUTIONS OF CRIMINAL JUSTICE

The criminal-justice system in colonial society was hardly a system at all. Compared with those of our society, the basic institutions were small and nonbureaucratic. The police, the prison, probation, parole, and the juvenile-justice system as we know them did not yet exist. They would appear during the great institution-building period between 1815 and 1900. The county was the basic unit of government, assuming responsibility for maintaining the agencies of law enforcement, the courts, and the jail. By the end of the colonial period, however, the cities on the eastern seaboard had begun to maintain separate institutions to cope with the growing problems of urban society.

The County Sheriff

The county sheriff was the most important law-enforcement official in colonial America, but enforcement of the laws comprised only a small part of his duties. The sheriff was also responsible for collecting taxes, supervising elections, and handling much of the other legal business of county government. As a consequence he was also the most important political figure in the county, a situation that continues even today in many rural areas.

Nominally, the sheriff represented the governor and the English government. In most colonies the governor appointed the sheriffs. Local political factions curbed the power of the governor, however. In Virginia and North Carolina, for example, the governor deferred to the recommendations of the county court. Members of the court, meanwhile, became a powerful and self-perpetuating elite, at least in Virginia. Thus, the two most important criminal-justice institutions represented the interests of a local power elite.[13]

In the enforcement of the laws, the sheriff was a *re*active agent. He acted upon a formal complaint or information about an offense. The initiative lay with the public and the sheriff did not engage in patrol or any other technique to attempt to prevent crime. Inevitably, this system was extremely inefficient. In sparsely settled rural communities, the practical problems of investigating a crime, serving a subpoena, or making an arrest were enormous. At best the sheriff might be assisted by a few deputies. But there were great distances to be traveled over poorly maintained roads. For similar reasons it is likely that many offenses simply went unreported.

The sheriff was paid through a system of fees rather than a salary. For example, he would be paid a fixed amount for serving a subpoena, making an arrest, appearing in court, and so on. Because he could generate larger fees through his tax-collecting responsibilities, the sheriff was discouraged from giving primary attention to law enforcement. Corruption soon became a major problem. There were persistent and widespread charges of embezzlement and other irregularities in tax collections and the charging of fees. Julian Boyd's study of the North Carolina sheriff indicates that the colony passed numerous laws in a futile attempt to bring the sheriff's office under control. Douglas Greenberg's study of New York reveals a large number of criminal cases involving both malfeasance in office and contempt of authority by civilians. In short, contemporary police problems have a long history indeed.[14]

The inefficiency of law enforcement was compounded by the fact that in many areas there were no agents at all. North Carolina did not provide for a system of county sheriffs until 1739, and the back country was perpetually short of the basic institutions of government. There were no sheriffs in western South Carolina until 1769—and even then only after the insurrection known as the Regulator movement.

Protecting the Cities

The villages and cities added other law-enforcement agents to help maintain order. As the cities grew, the number of agencies increased, creating new problems of conflicting authority. James Richardson writes in his history of the New York City police that in the colonial era "the mayor, Common Council, high constable, police justices, constables, marshals and night watch all bore some responsibility for the police protection of the city." The mayor was nominally the chief law-enforcement officer, but usually acted only in cases of extreme emergency, such as a riot. The mayor appointed the high constable and various lesser constables and marshals to assist him.[15]

Both the marshals and the constables possessed law-enforcement powers similar to those of the sheriff. They could serve warrants, make arrests, testify in court, and so on. In New York City constables were popularly elected. In 1800, for example, six wards elected two constables annually while a seventh ward elected four. In Boston, where the constables were paid by fees, the job was lucrative and highly sought after. In 1802 it became an appointive office and thereafter grew into a more professional occupation. Other cities, however, had difficulty finding people to serve as constables. Philadelphia had so much trouble that the colonial Assembly passed a law in 1712 specifying a fine of £10 for anyone refusing to serve.

To provide protection at night the cities added the institution of the night watch. Inherited from Europe, the night watch consisted of a group of civilians who patrolled the city to watch for fires, suspicious individuals, or possible riots. Fires were a particularly serious problem. The night watch was a collective responsibility, and in Boston all men over the age of eighteen were eligible for service. Because many men were unwilling to serve, the cities had to impose fines upon those who refused. Eventually the night watch, like the office of constable, became more of a permanent profession. New York experimented with a paid night watch on two occasions (1684–1689 and 1734), but the expense of maintaining a large paid force of this type usually outweighed fears of lawlessness.[16]

The night watch served only during the evening hours. During the day, the constables and marshals were the only law-enforcement officials on duty. Eventually cities added a day watch; Boston experimented with an eight-person "ward" in 1712. Southern cities developed more elaborate systems of police patrol in an effort to control the slave population. Charleston, South Carolina, maintained a mounted daytime patrol as early as the 1740s. Northern cities did not establish "modern"-style police forces until the 1830s and 1840s. These represented a consolidation and coordination of the existing day- and night-watch systems.

In the event of serious disorders, colonial communities had to call out the militia. English law bequeathed the riot act. At the sign of a riot the mayor or some other official would appear and literally read the riot act to the assembled crowd. This constituted an order to disperse. Only after the passage of a specified period of time could the authorities begin to make arrests or call out the militia. This was of course a cumbersome and inefficient method of coping with disorders. And riot was a common phenomenon in colonial America. Mobs took to the streets to contest elections (Philadelphia, 1742), to protest economic conditions (Boston, 1713), or to enforce standards of morality (the "doctors' riots" in Philadelphia, 1765, and New York, 1788). An even more serious wave of riots in the 1830s provoked the creation of modern police forces.

The Courts

Courts in colonial America assumed a wide range of responsibilities. They generally served as the legislative, executive, and judicial branches of county government, conducting the full range of its business. In this respect they reflected the highly unspecialized nature of government agencies during the period.

The courts also played an important informal role in the social and economic life of the county. In Virginia "Court Day," when the county court convened once a month, was a major event. The business of the court brought large numbers of people into town. There they conducted business, talked politics, and socialized with other residents of the area. Even today the county courthouse remains a focal point of life in many rural communities.[17]

The justice of the peace (JP) handled the bulk of the court cases. The office of the JP could be traced far back into English legal history. In colonial America the JPs were appointed by the governor and served at the county level. In Virginia, for example, selection of the JPs was effectively controlled by the local power elite, and many justices served for twenty or thirty years. One did not have to have any legal training to serve as a JP. This established a firm tradition of nonprofessional lay participation in the judicial process, one that still lingers even today.

Generally, JPs could try minor cases individually. The more

serious cases were heard by courts composed of several justices. These courts, however, met only periodically. In the colony of New York the sessions courts met semiannually in many areas and quarterly in the more populous regions. The Virginia county courts met once a month by the eighteenth century. A county court consisted of between ten and fifteen justices, with four needed for a quorum for conducting business. The infrequent sessions of the courts, and their complete absence in many back-country areas, was the cause of many problems. Obviously, it was impossible to conduct legal business in a speedy and efficient manner. The absence of legal machinery aroused frequent complaints and, on occasion, led to the complete breakdown of law and order.

The prosecution of cases was handled by the district attorney, usually appointed by the governor and assigned to a particular county or region. In this respect colonial practice diverged from the custom in England, where private prosecutors handled all but the most important cases. The public prosecutor in this country— known variously as the district attorney, the county attorney, or by some other title—became a key figure in the criminal-justice system. Because prosecutors were often elected, the office became one of the most important political positions in county government.

American practice also began to diverge with respect to the role of the defense counsel. The English legal tradition sharply restricted the role of the defense to challenging narrow points of law. Gradually, American practice allowed a broader and more vigorous role. In any event there were few trained lawyers in the colonies, and only a few defendants could afford them. In the nineteenth century, the "age of the common man," formal barriers to entry into the legal profession fell, and the practice of law became an important occupation, followed by many.[18]

The County Jail

The county jail was less a place for punishment than a holding facility for those awaiting trial (except for those released on bail, of course). Jails had no distinctive architecture; they resembled ordinary houses both externally and internally. Prisoners were placed in rooms (often there was only one) rather than cells, and the jailer made no attempt to classify and segregate them. Thus, women and even children were thrown in together with men who had committed violent crimes. Scandalous conditions existed in almost all jails, and the problems of overcrowding and lack of adequate sanitation developed immediately. Moreover, the jails were extremely inefficient in terms of their basic purpose, holding people. Escapes were frequent, and many repeat offenders, according to their own testimony, escaped from several jails.[19]

The financial arrangements of the jail resembled those of the office of sheriff. The county paid the jailer (who was often the sheriff as well) through a system of fees. The jailer submitted to the county commissioners bills for specific items such as food, clothing, removing a set of leg irons, and so on. In some counties the jailer sold meals to the prisoners, and the prisoners had to rely on family, friends, or public charity for money. Corruption pervaded the management of the jails, whose keepers acquired a notorious reputation for embezzling public funds, soliciting bribes from prisoners and their families, selling whiskey in the jails, and physically abusing prisoners.

THE ADMINISTRATION OF JUSTICE

The Crime Problem

The institutional network of the colonial criminal-justice system, compared with that of our own, was extremely small and unspecialized. There was no large law-enforcement establishment, no separate juvenile-justice system, and the prison and the institutions of probation and parole also had not yet been created. Criminal matters occupied only a part of the work of both the sheriff and the courts. The lack of a large institutional framework was due in part to the fact that colonial communities were relatively small and homogeneous. Historians have called these communities *self-policing*. Social control was maintained by a pervasive set of informal sanctions, and community pressure was an important means of regulating human conduct.[20]

Despite these differences, however, the administration of justice in practice resembled our own. The system was inefficient in dealing with crime, and a high degree of informal decision-making characterized the criminal process. While colonial criminal codes were seemingly harsh, the colonists themselves found many ways to mitigate punishments and evade the intent of the laws.

How serious was the crime problem in colonial America? It is impossible to give a definitive answer to this question. Surviving records are fragmentary at best, and officials did not always maintain complete records to begin with. Douglas Greenberg has attempted a systematic study of crime patterns in *Crime and Law Enforcement in the Colony of New York, 1691–1776,* using more than five thousand criminal cases. But even his conclusions must be regarded as tentative at best. It is even more difficult to draw comparisons with our own society, since community standards change over time. Types of behavior regarded as extremely serious in one era (blasphemy, for example) often diminish greatly in importance in later periods. As historian Roger Lane has argued, we do not have an "index of disorder" that would permit us to make systematic comparisons of the historical patterns of crime.[21]

It is possible, however, to draw some general conclusions about life in colonial America. Crime, disorder, and deviance were indeed serious problems—at least as perceived by the colonists themselves. Contemporary accounts are filled with cries of alarm about rising crime, both in the cities and in the back country. Civic leaders complained about drinking, gambling, prostitution, robbery, and a general sense of lawlessness in all of the colonial cities. And in the back country, law enforcement was often completely nonexistent. Not only were the cities wracked by periodic riots, but as the New York tenants' riot of 1766 suggests, mob violence existed in rural areas as well. Colonial communities had little tolerance for deviant behavior, and serious conflict erupted over different religious or cultural practices. Douglas Greenberg's study of New York reveals that hostility between various ethnic groups was a major source of discord. "Demographic complexity shaped every aspect of life in the province," he observes, and the crime problem was significantly worse in the more heterogeneous counties.[22] Finally, the quality of the administration of justice was itself a problem.

An Inefficient System

A number of factors hampered the effectiveness of the criminal-justice system in detecting, apprehending, prosecuting, and punishing criminals. As we have already noted, the resources of the system were extremely limited. Law enforcement was a *reactive* process. Sheriffs and constables had few men at their disposal. The dispersal of the population and poor roads made it difficult to carry out even the most routine assignment. Courts met infrequently, and the jails had difficulty in holding those awaiting trial.

The attitudes of citizens also undermined efficient law enforcement. The number of court cases involving disrespect for authorities suggests that officials were not held in high regard. The practical difficulties of reporting a crime probably led to a high degree of "underreporting." Perhaps most important, people did not always want all the laws enforced in the first place. In his essay on "Law and the Enforcement of Morals in Early America," David Flaherty argues that the colonists were far less moralistic in practice than they were in theory. Illicit sex provides a good illustration. While the laws prescribed heavy penalties, individuals were understandably reluctant to lodge formal complaints against friends or neighbors. Flaherty also believes that standards were weakened by the sheer prevalence of immorality. Seventeenth- and eighteenth-century Americans enjoyed strong drink and took an often lusty attitude toward sex (temperance and sexual prudishness were nineteenth-century phenomena). Only the grossest excesses provoked formal complaints. To a great extent the colonists adopted a live-and-let-live attitude, despite what the laws said.[23]

The discrepancy between principle and practice was evident even where criminal charges were filed. Officials exercised broad discretion in disposing of cases. Greenberg argues that a major feature of the criminal process in New York was "the extent to which its procedures were personalized and suited to individual criminals as well as to particular categories of crime." The phenomenon of plea bargaining had not yet become a formal process, but officials achieved the same results nonetheless. Greenberg found that almost a third of the cases filed simply vanished from the records. Many of these were undoubtedly instances where charges were dropped.[24]

Juries exercised great freedom in reaching their verdicts. A tradition of jury "lawlessness," in which juries ruled on the appropriateness of the law as well as the facts of the case, developed and lasted until well into the nineteenth century. The records show many cases in which the jury arbitrarily lowered the estimated value of stolen goods and thereby found the defendant guilty of petit rather than grand larceny. As the struggle for American independence gained momentum, both grand juries and trial juries became bulwarks of patriot sentiment, blocking royal attempts to prosecute rebel leaders. Thomas Jefferson defended the right of a jury to invoke community sentiment and to either disregard the law or the instructions of a judge.[25]

The sentences handed down by judges also relected an arbitrary and individualized form of justice. Some penalties were not even those prescribed by law. In their detailed study of the criminal process in New York, Julius Goebel and Raymond Naughton found many such examples: a woman suspected of theft was ordered out of the county; a woman charged with being a "common disturber" was ordered kept at home by her husband; a sentence of twenty-one lashes was to be suspended if the thief left the county; a youth was "remitted to the correction of his father." The courts also used peace bonds as early forms of probation and parole. Thus, an offender was ordered to post a cash bond and report periodically to the court in lieu of punishment. Occasionally, peace bonds were ordered for individuals when the criminal charges against them had not been sustained. In this manner the court maintained control and supervision over individuals regarded as suspect or undesirable. Clearly, it was an arbitrary and unjust use of the criminal-justice system.[26]

The most obvious mitigation of punishment occurred with respect to the death penalty. Not only did the colonies prescribe death for a relatively few number of crimes, but they imposed it infrequently. Juries simply found defendants guilty of manslaughter rather than murder. It is doubtful that many third-offense thiefs suffered the death penalty. Even those convicted and sentenced to death avoided their fate through pardon or "benefit of clergy." According to Greenberg 51.7 percent of those sentenced to die in New York were pardoned. Some pardons were granted conditionally, upon promise that the individual would either leave the area or enlist in the army or navy. The "benefit of clergy" was an ancient practice inherited from the Middle Ages, when clergymen were exempted from many civil punishments. Gradually, the "benefit" was extended to laymen who could demonstrate their religiosity by either reading or reciting from memory a passage from the Bible. In the colonial period this provided exemption from the death penalty.[27]

In short, the administration of criminal justice with respect to "routine" or "ordinary" crimes resembled procedures existing today in important respects. Clearance rates were low, large numbers of cases were dismissed, and convicted offenders frequently received lighter penalties than prescribed by law. Not only were the resources of the criminal-justice system extremely limited, but citizens routinely preferred not to invoke the criminal process at all. Officials exercised enormous discretion, and the net result was an inconsistent and often unjust use of the criminal process.

Deviance and Vigilantism

The nature of a criminal-justice system is revealed not only by how it responds to ordinary crime, but also by how it operates in extreme situations. The atypical incident often illuminates important underlying aspects of society's attitude toward deviance, crime, and the administration of justice. We turn our attention now to several extreme situations: the persecution of the Quakers in Massachusetts, the Salem witch trials, and the vigilante movement led by the South Carolina Regulators in 1767–1769. These incidents reveal aspects of the administration of justice in America that persist even to the present day.

PERSECUTION OF THE QUAKERS

The Puritans of Massachusetts Bay Colony, in their effort to establish a righteous community of believers, had little tolerance for different religious beliefs. Much of the early history of the colony, in fact, can be told in terms of doctrinal disputes. Given their strong sense of mission in the world, the Puritans easily viewed alternative religious beliefs and practices as "deviant" behavior—a threat to the order and stability of the community.

The arrival of the first handful of Quakers in Massachusetts in the mid-1650s was viewed by the Puritans as a virtual "invasion." The Quaker belief in the "inner light," the idea that the individual could personally know God's will, was heretical to Puritan doctrine. Thus, the Puritans banned Quaker literature and ordered that it be burned. For their own part, the Quakers were determined believers, as militant in their own orthodoxy as the Puritans.

A crisis arose in 1656 when two Quaker women were discovered in Boston and immediately arrested. Eight or nine other arrests soon followed, and eventually the entire group was placed on a ship bound for the West Indies. In October 1656 the general court passed a new law establishing fines for ship captains who knowingly brought Quakers to Massachusetts. The law also specified punishment of whipping and a five-pound fine for mere belief in Quakerism. This attempted suppression only aroused the missionary zeal of the Quakers. More arrived from other colonies, and a number of sympathizers became converts. Massachusetts Bay responded with an even harsher law in 1657. It provided that "every such male Quaker shall for the first offense have one of his ears cut off, and be kept at work in the house of correction till he can be sent away at his own charge." Second offenders would have the other ear cropped. Women were to be whipped. Third offenders, male or female, "shall have their tongues bored through with a hot iron."[28]

The confrontation escalated, and in 1658 the Massachusetts general court ruled that Quakers would be put to death if they failed to leave the colony. This action only provoked more Quakers to rush forward to test the new law. With the jails filling up, the authorities selected three for execution. The one woman among the three, Mary Dyer, had her sentence commuted as she stood on the gallows, but the two men were hung as ordered (Mary Dyer was executed the next year for a repeat offense). Still more Quaker missionaries came forward. The colony responded with the "vagabond act" of 1661, which called for Quakers to be stripped naked, whipped, and run out of town.

Later in 1661, King Charles II forbade the use of either corporal or capital punishment against Quakers. This action halted the growing conflict in Massachusetts, and shortly afterward the crisis disappeared. The Puritans apparently learned to live in peace with the Quakers. Historians have attributed the persecution of the Quakers to a crisis of confidence in the Massachusetts Bay Colony. The passing of the first generation of leaders and isolation from sources of support in England caused grave doubts about the Puritan "mission," and the Quakers became scapegoats for other problems.

The persecution of the Quakers illustrates a recurring theme in the history of American criminal justice: the use of the criminal-justice system to suppress real or imagined threats to the community. Popular justice, in this sense, has meant the suppression of political dissidents, racial and religious minorities, or simply different cultural lifestyles by the majority. As Kai T. Erikson argues in his book *Wayward Puritans*, "the shapes of the devil" can take many forms.[29] The Salem witchcraft trials further demonstrate the point.

THE WITCHES OF SALEM, MASSACHUSETTS

The witchcraft episode in Salem, Massachusetts, began in early 1692. A group of girls and young women began meeting with a slave woman named Tituba, servant to the Reverend Samuel Parris. Recently arrived from the West Indies, Tituba had a reputation for her knowledge of the "magic arts." Some of the women began to exhibit bizarre behavior—incoherent screaming, convulsions, crawling on the ground and barking like a dog— and other members of the community concluded that the devil himself had come to Salem.

Three of the women, including Tituba, were immediately brought to trial. Witchcraft was punishable by death, and the village leaders hoped that speedy justice would end the threat. But the trial only worsened matters. The suspects were urged to identify other witches, and they took up their assignment enthusiastically. The search for witches spread throughout Salem and into neighboring towns as well. The girls were invited to Andover, and even though they did not know anyone in the town they managed to identify more than fifty "witches" in a matter of hours. Forty warrants were signed, and when the justice of the peace refused to sign any more, doubting the validity of the accusations, he became suspect himself.

By the end of the summer, nineteen people had been executed, seven more had been sentenced to die, and one person had been pressed to death under a pile of rocks for having stood mute at his trial. Then the witchcraft scare began to disappear almost as quickly as it had begun. The wild accusations, which left almost no one free of suspicion, provoked a sober reaction. The governor appointed a new session of the superior court which then proceeded to acquit most of the accused. He then brought a swift end to the matter by signing reprieves for the last eight sentenced to die and by granting a pardon or discharge to every prisoner in custody for suspected witchcraft.[30]

Why the witchcraft hysteria? Historians tend to offer a social and economic explanation. Social change had altered the fortunes of the community, creating new divisions and arousing fears that the Puritan consensus was in danger of being lost. The witchcraft

scare offered convenient scapegoats for larger community problems. Like the persecution of the Quakers, the incident illustrated
the repressive potential of the criminal-justice system in a community caught in the grip of hysteria. The term *witchhunt* entered
the American language to describe the persecution of imaginary
social or political threats.[31]

THE ORIGINS OF AMERICAN VIGILANTISM

As we have already noted, the weakness or complete absence of
constituted authority in newly settled areas became a major problem in the American colonies. Conflict with the Indians often
accentuated this problem. Two major conflicts, Bacon's Rebellion
(1676) in Virginia and the revolt of the Paxton Boys (1763–1764)
in Pennsylvania, arose from demands by frontier settlers for greater
protection. In other cases settlers simply took the law into their
own hands because of a general lawlessness. The vigilante committee, a form of ad hoc community justice, became an important
part of American criminal-justice history. Richard Maxwell Brown
has examined American vigilantism in depth and argues that the
South Carolina Regulator movement of 1767–1769 marked the
birth of a long tradition of vigilante movements.[32]

The Regulator movement arose from the absence of effective
law enforcement in the backwoods regions of South Carolina.
There were no sheriffs in the western counties, and all courts met
in Charleston. Local JPs could settle civil disputes involving
small amounts of money, but major cases, both civil and criminal,
required an arduous and time-consuming trip to Charleston.
Settlers in the backwoods demanded greater government services,
and the Regulator movement was essentially a political conflict
between the seacoast and western regions. The sparsely settled
areas provided a haven for criminal bands who victimized other
settlers; additionally, settlers demanded greater protection from
the Indians upon whose land they were steadily encroaching.

The crisis arose when the governor of South Carolina pardoned
five of six criminals who had been convicted and sentenced to die
for robbery and horse-stealing. Outraged, the more substantial
residents of the back country took the law into their own hands by

organizing a vigilante committee and setting out to purge the area of both known and suspected criminals as well as anyone they deemed lazy or shiftless. Known as the Regulators, this vigilante committee tried, convicted, and executed individuals, administered whippings, and ordered people to leave the area. The movement was, in short, swift and speedy community justice with a vengeance.

The Regulator movement provoked a major political crisis in the colony, bringing to a head the long-standing conflict between seacoast and back-country regions. Initially the colonial government sought to suppress the Regulators, but found this impossible to accomplish. By 1768 the Regulators maintained the only effective governmental authority in the back-country. Their actions became excessive, however, and an opposition group, the "Moderators," arose in 1769. A virtual civil war existed as both vigilante groups acted in the name of "law and order."

The crisis ended with the passage of the Circuit Court Act of 1769. This law answered the major grievances of the Regulators by bringing the presence of legal authority to the back-country through a system of circuit courts in the areas outside of Charleston. The courts met twice a year with justices of the court of general sessions "riding the circuit" to conduct business. The new law also provided for a sheriff in each of the six districts outside of Charleston and mandated the construction of jails and courthouses.

While the immediate crisis in South Carolina passed, the story was repeated again and again as the American frontier advanced across the country. Vigilantism became an important part of the American experience through the end of the nineteenth century. Brown has identified a total of 326 vigilante movements, and undoubtedly many more went unrecorded. The "lawlessness" of vigilantism was a curious phenomenon, for it represented an effort to impose law and order. Brown argues that the elite of the community—the wealthy and the politically powerful—took the lead in most vigilante movements. They acted to impose their own notions of what constituted the good community. Thus, vigilantism as the most direct expression of "popular justice" was often directed not just at criminals, but at political opponents, racial, ethnic, and religious minorities, the poor, and other alleged "undesirables" as well. Vigilantism formed a violent and ugly scar on the history of American criminal justice.[33]

THE QUAKER EXPERIMENT, 1682–1718

The colony of Pennsylvania adopted a criminal code in 1682 that differed substantially from the approach to crimes and punishments prevailing elsewhere. In terms of both philosophy and practice, the law was extremely "modern," foreshadowing developments that would become universal nearly a century later. Quaker leadership, in fact, thrust Pennsylvania into the forefront of subsequent penal-reform efforts.[34]

Pennsylvania was a proprietary colony, which is to say that the English Crown granted it to William Penn, who served as proprietor. Penn sought to establish a model Quaker community. In December 1682 the colonial Assembly adopted the "Great Law of Pennsylvania" in place of the laws of the Duke of York, which had prevailed to that time. The new criminal code eliminated the death penalty for all crimes except murder and substituted incarceration for corporal punishment for most other serious crimes. The most notable innovation was the use of imprisonment at hard labor in the "house of correction" for many crimes. Punishment for arson involved restitution to the victim of twice the value of the lost property, one year of imprisonment, and any corporal punishment deemed appropriate by the court. Breaking, entering, and theft of goods called for restitution of up to four times the value stolen and three months imprisonment. A rapist could suffer a fine equal to one third of his property and one year of imprisonment for the first offense and life imprisonment for a repeat offense.

Imprisonment introduced an endless series of problems related to maintaining an adequate facility. A supplementary law of 1683 directed each county to construct "a sufficient house, at least twenty foot square, for restraint, correction, labour, and punishment of all persons as shall be thereunto committed by law." Thus, the Quakers sought to use imprisonment for the multiple purposes of incapacitation, rehabilitation, and punishment. The first prison in Philadelphia was nothing more than a cage, seven feet long and five feet wide. It was replaced by a slightly more elaborate structure, but three years later officials simply rented one half of the residence of Patrick Robinson. Then the county constructed a two-story brick "prison," twenty feet by fourteen feet. Completed in 1695, it was deemed inadequate in less than a decade. This prefigured the subsequent history of American jails and prisons, for the problems of maintaining adequate, secure, and sanitary facilities would always remain paramount.

The Quaker experiment did not endure in its initial trial. Gradually, Pennsylvania officials retreated from their more humane approach to punishment. A series of laws between 1700 and 1706 reintroduced branding and reinstituted the death penalty for crimes other than murder. Even the Quakers were not free of racial prejudice. They prescribed the death penalty for blacks convicted of murder, rape, buggery, or burglary. The Quaker experiment ended completely in 1718 when the Quakers became engaged in a conflict with the English government over their refusal to take sworn oaths. The struggle resulted in a compromise which called for the adoption of the English criminal code.

The brief experiment with imprisonment in Pennsylvania anticipated later developments in penology. Before the end of the eighteenth century, similar ideas about crime and punishment would emerge in Europe and elsewhere in the United States. Penal reform flourished in America, and experiments with the penitentiary reached their most elaborate development here. The ideas that shaped and accompanied the American Revolution had an important effect on the evolution of criminal justice. As a new nation, unfettered by established institutions, the United States was particularly receptive to emerging ideas and practices. We now turn our attention to the era of the American Revolution.

2

THE NEW NATION AND
CRIMINAL-JUSTICE REFORM

THE ENLIGHTENMENT INFLUENCE

The eighteenth century has been called the *age of Enlightenment*.
Revolutionary new ideas emerged about the natural world and
the nature of man and civil society. These ideas were revolutionary
because they challenged existing institutions. Both the American
and French Revolutions drew their inspiration from Enlightenment ideas. The established institutions and processes of criminal
justice also came under attack, and these criticisms spurred an international wave of criminal-justice reform. By the late 1700s,
criminal codes were being revised in both Europe and the United
States.[1]

Enlightenment philosophers viewed man as a rational creature.
Moreover, the natural world was guided by rational principles
which man could discover through the use of his intelligence.
Civil society, therefore, should reflect the fundamental rationality
of the universe. Monarchy, the traditional form of government,
was irrational and should be abolished. The American Declaration of Independence expressed the Enlightenment belief that
existing institutions could be swept aside and new ones created in
their place.

When they turned their attention to the administration of
criminal justice, the Enlightenment philosophers found a savage
and irrational system. Montesquieu, Rousseau, Voltaire, and the

other leading philosophers condemned the wide use of capital and corporal punishments. "To impose suffering upon anyone simply because he has made another suffer is an act of pure cruelty, condemned by Reason and Humanity," argued the French *Encyclopedia*. Excessively severe punishments were not only barbaric, but contributed to the capriciousness of the administration of justice. Judges were reluctant to impose death for minor crimes, and even when the sentence of death was imposed, the king frequently pardoned the offender. Pardons both mitigated the severity of the law and reinforced the absolute power of the Crown.[2]

Enlightenment thinkers did not oppose punishment per se. Indeed, they saw it as a necessary and proper function of government. The French *Encyclopedia* stated that "the main and ultimate purpose of punishments is to secure the safety and good order of the community." Punishment had a utilitarian function and, like all aspects of government, should promote human happiness, liberty, and the general progress of society. But reason dictated that specific penalties had to be proportional to the crime. According to Montesquieu, "It is essential that there be a *proportion between* crime and punishment, because it is essential that the restraint upon commission of a major crime be more powerful than the restraint upon commission of a less serious one." Since man was a rational creature, a person would calculate the relative costs and benefits of any act and, if the cost were too high, refrain from it.

Crime prevention was a basic Enlightenment goal. Voltaire wrote, "It were much better to prevent than to think only of punishing these frequent misfortunes. The proper subject of jurisprudence is, to hinder the commission of crimes." Jeremy Bentham listed four specific aspects of deterrence: "to prevent all offenses"; "to prevent the worst"; "to keep down the mischief"; and, "to act at the least expense." These Enlightenment ideas set in motion a general revision of criminal codes throughout Europe and America. Capital punishment was limited, and corporal punishments nearly vanished. In their place arose the prison as the cornerstone of a new system of punishment.

Enlightenment ideas eventually spawned the modern police.

London police magistrate Patrick Colquhoun, in *The Police of the Metropolis* (1795), argued that a systematic and efficient law-enforcement system would serve to prevent crime. This extension of the police power of the state throughout society was an inherent feature of Enlightenment thinking. All criminal-justice reforms arising in the late eighteenth century, Michel Foucault contends, represented "a new strategy for the exercise of the power to punish": the goal was "not to punish less, but to punish better; to punish with an attenuated severity perhaps, but in order to punish with more universality and necessity; to insert the power to punish more deeply into the social body."[3]

Beccaria's Criminology

Cesare Bonesana, Marquis of Beccaria, was the single most important Enlightenment thinker on the subject of criminal justice. Known simply as Beccaria, he distilled emerging ideas into a single essay, *On Crimes and Punishments*, published in 1764. The essay had an immediate and profound international impact. Translations into German, Dutch, Polish, and Spanish appeared very quickly, and in 1777 the first American edition was published in Charleston, South Carolina. Because of his comprehensive treatment of the subject, Beccaria has been called the "father of modern criminology." His ideas continue to influence our thinking, and *On Crimes and Punishments* merits reading and careful study.[4]

Beccaria opened with a discussion of the right to punish. The contract theory of government justified punishment; for "laws are the conditions, under which men, naturally independent, united themselves into society." The pursuit of order and liberty made it "necessary to prevent the despotism of each individual from plunging society into its former chaos. Such motives are the punishments established against the infractors of the laws." But the laws could not be arbitrary nor could judges be allowed too much discretion. Criticizing contemporary practice, Beccaria argued that "judges, in criminal cases, have no right to interpret the penal laws, because they are not legislators." Once the criminal code was written, judges should apply it mechanically in each case.

In his fifth chapter, Beccaria advanced the utilitarian concept of crime prevention: "It is better to prevent crimes, than to punish them. This is the fundamental principle of good legislation, which is the art of conducting men to the maximum of happiness, and to the minimum of misery." To accomplish this Beccaria proposed various ideas for improving public safety, including "the illumination of the streets, during the night," the posting of "guards stationed in different quarters of the city," and a new institution, "which the French call *Police*."

The sixth chapter of *On Crimes and Punishments* dealt directly with the question of deterrence. Speedy justice was essential: "An immediate punishment is more useful; because the smaller the interval of time between the punishment and the crime, the stronger and more lasting will be the association of the two ideas of *Crime* and *Punishment*." Beccaria also proposed a number of reforms to ensure the fairness of the criminal process. It was important to guarantee the credibility of witnesses and the certainty of the facts in a case. Trial by a jury of one's peers was also essential: "It is an admirable law which ordains, that every man shall be tried by his peers. . . . All trials should be public, that opinion, which is the best, or perhaps the only cement of society, may curb the authority of the powerful and the passions of the judge." In short, fairness in the criminal process was closely related to democratic government; justice and liberty would be advanced by placing checks upon the arbitrary and tyrannical authority of government officials, especially judges.

Beccaria concluded with a discussion of punishment. To make punishments proportional to offenses, he suggested a "scale of crimes." "Crimes are only to be measured by the injury done to society." Thus, "first-degree" offenses would be those "which immediately tend to the dissolution of society." Disproportionate penalties undermined the deterrent effect. "If an equal punishment be ordained for two crimes that injure society in different degrees, there is nothing to deter men from committing the greater, as often as it is attended with greater advantage."

Beccaria took a firm stand against the death penalty. While most Enlightenment thinkers criticized only its misapplication to minor crimes, Beccaria opposed it altogether. "The punishment of death," he argued, "is pernicious to society, from the example of barbarity it affords." He suggested that "perpetual slavery" (life imprisonment) carried a far stronger deterrent effect: *"If I commit such a crime, says the spectator to himself, I shall be reduced to that miserable condition for the rest of my life. A much more powerful preventative than the fear of death, which men behold in distant obscurity."* Beccaria conceded the possible utility of capital punishment only in the case of treason where the offender "has such power and connections as may endanger the security of the nation." Only this most serious breach of the social contract was sufficient to warrant taking a person's life.

The question of pardons greatly concerned Beccaria. He and most other Enlightenment thinkers were convinced that their frequent use undermined the consistent and rational administration of justice. Pardons were frequently granted in most countries at that time for capital crimes, and grave injustices arose from their inconsistent application. The heart of the problem, Beccaria argued, was the fact that penalties were too severe for many crimes. The solution was a rational and proportionate scale of punishments: "As punishments become more mild, clemency and pardon are less necessary. . . . Clemency . . . would be excluded in a perfect legislation, where punishments are mild, and the proceedings in criminal cases regular and expeditious."

Beccaria's Impact

On Crimes and Punishments was the first systematic discussion of the full range of criminological issues: the cause of crime, the administration of justice, the role of the criminal law, and the meaning of punishment. Beccaria's ideas included theories of human behavior and the nature of government. He and the other Enlightenment thinkers are generally labeled the *classical school* of criminology. They put their main emphasis on the reform of the laws. Since man was a rational creature, a rational legal code would influence human behavior. The classical school of thought reflected the ideas emerging in the eighteenth century, just as subsequent criminological theories would reflect the dominant ideas of their times.

Beccaria's ideas helped to stimulate criminal-law reform throughout Europe, beginning in the 1770s. Frederick II of Prussia ordered his chancellor to begin drafting a new criminal code in 1779. According to Frederick, "Beccaria has left nothing to glean after him; we need only to follow what he has so wisely indicated." In Sweden King Gustavus III abolished the use of torture in 1772 and invoked a new criminal code in 1779 which greatly reduced the use of the death penalty. Leaders in Poland expressed great interest in Beccaria's ideas, but the end of Polish independence in 1794 thwarted the movement for reform. Joseph II in Austria incorporated some but not all of Beccaria's ideas in a new criminal code. In Russia, meanwhile, Catherine the Great issued her famous *Instructions* calling for a new civil and criminal code. The commission of fifteen hundred people assigned to the project never completed its work, but many of the proposed changes were taken almost verbatim from Beccaria and Montesquieu.[5]

The French Revolution, which swept aside the old regime, offered an unparalleled opportunity for law reform. The 1789 Declaration of the Rights of Man contained passages taken directly from Beccaria. In 1791 the revolutionary government enacted a new penal code based on Enlightenment ideas. The new law contained a graduated scale of punishments and reduced the number of capital crimes from 115 to 32. The more brutal forms of execution were also abolished. Criminal-law reform took much longer in England. While agitation for reform began in the 1770s, it did not reach fruition until the 1820s. Indeed, the English criminal code became steadily more barbaric during the late eighteenth century as the number of capital crimes increased to nearly 200. This illustrated the complex and contradictory forces at work during the age of Enlightenment. The beginnings of industrialization in England generated new social problems, and

English leaders responded by seeking to suppress the lower classes through harsher penalties for a wider range of property crimes.

John Howard and The State of the Prisons

While Beccaria was developing new theoretical perspectives on criminal justice, English reformer John Howard (1726–1790) aroused public opinion with his examination of prison conditions in England and Europe. First published in 1777, *The State of the Prisons* attracted enormous attention. Howard published three editions during his lifetime, and a fourth appeared in 1792 after his death. Howard's interest in prison reform began in 1773 when he was elected high sheriff of Bedfordshire, England. Horrified by the conditions he found in the jail under his control, he embarked on a campaign of investigation and agitation that consumed the remainder of his life.[6]

The State of the Prisons had a twofold impact. It shocked public opinion with its report on the appalling conditions in most jails and prisons, and it indicated the direction of prison reform by describing a few "model" institutions. The book established the format for a long history of prison-reform literature. Howard began his report with the observation that

> There are prisons, into which whoever looks will, at first sight of the people confined, be convicted, that there is some great error in the management of them: their sallow meagre countenances declare, without words, that they are very miserable. Many who went in healthy, are in a few months changed to emaciated dejected objects. Some are seen pining under diseases, "sick and in prison;" expiring on the floors, in loathsome cells, of pestilential fevers, and the confluent small pox: victims, I must not say to the cruelty, but I will say to the inattention of sheriffs, and gentlement in the commission of the peace.

Through the next several hundred pages, *The State of the Prisons* provides the details that supported this indictment. Most prisons lacked even the basic necessities of life: "There are several . . . in which prisoners have no allowance of *food* at all." And "many prisons have *no Water*." Ventilation was usually inadequate, thereby contributing to the spread of disease, and medical attention was virtually unknown. Howard was "fully convinced that many more prisoners were destroyed by Gaol-fever than were put to death by all the public executions in the kingdom."

Howard condemned the administration of the prisons (the terms *prison, jail,* and *bridewell* were virtually interchangeable). Sheriffs and bailiffs were notoriously corrupt and extorted money from prisoners who had any. The prisons confined all persons together indiscriminantly: "Few prisons separate men and women in the day-time," and "in some gaols you see . . . boys of twelve or fourteen eagerly listening to the stories told by practiced and experienced criminals, of their adventures, successes, stratagems, and escapes." Moreover, prisoners remained completely idle: "It will perhaps be asked, does not their work maintain them? for everyone knows that those offenders are committed to *hard labour.* The answer to that question, though true, will hardly be believed. There are few bridewells in which any work is done." Rather, the prisoners "spend their time in sloth, profaneness and debauchery, to a degree which, in some of those houses that I have seen, is extremely shocking."

Howard then proposed a few basic principles of prison administration. This marked the beginning of the modern "science" of penology. In his travels he found two institutions that impressed him as models for the future. The "prison discipline" of the Hospital of San Michele in Rome particularly excited Howard. Inscribed over the door was a statement of San Michele's philosophy: "It is of little advantage to restrain the bad by punishment, unless you render them good by discipline." The institution taught young delinquents "various manufactures and arts," including bookbinding, carpentry, shoemaking, and other trades. In other words, "prison discipline" meant teaching delinquents useful trades and the value of work in hopes that this would lead them away from lives of crime.

John Howard's model institution was a hospital, treating the sick, the impoverished, and the young delinquent. The idea of incarceration did not originate with the modern penitentiary. It developed, as we have already noted, in the sixteenth and seventeenth centuries from a number of sources, including institutions of social welfare. The creation of the modern prison in the late eighteenth and nineteenth centuries represented the extension of the principles of confinement and rehabilitation to a new type of client: the adult felon.[7]

English philosopher Jeremy Bentham made another important contribution to prison reform in the late eighteenth century. Bentham discussed the full range of criminal-justice issues in his writings, but his unique contribution was the design of a model prison, the *panopticon*. The name derived from its circular design, which permitted prison officials, placed in the center, to continuously observe the inmates whose cells were arranged along the outside perimeter. Bentham argued that this constant surveillance—and the prisoners' knowledge that they were being watched—would greatly enhance the "corrective" process of imprisonment. The *panopticon* represented the application of utilitarian principles to the practical question of prison design. The British government declined to build an institution utilizing Bentham's design, but Thomas Jefferson's plan for the Virginia state prison (1800) involved a modified *panopticon*. And today one can see the idea in the Illinois state prison at Stateville, constructed between 1916 and 1924.[8]

THE ERA OF THE AMERICAN REVOLUTION

The struggle for American independence and the subsequent creation of a new nation had an important effect on the history of American criminal justice. On the one hand, the fight for independence enshrined Enlightenment ideas about liberty in the American political tradition. Also, as a self-consciously new nation, the United States proved to be a very fertile ground for criminal-justice reforms, especially with regard to the improvement of prisons and the development of the modern penitentiary.

But on the other hand, the revolutionary struggle established a tradition of vigilante-style violence and lawlessness that haunted the subsequent history of American criminal justice.

Enlightenment ideas about human rights underpinned the American Revolution. The Declaration of Independence, like the French Declaration of the Rights of Man, expressed the fundamental idea that human liberty was paramount and that people could make and remake governments to serve that end. The U.S. Constitution embodied the ideas of Locke, Montesquieu, Beccaria, and others that liberty could best be served by defining and limiting the powers of goverment. The Bill of Rights contained in the first ten amendments to the Constitution defined specific limitations upon government authority. The Fourth, Fifth, Sixth, and Eighth Amendments became the cornerstones of individual liberty with respect to the criminal process. According to historian William Nelson, the founding fathers defined liberty to mean that "government ought not to be able to punish an individual for a crime except after a proceeding in which the accused had been given the same procedural opportunities to prove his innocence as the state had been given to prove his guilt."[9] To be sure, the guarantees of the Bill of Rights were frequently ignored. But they proved to be an irreducible touchstone defining the parameters of the criminal process.

Blackstone's *Commentaries on the English Law*, written between 1765 and 1769, exerted an enormous influence on legal thought in the new nation. The first American edition appeared in 1771-1772 and was an immediate success. Americans subscribed to 1,557 sets of the *Commentaries*. In his history of American law, Lawrence Friedman terms this "an astounding response." The basis for Blackstone's popularity was simple. The *Commentaries* provided a convenient codification of the full scope of the law. This was indispensable in a country that lacked both trained lawyers and the law schools to train them. Through the nineteenth century the bulk of the lawyers were trained by means of apprenticeship, and subsequent editions of Blackstone served as an invaluable text.[10]

Given the popularity and influence of the *Commentaries*, it was significant that Blackstone adopted Enlightenment ideas on crimes and punishments, thereby greatly furthering the spread of these ideas in the United States. Blackstone argued that "punishment ought always to be proportioned to the particular purpose it is meant, and by no means to exceed it." He accepted the death penalty for the most serious crimes but not for lesser ones.

The era of the American Revolution, then, was a time of significant change in American law. Concepts of individual liberty acquired a more precise definition and were written into federal and state constitutions. Enlightenment ideas on law reform gained considerable popularity and gave impetus to prison reform. Finally, it was a time of a more general secularization of attitudes. Crimes of a religious nature, such as blasphemy, declined in significance; crimes against property assumed a larger place in the role of criminal justice.[11]

Violence and the Revolution

The American Revolution was accomplished through violence: civil disobedience, mob violence, the harassment of British officials, the intimidation of real or suspected Tories, and, of course, the war itself. This aspect of the Revolution left an ambiguous legacy. According to Richard Maxwell Brown, the Revolution "contributed to the demonic side of our national history." Violence, even vigilante-style actions against individuals and groups, became enshrined as a legitimate means to defend freedom and liberty.[12]

Mob violence was nothing new, either in American or Europe, by the second half of the eighteenth century. Over the previous two hundred years, riot had become "a purposive weapon of protest and dissent in both Great Britain and America."[13] It was a particularly common device in Europe to protest economic injustice, such as a rise in the price of grain. American colonists inherited this tradition and used it for their own purposes. The history of mob violence in the colonial era includes not only protests against economic problems, but conflicts between racial and religious groups, battles between political factions, and collective protests against violations of public morality.

The colonial period was also marked by a substantial number of insurgent movements against colonial governments. Historian Brown has identified eighteen insurrections between 1645 and 1760; six of these were successful, six failed, and six others had a mixed outcome. Several of these movements were major political crises, including Bacon's Rebellion in Virginia (1676–1677) and the overthrow of Governor Andros of Massachusetts (1689). By the time of the American Revolution, the colonists were well versed in the theory and practice of insurgency.

As the struggle for independence gained momentum, the colonists turned to mob action. Brown has counted a total of forty-four riots in the fifteen years between 1760 and 1775, with thirty of them being clearly anti-British. Seventeen of the riots, for example, protested the enforcement of customs laws. The "mobs" did not consist of disorganized rabble. They represented relatively well-organized social clubs and political factions who were led by patriot leaders with very definite political purposes. The technique of tarring and feathering became a particularly common weapon against suspected Tories. The victim would be stripped naked, covered with hot tar, sprinkled with feathers, and then usually carried out of town on a rail. It was a brutally effective means of dealing with opponents of the Revolution.

The patriots justified revolutionary violence as an expression of "popular sovereignty" and the will of the majority. Thus, civil disobedience, mob action, collective protest, and vigilante action against individuals entered the national folklore as legitimate political techniques. The long-term result has been a tradition of political lawlessness for both good and bad purposes. Following the Civil War, for example, Ku Klux Klan activity against blacks closely resembled the various actions of the American Revolution. White southerners, moreover, justified their attacks as an expression of the will of the popular (i.e., white) majority. Yet, insurgent action was also used in defense of black rights: northerners attempted to block enforcement of the Fugitive Slave Act in the 1850s and, more recently, the civil disobedience of the 1960s civil-rights movement found inspiration in the American Revolution. The legacy of the Revolution was an ambiguous tradition of popular justice.[14]

Criminal-Justice Reform

With the arrival of American independence, each of the former colonies drafted state constitutions. This provided an opportunity to implement new concepts of criminal justice. The most significant innovations again occurred in Pennsylvania, where Quaker influence and the previous experiment with a more humane criminal code accounted for some, but not all, of the leadership in the area of criminal-justice reform.

The Pennsylvania constitution, dated September 28, 1776, directed future legislators to compose a new and more humane criminal code: "The penal laws as heretofore used, shall be reformed by the future legislature of the State as soon as may be, and punishments made on some cases less sanguinary, and in general more proportionate to the crimes." In Pennsylvania and the other states there was a pervasive feeling that existing laws were too English and that it was appropriate for the new nation to be governed by indigenous laws. William Bradford, an early U.S. attorney general, justice of the Pennsylvania Supreme Court, and major author of Pennsylvania criminal-code revisions, expressed this sentiment by saying that "the severity of our criminal law is an exotic plant, and not the native growth of Pennsylvania." Citing Montesquieu, he too called for a more humane criminal code: "As freedom advances, the severity of the penal law decreases."[15]

The Quakers had a great deal of influence on the developing science of penology. William Penn's "Great Law" of 1682 provided considerable inspiration. Just prior to the War for Independence, Richard Wistar, a prominent Philadelphia Quaker, became concerned about conditions in the local jails. In 1776 a number of Quakers formed the Philadelphia Society for Assisting

Distressed Prisoners. This led to the formation two years later of one of the most famous organizations in the history of American criminal justice, the Philadelphia Society for Alleviating the Miseries of Public Prisons. Harry Elmer Barnes has called it "the first of the great modern reform societies."[16]

Dr. Benjamin Rush of Philadelphia was one of the most important advocates of reform. A signer of the Declaration of Independence, Rush was a founding member of the Philadelphia Society for Alleviating the Miseries of Public Prisons. He was also the first prominent American to oppose capital punishment. At the home of Benjamin Franklin on March 9, 1787, he read his essay *An Enquiry into the Effects of Public Punishments Upon Criminals and Upon Society*. In this and subsequent writings, he elaborated upon ideas borrowed from Beccaria: "The punishment of murder by death, is contrary to *reason*, and to the order and happiness of society." To Beccaria's secular argument Rush added a characteristically religious overtone: capital punishment was also "contrary to *divine* revelation. A religion which commands us to forgive, and even to do good, to our enemies, can never authorise the punishment of murder by death."[17]

Because of the exigencies of the war, ten years passed before Pennsylvania began to revise its criminal code. There followed a series of laws which not only implemented Enlightenment ideas but, most notably, initiated the development of the modern prison. A law of 1786 eliminated the death penalty for robbery, burglary, and sodomy, substituting a maximum penalty of ten years imprisonment plus forfeiture of all of the offender's property. Theft of property worth more than twenty shillings carried a penalty of full restitution and up to three years imprisonment at hard labor in the county jail.

The 1786 law defined the purpose of confinement as "to correct and reform the offenders, and to produce such strong impressions on the minds of others as to deter them from committing the like offenses." The explicit statement of the correctional and reformative aims of punishment marked a significant departure from colonial-era thinking. Carrying out these new objectives, however, posed new problems. Where and how would "hard labor" be imposed? The law combined old practices with new. It called for "continued hard labor, publicly and disgracefully imposed . . . [in prisons and] in streets of cities and towns, and upon the highways of the open country and other public works." Thus, hard labor was intended to be a form of public humiliation. And by putting prisoners to work on the streets, highways, and other public works, officials hoped to keep down the cost of government services.

Having prisoners work in public did not meet with everyone's satisfaction, however. Soon there were complaints that citizens taunted the prisoners and that prisoners responded in kind. Social values had changed considerably since the early colonial period. The public humiliation of offenders was no longer believed useful; urban residents preferred a quiet and orderly environment, and many were offended by the presence of prisoners and the disorder it created. At the same time other people were exploring different reasons for confining all prisoners within institutions. The emerging concept of imprisonment stimulated thinking about the best means of accomplishing its correctional goals. This led to the development of solitary confinement and the modern prison.[18]

The Philadelphia Society sharply criticized the failure of jails to segregate men from women, juveniles from adults, and felons from misdemeanants. Moreover, it suggested that punishment *"by more private or even solitary labour,* would more successfully tend to reclaim the unhappy objects." In 1788 the legislature requested a detailed report from the society and this report helped to bring about major changes. A 1790 law converted the Walnut Street Jail in Philadelphia to solitary confinement. Historians have generally regarded the Walnut Street Jail as the first penitentiary. It had statewide responsibilities: other counties across the state could send their "more hardened and atrocious offenders" there for confinement. While each county paid for its own prisoners, this marked the beginning of a genuine state-prison system.

From the outside, one would never guess that the Walnut Street Jail represented such a radical innovation. Like other jails of the period, it was simply a conventional dwelling. Inmates were placed in groups in the large rooms. The conversion of the jail in 1790 involved building thirty-six solitary confinement cells in the yard (twenty-four for men, twelve for women). The experiment in penology, however, was not a success. Overcrowding immediately undermined the goal of solitary confinement, and the jailer placed more than one prisoner in each of the cells. Moreover, the jail offered no regular work to the inmates and they remained confined in idleness.

Despite the early difficulties of the Walnut Street Jail, other states borrowed the idea over the next few years. New York built Newgate, a state prison, in the Greenwich Village section of New York City in 1791. New Jersey erected a state prison in Trenton in 1798 while Kentucky and Virginia built prisons in 1800. As noted previously, the Virginia prison, designed by Thomas Jefferson, represented a modification of Jeremy Bentham's *panopticon* plan.

Pennsylvania, meanwhile, continued to lead the way in law reform. In 1791 it abolished the death penalty for witchcraft and eliminated branding and whipping for adultery and fornication. Three years later it took another major step toward abolition of the death penalty by eliminating it for all crimes except murder. The 1794 law included another major innovation with the development of "degrees" of murder. First-degree murder carried the death penalty, while second-degree murder was punishable by a prison sentence of between five and eighteen years. Eventually, of course, other states copied this approach to the crime of murder.

The Legacy of Early America

The first two hundred years of the American experience bequeathed an ambiguous legacy for criminal justice. The European settlers brought with them the foundations of a legal system. The role of the criminal law, the nature of the criminal process, and the formal structure of the courts changed remarkably little during the following two hundred years. Some important changes were evident, however. By the time of the American Revolution, Americans had refined their concepts of individual rights, and they included specific protections in the U.S. Constitution. Also, they had begun to move away from the use of corporal punishments and had taken the first tentative steps toward the development of the prison.

Practice did not always conform to ideology, however. The first half of American history also bequeathed a legacy of intolerance and injustice. Americans did not hesitate to use the apparatus of the criminal-justice system against those who did not conform to their values. Racism also became an ingrained part of the American tradition: native Americans and black slaves were regarded as being beyond the pale of society and its ideals of law and justice.

The apparatus of the criminal-justice system remained extremely small. The administration of justice was both inefficient and informal. The existing institutions were completely inadequate to demands of a growing society. Beginning roughly in 1815—an admittedly arbitrary date—American society underwent a complete transformation as a consequence of westward expansion, industrialization, immigration, and urbanization. In response, new institutions of social control were created. We turn our attention now to the building of the modern criminal-justice system.

II

BUILDING A CRIMINAL-
JUSTICE SYSTEM, 1815–1900

3

POLICE AND PRISONS:
A NEW CONTROL APPARATUS

AN AGE OF DISORDER AND CHANGE

The Dimensions of Social Change

Between 1815 and 1900 the United States created its modern criminal-justice system. In 1815 key institutions—the police, the prison, probation, parole, did not yet exist in their modern form. By 1900 they were parts of a new apparatus of social control. To be sure, not every state had adopted all of the new institutions by 1900, but the idea of a criminal-justice *system* was firmly established. This system involved a set of interrelated bureaucratic agencies performing specialized tasks for the purpose of controlling crime, deviance, and disorder.

The new criminal-justice system did not appear all at once, nor did the people who created the new agencies think in terms of a system at first. Instead, they created separate agencies in a halting and uncertain attempt to deal with immediate problems. Not until late in the nineteenth century did a few individuals begin to understand the interrelationships and to think in terms of a systematic approach to social control.

The United States was not alone in creating its criminal-justice system. The industrializing countries of Europe devised similar solutions to similar problems. The nineteenth century was a period of remarkable international cross-fertilization. Ideas and institutions crossed the Atlantic with ease. Americans borrowed the police idea from England, while many Europeans came to study the American prison. A series of international conferences on penology facilitated the process of exchange.[1]

The development of a criminal-justice system in the United States was a response to the extraordinary disorder wrought by social change. As westward expansion, urbanization, immigration, industrialization, and the conflict over slavery remade the face of American society, uprooting established patterns of life and challenging old values, Americans launched what historian Robert Wiebe called a "search for order." The search led to the creation of a network of specialized bureaucratic agencies, each designed to deal with a particular social problem. The criminal-justice system was only one part of this new network.[2]

Three new institutions developed between 1820 and 1870: the police, the prison, and the first juvenile institutions. Each was designed to regulate, control, and shape human behavior. Regarding the police, Allan Silver points out that they represented an unprecedented social and political event: "the penetration and continual presence of central political authority throughout daily life." Life was subject to constant surveillance; "unacceptable" behavior was punished. In the same manner, the prison subjected the life of each prisoner to constant observation and control. The French historian Michel Foucault, in his history of the prison, argues that the factory, the school, the police, and the prison had a common purpose: to control behavior, or to "discipline and punish."[3]

Sources of Disorder

Several different sources of disorder contributed to the chaos of American life in the nineteenth century. Each was a disruptive force by itself, but the effects of westward expansion, urbanization, immigration, industrialization, and the slavery controversy also reinforced each other, accentuating and compounding the problem of disorder.

Expansion westward across the continent was an especially

lawless process. Settlement preceded society, and individuals with a vested interest in "law and order" often had to take the law into their own hands. The South Carolina Regulator movement provided a glimpse of things to come. Again and again, vigilante groups imposed their own law and order in the absence of effective government. Racism added another dimension to the lawlessness. To justify taking Indian lands, white settlers developed a dual standard of justice. By viewing Indians as savages, whites effectively put them beyond the protection of the law. At the same time, white settlers could not always agree among themselves. The 1892 Johnson County (Wyoming) war was essentially a civil war between rival groups of cattlemen. In this and similar conflicts, it was never clear who had a legitimate claim to the land. In the absence of law, violence arose.[4]

The anarchy on the frontier was matched by riotous disorder in the cities. The seaport cities had experienced numerous riots throughout the colonial period, but in the 1830s an unprecedented and frightening wave of riots swept over urban areas. Philadelphia and Baltimore competed for the dubious title of "mob city," as both had a dozen major disturbances between 1834 and 1860. New York experienced three major riots in 1834 alone. Nor was the problem confined to the East; Cincinnati, St. Louis, and Chicago had their own riots. To many Americans, the survival of the new nation seemed to be at stake. In 1838 Abraham Lincoln warned about the "increasing disregard for law which pervades the country."[5]

Immigration was the source of much of the violence. Its steadily increasing volume brought a new mixture of religions, languages, and lifestyles to America. From the 1830s through the 1880s, Irish and Germans comprised the bulk of the migrants, but toward the end of the century they were replaced by arrivals from southern and eastern Europe: Italians, Jews, Poles, Hungarians, and others.

Contrary to popular folklore, the "melting pot" did not exist. American society was more a boiling caldron of ethnic suspicion and hatred. Americans of English descent hated the Irish for their poverty, their Catholicism, and their alleged love of drink. According to Charles Loring Brace, they were "the dangerous classes." Anglo-Saxon Americans disliked the Germans for their "foreign" language, their fondness for Sunday drinking, and (for some Germans) their Catholicism. Subsequent immigrant groups encountered a similar mixture of class, cultural, and religious hostility.[6]

Urban riots frequently pitted bands of Anglo-Saxon Protestant Americans against bands of Irish Catholics. This was perhaps the most common cause of riots between 1834 and 1870. Economic problems also generated violent disorders. Investors destroyed banks that had failed and lost their savings, and workingmen retaliated with violence against the injustices of the new industrialism. By the second half of the century, industrial violence began to take on the aspect of class warfare. The worst episode was the railroad riots of 1877, when angry workers attacked and destroyed railroad properties in dozens of cities across the country. In Pittsburgh law and order completely collapsed, and the mob destroyed an estimated $5 million worth of property.[7]

The struggle over slavery accentuated the lawlessness and violence. As early as the 1830s the antislavery movement aroused racial passions and provoked vigilante actions in both North and South. In Boston, Cincinnati, Philadelphia, and other cities, mobs attacked both white abolitionists and free black citizens. In the South, vigilantes suppressed all opposition to slavery. Violence erupted in the western territories, where "Bleeding Kansas" was the scene of a virtual civil war between proslavery and antislavery forces. Finally, antislavery leaders in the North forcibly resisted enforcement of the 1850 Fugitive Slave Act, challenging the authorities with mob action.

The Civil War and Reconstruction period unleashed other forms of violence. Between five hundred and one thousand persons died in the 1863 New York City Draft Riot, the worst urban riot to that time. Rioters overwhelmed both the police and the militia and were suppressed only on the fourth day by regular army units. Meanwhile, in southern and border states the war divided communities into pro-South and pro-Union factions. Many of the legendary feuds in American history—the Hatfields and McCoys (West Virginia and Kentucky, 1873–1888), the Suttons and Taylors (Texas, 1869–1877)—grew out of Civil War passions. Finally, during Reconstruction white southerners used the Ku Klux Klan as a violent weapon for reestablishing white supremacy.[8]

THE NEW POLICE

The chaos and disorder of a changing America evoked demands for more effective social control. The crisis was most evident in the growing cities. It was not simply a matter of periodic riots; urbanization brought new expectations about permissible levels of disorder. The urban ethos demanded order and tranquility, and these demands led to the creation of the modern-style police.

As a new mechanism of social control, the police did not appear overnight. What we consider the modern style of law enforcement evolved out of earlier institutions through a gradual process of adaptation, consolidation, and expansion. In fact, it is difficult to pinpoint the exact date of the first American police department. Historians generally cite the establishment of a day watch in Boston in 1838. Philadelphia, however, had experimented off and on with temporary arrangements between 1833 and 1854.[9]

The police had several antecedents. The most obvious was the old night watch, which had traditionally engaged in a form of preventive patrol. In many cities the creation of a modern police department involved adding a day watch or consolidating the various law-enforcement agents (night watch, day watch, constables) into a single agency. Employing police officers on a full-time, paid basis was another important step in the direction of "professional" law enforcement. Another main precursor was the slave-patrol system in the South. Charleston, South Carolina, had a police force of one hundred officers in 1837. In the rural areas, mounted patrolmen maintained control over slaves who were away from their plantations.[10]

The London Model

The London Metropolitan Police, established in 1829, provided a model for the new approach to law enforcement. In London as in American cities, the new police emerged only after many years of debate and had many predecessors. The need for more effective law enforcement and protection of public safety in London was evident even by the late 1700s. The Gordon Riots, a major clash between English and Irish immigrants, dramatized the crisis in 1790 but did not hasten reform.

The police devised by Robert Peel (hence the popular name *Bobbies*) represented a new strategy of social control. The police would maintain a continuous presence throughout society for the purpose of preventing crime and disorder. In modern terminology, they were *pro*active rather than *re*active. To achieve their ends, officers would patrol regularly over assigned routes, or "beats." To maintain effective supervision over the police themselves, Peel borrowed the administrative structure of the military. Officers wore uniforms, held military-style ranks, and were commanded by superior officers in an authoritarian manner. Thus, the "military model" became the cornerstone of modern police administration.[11]

The Americans borrowed freely but selectively from the English experiment. They adopted the strategy of crime prevention through patrol and the more superficial aspects of the military model. But the London Metropolitan Police was too elitist for American tastes. It was an agency of the national government, controlled by the home secretary (equivalent to the American attorney general). Since suffrage was highly restricted in England at the time, the citizens of London had no effective voice in police administration. Insulated from the people, the London police commissioners had a free hand to establish high standards of professionalism. The Americans opted for a more democratic approach. Police departments in the United States were deeply embroiled in the passions of local politics, and policing became a job for amateurs rather than professionals. In short, the London and American police systems reflected prevailing differences in

political structure. These differences had enormous consequences
for the quality of policing in the two countries.[12]

Policing the City

The quality of policing in nineteenth-century America was a
continuing scandal. In the words of August Vollmer, it was "an
era of incivility, ignorance, brutality and graft." In addition to
the pervasive brutality and corruption, the police did little to
effectively prevent crime or provide public services. Politics lay at
the heart of the problem. Officers were primarily tools of local
politicians; they were not impartial and professional public servants.[13]

Politics dominated the recruitment of officers. In most cities
aldermen or city councilmen nominated police officers for their
own wards. A change in political fortunes could result in a
complete housecleaning of the department. In Cincinnati, for
example, 219 of the 295 officers were dismissed after the 1880
elections. Six years later another shift at the polls caused the
dismissal of 238 of the 289 patrolmen and 8 of the 16 lieutenants.

The ethnic and racial composition of police departments was a
constant source of controversy. Anglo-Saxon Protestant Americans worried openly about the Irish "takeover" of the cities. In
1855 the New York City Council ordered an investigation into the
number of Irish-born officers on the police force. Other ethnic
groups won places on the police force in those cities where they
had political power. Thus, large numbers of German-Americans
could be found among police officers in Cleveland, Cincinnati,
and St. Louis. Even blacks were able to gain a foothold in the
police departments of some cities through their political power. A
Republican mayor appointed the first black police officer in
Chicago in 1872, and by 1894 Chicago had twenty-three black
officers.

Ignorance, poor health, or old age was no barrier to employment. An individual with the right connections could be hired
despite the most obvious lack of qualifications. Recruits received
no formal training. A new officer would be handed a copy of the

police manual (if one could be found) containing the local ordinances and state laws, and sent out on patrol. There he would receive on-the-job training from experienced officers who, of course, also taught the ways of graft and evasion of duty.

Policing was an attractive job because officers were relatively well paid. A policeman could expect to make an average of $900 a year in 1880 when skilled craftsmen averaged $774 and factory workers made $450. The majority of police officers were skilled craftsmen (blacksmiths, carpenters, machinists, etc.) who fully expected to return to their original trade.

Patrol duty was nominally an onerous task, but officers found many opportunities to evade their assignments. Until the twentieth century, departments used the two-platoon system. Officers spent long hours alternating between patrol and "reserve" duty at the station house. Reserve duty was necessary because there was no other way to mobilize large numbers of officers in case of emergency. In Philadelphia, for example, an officer would spend eighteen and one-half hours on the street and eleven and one-half hours on reserve during any forty-eight-hour period. The station houses were filthy places where officers slept, ate, played cards, and talked politics.[14]

Police officers were essentially unsupervised while on patrol and, as a consequence, were able to lighten their burdens considerably. Rather than patrol on foot through rain or snow they spent many hours in saloons and barbershops, drinking and gossiping. If some critics are to be believed, officers spent most of their time on duty drunk. The primitive state of communications technology inhibited effective supervision. In the early years, the "roundsman" (i.e., sergeant) attempted to monitor the activities of patrol officers. Later, the development of the call box and other devices contributed to internal communications. But police officers proved extremely ingenious in sabotaging these communications systems.[15]

Primitive technology also undermined the ability of the police to combat crime or provide public services. A citizen simply had no way to summon the police quickly. If an officer was not in the immediate vicinity, it was necessary to run to the nearest call box or station house. Nor could the police department itself mobilize its officers rapidly. Many if not most of those on patrol were evading their duties, and those who were on the job could not be contacted quickly. Despite Robert Peel's dream of a continuous police presence, the police were spread extremely thin. Patrol coverage was a token gesture at best. A Chicago patrolman in 1880 was required to cover a beat of three and one-half miles at night or four and one-half miles in the daytime. "It should not be surprising if the cry 'where are the police?' is occasionally heard," explained the superintendent of the Chicago police.[16]

Police and the Public

Mutual disrespect and brutality characterized relations between the police and the public. The problem could be traced to the very origins of the American police. The social and political conflicts that brought the police into being continued to shape their destiny. The police were immersed in political conflict and never gained full public acceptance. Citizens viewed them as political hacks and made them frequent targets of abuse, while youth gangs took great delight in taunting or throwing stones at police officers. When an officer made an arrest (as many as 80 percent of the arrests were drunkenness-related), he often had to physically subdue the suspect.

A tradition of police brutality developed out of this reciprocal disrespect. Officers sought to gain with their billy clubs the deference to their authority that was not freely given. The lack of training and supervision only aggravated the problem, and officials openly tolerated the "curbside justice" of the nightstick. Lincoln Steffens recalled his years as a police reporter: "Many a morning when I had nothing else to do I stood and saw the police bring in and kick out their bandaged, bloody prisoners, not only strikers and foreigners, but thieves too, and others of the miserable friendless, troublesome poor."[17] Police brutality was a form of "delegated vigilantism" by which the middle class tolerated and even approved violence against the outcasts of society.

The London police provided a striking contrast to their American counterparts. According to Wilbur Miller in *Cops and Bobbies*, the professionalism of the London police was the result of the different institutional arrangement. The London Bobby appeared on the streets as the representative of the national government, a vast impersonal authority backed by the majesty of the law. A highly centralized administration facilitated the control of misconduct. Thus, a tradition of professional self-restraint developed among the London police.[18]

Violence in the cities escalated during the 1860s. Initially, American police officers had not been armed. Standard equipment included a billy club, a whistle, and a pair of handcuffs. Even as late as 1880, the police of Brooklyn, New York, then a separate city of five hundred thousand persons, did not carry firearms. But gradually the police took up arms, largely in response to the growing violence around them.

Corruption and Politics

Corruption pervaded the American police. In fact, one could almost say that corruption was their main business. The police systematically ignored laws related to drinking, gambling, and prostitution in return for regular payoffs; they entered into relationships with professional criminals, especially pickpockets, tolerating illicit activity in return for goods or information; they actively supported a system of electoral fraud; and they sold promotions to higher rank within the department.

There was a method to the madness of police corruption, however. Corruption pervaded not just the police, but the rest of the criminal-justice system and all of municipal government. It flourished because it was functional, serving the needs of particular groups. Protection against law enforcement was a valuable piece of patronage for political machines. Appointments to the force were an equally important form of patronage. Protection of vice-related businesses also helped low-income groups to enter business careers. The political machines viewed the whole of city government as a vast field of opportunity. Tammany Hall leader

George Washington Plunkitt summed it up best when he said, "I seen my opportunities and I took them."[19]

Corruption did arouse public outrage from time to time. In city after city, reform movements arose because of scandals associated with the police. Police reform, however, made little headway. The main problem was the lack of an alternative vision of a professional police. Most of the reform movements were simply partisan attacks which did little more than replace one crooked group with another. Police reform prior to 1870 did not involve improvements in recruitment, training, or supervision. Instead, there developed a long struggle over the structure of administrative control. This culminated in the creation of the police board of commissioners. New York led the way, establishing a three-person board of commissioners in 1853. Four years later the state legislature took control of the New York City police by appointing a board of commissioners. These changes were politically inspired; each faction sought to enhance its own control by changing the rules of the game. Cincinnati experienced ten major changes in administrative structure between 1859 and 1910. But in most cities these changes did not result in improvements in policing.[20]

By 1870 the American police were a long way from fulfilling Robert Peel's idea of police service. The police were hopelessly corrupt, scandalously brutal, and incapable of effectively dealing with crime. Immersed in partisan politics, they also seemed incapable of reforming themselves.

THE MODERN PRISON

The prison emerged as the principal instrument for punishing criminals by the 1820s. Following European practice, American colonists had employed incarceration as part of the social-welfare system when they sentenced indigents to terms at hard labor. The important new development of the period up to and including the 1820s was the emergence of a coherent theory of correctional treatment. Incarceration was seen as a way to prevent crime by rehabilitating offenders, and it was extended to a whole new category of clients: adult felons. Existing practices were adapted and extended for this purpose.

The idea of correctional treatment rested on new theories of man and criminal behavior. An intellectual revolution accompanied and made possible the development of the prison. Crime was no longer equated with sin; instead, crime was a social phenomenon caused by harmful influences. The prison would rehabilitate by creating a better environment, separating the individual from harmful influences and subjecting him to a corrective "prison discipline" of solitude, silence, hard work, and religious study. The prison was only one of several new institutions that appeared around the 1820s. David Rothman argues that the people who created the prison also believed that "the insane asylum would cure the mentally ill . . . [and] the almshouse would rehabilitate the poor."[21]

The Pennsylvania and Auburn Systems

The idea of rehabilitation fired the imaginations of prison reformers. As Americans set out to transform this idea into reality, two rival concepts of prison design emerged. A furious battle developed between the advocates of the Pennsylvania and Auburn systems of prison discipline. In fact both were quite similar. But in the context of the period, the differences seemed to be large.

The Pennsylvania system rested on the principle of uninterrupted solitary confinement. The initial experiment at the Walnut Street Jail (1790) had failed, largely because of overcrowding. The new theories of correctional treatment developed slowly over the next three decades, as authorities wrestled with the problem of what to do with criminal offenders. The modern prison emerged first with the Western State Penitentiary (authorized by the Pennsylvania legislature in 1818, opened in 1826) and the more famous Eastern State Penitentiary at Cherry Hill (authorized in 1821, opened in 1829). Cherry Hill represented the architectural fulfillment of the new theories. The design of the prison denied the inmate contact with any person. Prisoners remained in their cells except for one hour of exercise per day. The exercise yard, moreover, was surrounded by a high wall which prevented contact with other prisoners.

The Auburn system took its name from the prison in the town of Auburn, New York. It too emerged out of a succession of earlier experiments and failures. New York opened the Auburn prison in 1819. In 1821 the New York legislature ordered inmates divided into three groups, with the most "hardened" criminals committed to uninterrupted solitary confinement. The results were disastrous. Soon reports circulated that inmates in solitary suffered nervous breakdowns and died from either suicide or disease. The governor inspected Auburn in 1823 and, shocked at what he found, ended the experiment by pardoning all those remaining in solitary confinement.[22]

Out of the ashes of this failure, Warden Elam Lynds devised a new system of prison discipline. Prisoners would sleep in individual cells but work and eat together in groups. Thus, the Auburn system was also known as the *congregate* system of prison discipline. The inmate was insulated against supposedly corrupting influences through a regimen of total silence. Prisoners were forbidden to speak to each other and marched to and from their cells in "lockstep," with eyes downcast and one hand on the shoulder of the man ahead. Violations of the rule of silence were punished by whippings, solitary confinement, or even torture.

Despite their similarities, the Pennsylvania and Auburn systems stimulated a vigorous national debate. Each side had its partisans in a furious "pamphlet war." The Auburn system enjoyed the support of Louis Dwight, leader of the Boston Prison Discipline Society, the most important prison-reform group in the country between 1825 and 1854. European governments sent delegations to study the two systems. The most famous visitors were Alexis de Tocqueville and Gustave de Beaumont, sent by France in 1831. Their report, entitled *On the Penitentiary System in the United States and Its Application in France* (published in America in 1833), was a thorough review of the two systems.[23] England and Prussia sent their own delegates and France dispatched a second group in 1836.

The debate over the two systems of prison discipline took on an unreal quality. First, both approaches agreed on the essential elements of correctional treatment: isolation from corrupting influences, hard work, and religious instruction. They disagreed only over the question of whether inmates should be physically isolated or allowed to work in groups. The Auburn system eventually triumphed for the simple reason that it facilitated profitable prison industries.

The second problem with the debate was that it was divorced from the practical realities of the administration of criminal justice. The pamphleteers could describe the reformative effect of prison discipline in glowing terms, but they could never prove that it actually worked. Moreover, the public and key actors in the criminal-justice system saw the prison in a different light. They were less interested in rehabilitation and saw the prison as a form of punishment—the more unpleasant the better. Legislators, judges, and much of the public also saw the prison as a means of removing undesirables from society. It was a convenient device for dealing with alleged threats to the social order.

Thus, the prison served conflicting goals simultaneously: rehabilitation, punishment, and incapacitation. In practice, the latter two were clearly the most important. The subsequent history of the prison, a story of endless failure, was a consequence of this hopeless confusion of purpose.

The Problems of Prison Administration

The practical problems of prison administration were at least as serious as the theoretical confusion. The advocates of the prison never envisaged the difficulties that would arise when hundreds of men (Auburn has 770 cells; Sing Sing had 1,000) were confined against their will in a single institution. Politics dominated prison administration just as it did police administration. With the exception of a few noted wardens, most prison employees obtained their jobs through political patronage. Turnover was extremely high: seven persons served as warden of Auburn penitentiary between 1840 and 1851. In their 1867 *Report on the Prisons and Reformatories,* Enoch Wines and Theodore Dwight com-

plained that "the controlling power given to party politics over
the management of the prisons" undermined correctional goals.[24]
Training was unheard of, and few individuals lasted long enough
to gain valuable administrative experience.

The idea of the prison was based on the concept of individualized treatment, which prison reformers firmly believed would
rehabilitate the offender and prevent further criminal activity. In
their *Report on the Prisons and Reformatories*, Wines and Dwight
called for *"individualization"* which they defined as "the thorough
study of the character of each prisoner, and the adaptation of the
discipline, as far as can be done consistently with a due regard for
general principles, to his personal characteristics."[25] Cut off from
contact with all other persons, with only a Bible to read, the
prisoner would have ample time to reflect upon his or her wrongdoing. The name *penitentiary* derived from the concept of peni-
tence, the feeling of sorrow or guilt.

The reality of prison life made a mockery of the promises of the
prison reformers. The prison never approached individualized
treatment and, in fact, destroyed ever vestige of individuality and
human dignity. The central concern of prison administrators
immediately became the problem of maintaining custody and
control over the inmates. The daily routine was a harsh and
brutal regimen. Wines and Dwight reported this description of
life in the Wisconsin penitentiary.

> In winter, the prisoners rise at 6 A.M., and without previous labor,
> breakfast at 6½. . . . Breakfast is served in the cells by assistants. On
> the ringing of a small bell in the morning, the prisoners rise, dress, put
> up their bedstead, bed and bedding, and wash themselves. On the
> ringing of a large bell, immediately after breakfast, they come out of
> their cells and march single file, taking the lock step, to their usual
> places of labor, where they remain until 12 P.M., working diligently
> and in silence.[26]

At the sound of another bell they would stop work, wash, and
return to their cells for lunch. The same routine would then be
repeated in the afternoon and evening.

This routine left no room for individualization. The staff,
moreover, had neither the resources, training, or inclination to
treat each prisoner as a unique human being.

The rule of silence proved impossible to enforce. One official confessed that "if a keeper were placed over every five men, communication would not be prevented."[27] Prisoners communicated through their cell walls by tapping out coded messages. And in the workshops they openly rebelled against their guards through the sheer weight of their numbers. Nonetheless, prison officials attempted to enforce the rule, and resorted to corporal punishment and even torture. Guards made liberal use of the whip, confined rebellious inmates to ghastly forms of solitary confinement, and devised iron gags, "shower baths," and other varieties of torture.

Prison brutality flourished. It was ironic that the prison had been devised as a more humane alternative to corporal and capital punishments. Instead, it simply moved corporal punishment indoors where, hidden from public view, it became even more savage. Like its counterpart, police brutality, prison violence was a form of "delegated vigilantism." For the most part the general public did not know what went on behind prison walls. But it regarded the prison as a form of punishment and believed that the undesirables confined there deserved whatever they got.

Out of necessity, prisons began to relax the rule of silence. By the 1860s Maine, Kentucky, and Missouri prisons allowed inmates to converse "in reference to their work." Other institutions simply abandoned the rule altogether. Wines and Dwight concluded in 1867 that the rule was more likely to "crush out every noble aspiration, every manly sentiment, from the breasts of those who were subjected to its operation" and counseled against it.[28] By the time of their report, the Auburn system had become the standard form of American prison discipline; only Pennsylvania clung to its own concept of complete solitary confinement.

Prison Industries

The laws creating prisons usually specified imprisonment "at hard labor." The exact meaning of this was not clear at first. Pennsylvania put its prisoners to work repairing streets and highways in 1786. The resulting disorder, as citizens and prisoners jeered at each other, stimulated the idea that it would be best to confine prisoners out of public view. Gradually, through a process of trial and error, officials developed a system of prison industries, employing inmates in organized and profitable labor. Prison industries quickly became a dominant feature of prison administration in the nineteenth century.[29]

Prison industries were popular because they served several purposes simultaneously. First, it seemed logical that hard work would teach the value of self-discipline, while teaching the inmate a useful trade would break the link between unemployment and crime—or so the reformers hoped. Second, prison officials found that the routine of work was an effective way of imposing order upon the daily life of the inmates. Under the Auburn system, inmates could be guarded while at work in large groups. Finally, and perhaps most important, officials discovered that prison industries could defray the cost of imprisonment and possibly even return a profit.

Prison industries took several forms. The most common was the *contract* system. Officials sold the labor of inmates to a private businessman who supplied the necessary tools and raw material. The contractor earned a profit on the difference between the sale price of the goods and whatever he had paid for materials and the price of the prisoners' labor. In some cases the contractor assumed direct supervision of the inmates inside the prison itself. Another variation was the *convict-lease* system, whereby the state simply leased the prisoners to a businessman for a fixed annual fee. In effect, the state abdicated all responsibility for its prisoners. For example, the terms of the lease made Captain H. I. Todd, lessee of the Kentucky prison, "warden or keeper [and] invested with its government and discipline."[30] A third variation was the *state-account* or *state-use* system, through which prisoners produced goods either for the use of state agencies or for sale by the state.

Whichever form they took, prison industries were a scandal. The heart of the problem was the profit motive, which superseded all concern for legitimate penal objectives or simple human decency. The lease system was unquestionably the worst. As Wines and Dwight argued, "the lessee is unrestrained by any authority, and is in the position of absolute master." As a result, "the temptation to excessive gains and to whatever abuses may be thought conducive to that end will only cease when self-interest itself cries 'Hold, enough.'"[31] The desire for profits and the fact that inmates were not free to take another job created an irresistible temptation to provide as little as possible in the way of food, clothing, and shelter. And the law offered no protection to the inmates against physical violence by the lessee.

The contract system was only slightly better. New York allowed contractors into the prison, thereby delegating the bulk of prison administration to "outsiders, having no interest in the discipline of the prison or the reformation of the prisoners, but only in making as much money out of them as possible." Contractors encouraged the practice of "overwork," by which prisoners who completed their assigned tasks early were allowed to work extra and keep the additional pay for themselves. Overwork privileges were granted through a pervasive system of bribes and favoritism.[32]

The appeal of prison industries lay also in the convenience to the state. The pamphleteers and reformers who supported the concept of prisons did not reckon on the unwillingness of state legislatures to provide adequate funds. The prisons never had either adequate facilities or staff. Legislators were eager to hear the claims of prison officials that the inmates could pay for their own incarceration. Officials at Auburn penitentiary in 1828 reported that "we are of the opinion that no further appropriations will hereafter be necessary to support this institution." The labor of 550 inmates generated $2,792 in October 1827, for an estimated annual rate of $33,307. The Clinton, New York, prison canceled its contract and, under the state-account system, generated a surplus of $3,000 over the cost of running the prison. Louisiana simply leased its prison system in 1844 for no fee whatsoever, simply to be free of the average annual cost of nearly $35,000. Five years later the state negotiated a new lease giving it 25 percent of the lessee's profits.[33]

Changes in the economy directly affected the development of prison industries. Before the Civil War inmates were generally employed in shoemaking and weaving. The prevailing handcraft style of production lent itself readily to the prison environment. But the increase in machine production and the demise of handcraft in these industries forced the development of new approaches. The manufacture of stockings became a principal prison industry after the Civil War. Prison labor was paid only one third or one fourth the wages earned by workers in the open market. This of course was the major source of prison-industry profits and, at the same time, the mainspring of organized opposition to the system.

Various groups opposed prison industries for different reasons. Many prison reformers were outraged on strictly humanitarian grounds. Others argued that the system undermined the goal of rehabilitation, especially when contractors or lessees assumed direct control of the inmates. These complaints had comparatively little effect in the face of the profit motive, however. Meaningful opposition began to appear in the 1880s, when organized labor and businessmen in related industries attacked prison industries on the basis of unfair competition. Carroll D. Wright, the new U.S. commissioner of labor, devoted his entire second annual report in 1886 to "Convict Labor." New York and other states began to pass a series of laws that gradually restricted prison industries.

Religion and Prison Reform

Religion dominated American thinking on prison reform throughout the nineteenth century. Tocqueville and Beaumont observed that "in America, the progress of reform has been of a character essentially religious. Men, prompted by religious feelings, have conceived and accomplished everything which has been undertaken." They doubted whether prison reform would enjoy the same degree of support in their own country, where evangelical protestantism was not a potent social force.[34] The Quakers played an especially prominent role, particularly in Pennsylvania, but Protestants of other denominations were numerically more important. Most were inspired by the biblical injunction: "I was in prison and ye came unto me . . . " (Matthew 25:36).

Religious instruction was one of the main components of prison discipline. Prisoners were confined to their cells with only a Bible to read. Further religious instruction was offered through chaplains, visiting ministers, and lay persons. Wines and Dwight also argued that religious commitment was the best qualification for the job of warden. "Prison officers," they wrote, "should be men of strict and uniform sobriety . . . men of mild temper, quiet manners and pure conversation . . . duly impressed with religious principles; men who fear God."[35] Just as there was no secular "science" of police administration, there was no science of prison administration.

The work of prison reform was led by a series of societies. The Philadelphia Society for Alleviating the Miseries of Public Prisons (1787) was instrumental in promoting the conversion of the Walnut Street Jail in 1790. The Society for the Prevention of Pauperism, a New York City group, played a major role in penal developments in New York state. On the national level, the single most important organization was the Boston Prison Discipline Society, founded and headed by Louis Dwight from 1825 to 1855. Dwight discovered prison reform through his religious work, distributing Bibles for the American Bible Society on a trip through southern jails in 1825. The New York Prison Association sponsored Wines and Dwight's 1867 *Report on the Prisons and Reformatories*.[36]

Individual reformers also played a key role. Particularly notable was the work of Dorothea Dix, who campaigned tirelessly to improve the treatment of the mentally ill. Dix discovered the issue that was to become her life work when asked to teach a Sunday school class at the East Cambridge (Massachusetts) House of Correction. Shocked at the conditions she found, she embarked on a two-year investigation of all the jails and almshouses in Massachusetts. In her 1843 report to the state legislature, she charged that the mentally ill were confined "in cages, closets, cellars, stalls and pens. Chained naked, beaten with rods, and lashed into obedience."[37] Her investigation eventually resulted in the creation of a state mental institution and, as a consequence, the removal of the mentally ill from criminal-justice facilities. Dix then took her campaign across the country, conducting similar investigations in other states until 1854.

The Question of Death

The penitentiary was designed as a humane alternative to capital and corporal punishments. Revulsion against the use of the death penalty was part of the humane spirit of the Enlightenment in the late eighteenth century. Opposition to the death penalty never completely disappeared, however, and concerted efforts to abolish it punctuate the history of American criminal justice.

The first wave of anti–capital-punishment activity began in the 1830s. The *antigallows movement,* as it was called, had the support of some of the most prominent individuals in the country, including former President John Quincy Adams, Horace Greeley, editor of the *New York Tribune,* and abolitionists William Lloyd Garrison and Wendell Phillips. The campaign drew upon the same reform spirit that inspired the temperance, women's rights, and antislavery movements.[38]

Part of the attack on the death penalty involved only objections to the traditional practice of public executions. Increasing numbers of persons were disturbed by the festivity, drunken brawling, and potential for serious rioting that accompanied these events. The hanging of Joseph Sager drew a riotous crowd of between ten and twelve thousand to Augusta, Maine, in 1835. Public attitudes reflected a growing squeamishness about officially sanctioned violence in public. Between 1833 and 1835 five states (Rhode Island, Pennsylvania, New York, Massachusetts, and New Jersey) moved all executions into the relative seclusion of the prison yard. By 1849 fifteen states had abolished public executions.

The movement for complete abolition of capital punishment was only partly defused by the compromise of ending public executions. The abolitionists scored their first major victory when Maine imposed a de facto moratorium on executions in 1837. After the Joseph Sager incident, the legislature passed a compromise law which said that an individual sentenced to die could not be executed for one full year, and then only on the specific order of the governor. The law fulfilled the expectations of its supporters as no one was executed in Maine for twenty-seven years.

The anti-capital-punishment movement reached its peak in the late 1840s. Michigan eliminated the death penalty for all crimes in 1846. In fact, no one had been executed there since 1830. In other states abolition narrowly failed. Vermont enacted a "Maine Law" moratorium in 1842, but repealed it two years later. In Connecticut, Ohio, and Iowa, abolition laws passed one house of the legislature but failed in the other. Rhode Island (1852) and Wisconsin (1853) abolished the death penalty, while other states greatly restricted its usage. Massachusetts, for example, eliminated it for the crimes of treason, rape, and arson in 1852, leaving only first-degree murder punishable by death. Still other states altered the sentencing procedure. In 1838 Tennessee allowed the jury to exercise its discretion in imposing a sentence of death. The intent, however, was to increase the number of convictions. It was believed that where death was mandatory, jurors were reluctant to return guilty verdicts.

The anti-capital-punishment movement declined quickly in the mid-1850s and soon disappeared. The question of slavery increasingly absorbed the energies of reformers and sapped the strength of other social-reform movements. Like prison reform itself, anti-death-penalty sentiment reappeared periodically: a weak movement developed in the late nineteenth century, but strong movements occurred both in the progressive era and the 1960s.

THE ORIGINS OF JUVENILE JUSTICE

The House of Refuge

No special institutions or procedures for juvenile offenders existed in colonial America: responsibility for the control and discipline of children rested primarily within the family. The law officially sanctioned stern parental discipline in extreme cases.

All of this began to change in the 1820s as a growing number of Americans began to view juvenile delinquency as a new and special problem. Urbanization and industrialization were already undermining patterns of family life, and increasing numbers of young persons appeared to be idle, troublesome, and beyond the scope of family discipline. In response, community leaders established separate institutions for juveniles in 1825. This marked the initial step in the eventual development of a complete juvenile-justice system.

The first juvenile institution was called the *house of refuge*. It appeared at the same time as the prison and for the same reason. Both represented an institutional approach to the solution of social problems: a special institution would provide a better environment and thereby correct the behavior of the individual client. At the same time, many people saw both the prison and the house of refuge as a way of simply removing troublesome or undesirable people from society. In that sense, both were warehouses for the unwanted. Finally, both represented the bureaucratization of criminal justice: the creation of a set of specialized agencies designed to control crime, deviance, and disorder.[39]

New York City, Boston, and Philadelphia pioneered with the house of refuge. In each city the story was essentially the same. Private charitable societies, usually led by the wealthy elite of the community, initiated reform. The first institutions were in some cases run wholly or in part as private charities; later they became publicly supported. In New York City the Society for the Prevention of Pauperism, organized in 1817, began investigating the relationship between poverty and juvenile crime. This resulted in the creation of the Society for the Reformation of Juvenile Delinquents in 1825. In the spring of 1825 the legislature chartered the New York House of Refuge as a private charity. Meanwhile, the Massachusetts legislature had begun to study juvenile crime in 1820 and authorized the Boston city council to establish a house of reformation in 1826. The Philadelphia House of Refuge also opened in 1826. Both the Boston and Philadelphia refuges were racially segregated, and Philadelphia opened a separate House of Refuge for Colored Juvenile Delinquents in 1849.

The laws chartering the houses of refuge included the first statutory definitions of juvenile delinquency. The New York law designated the refuge for "children who shall be taken up or committed as vagrants, or convicted of criminal offenses" where the judge thought they were the "proper objects" for such treatment. The Massachusetts law was broader, including "rogues, vagabonds, common beggars, and other idle, disorderly and lewd persons," as well as "all children who live an idle or dissolute life, whose parents are dead or if living, from drunkenness, or other vices, neglect to provide any suitable employment, or exercise salutary control over said children."[40]

These first laws established the central themes of the American approach to juvenile justice. A child could be sentenced for any one of three reasons: a criminal offense, a "status" offense, or parental neglect. The status-offense category was also extremely vague and broad. As a consequence the administration of the law required an equally broad exercise of discretion. These key elements of juvenile justice were firmly established in the mid-1820s, and the subsequent development of the juvenile-justice system represented their elaboration and refinement. The creation of the juvenile court in 1899 marked the fulfillment of this process, not something radically new.

The refuges were essentially conservative in purpose. They were designed to reaffirm traditional values of work and self-restraint. Thus, work comprised the main "discipline." Inmates were employed through a system of contract labor similar to that prevailing in the adult prisons. The houses of refuge, however, went a step further and incorporated the work discipline into release procedures. Ninety percent of the inmates discharged from the New York House of Refuge were released under an apprenticeship agreement. Apprenticeship was a common form of recruitment and training for many jobs, and the houses of refuge simply accommodated themselves to prevailing practice. Refuge officials believed that apprenticeships contributed to the goal of reformation by providing the child with a productive career.

The use of apprenticeships anticipated subsequent developments in American corrections. For all practical purposes the apprenticeship represented both an indeterminate sentence and a form of parole supervision. The inmate achieved an early release, based on conduct within the institution, and could be returned for misconduct or violating the terms of the apprenticeship. The apprenticeships could also be viewed as a forerunner of modern-day work-release programs. In general, correctional programs tended to appear first in the juvenile-justice area; later they acquired a more elaborate theoretical justification and were applied to adult felons.

The houses of refuge were not intended to be seen as penal institutions. Instead, they were designed to provide a warm, supportive atmosphere that combined the best features of the family and the school. In reality, however, they never fulfilled this noble ideal. Like the prisons, the houses of refuge quickly became warehouses for the unwanted.

The Children's Aid Society

As urbanization progressed, the image of the city as a dangerous and unhealthy environment for children prompted many of the efforts to deal with delinquency. No one expressed this antiurban bias better than Charles Loring Brace, author of *The Dangerous Classes* and leader of the New York Children's Aid Society. By the "dangerous classes" Brace meant the masses of poor, foreign-born immigrants filling the cities. As the second annual report of the Children's Aid Society put it in 1855, "the greatest danger that can threaten a country like ours, is from the existence of an ignorant, debased, permanently poor class, in the great cities. It is still more threatening if this class is of foreign birth."[41] (The anti-Irish bias of reformers like Brace in the mid-nineteenth century was nearly identical to the antiblack stereotypes of Americans one hundred years later. In both cases, "the city" served as a euphemism for ethnic, racial, and class prejudices.)

A private charity, the Children's Aid Society engaged in a variety of activities from 1853 onward. It managed lodging houses for newsboys, many of whom were homeless vagabonds, established separate lodging houses for girls, and conducted a number of industrial schools which taught basic literacy and specific trades. There were eight such schools in New York City in 1863, most of them serving children from specific ethnic groups. Brace sought to teach these working-class children what he perceived to be the middle-class virtues of cleanliness, godliness, and self-discipline.[42]

The most famous program of the Children's Aid Society was the "placing-out" system. It recruited city children, many of them orphans, and placed them with families. A total of 207 were placed the first year (1853). The next year the society undertook group emigration to rural areas. Forty-six children, under the supervision of the Reverend E. P. Smith, headed west in September 1854. The number of children placed rose to 863 that year, and over the next forty years the total was more than 91,000 children. Many were placed as apprentices, and the Society often arranged for a committee of leaders in the host community to handle the details of the actual placements.

State Reform Schools

The juvenile-justice system expanded gradually. The houses of refuge represented the earliest stage of development. The second stage included the creation of state reform schools. Massachusetts was the first to act, creating its State Reform School for Boys in 1847. New York had authorized a similar institution in 1838, but it did not open until 1848. By the 1850s reform schools became a general feature of the correctional system, with nine other states (in the Northeast and Midwest) following the lead of Massachusetts and New York. Massachusetts also pioneered with the creation of a separate reform school for girls in 1855. By 1860 there were approximately twenty juvenile institutions in the United States, and by 1876 the total number was fifty-one. Of these, twenty-three were state institutions, twelve were run by municipal governments, twelve operated as private charities, and three were mixed public-private agencies.[43]

In terms of theory and practice, the reform schools resembled the houses of refuge. They were designed to reform their inmates through a discipline of work, education, and religious instruction.

According to Connecticut officials, the reform school "is to be regarded as a school, not as a prison," and in Pennsylvania "the fact is impressively conveyed to the mind of each inmate, when received, that *reformation*, not *punishment*, is the *one object* of the institution." Despite the rhetoric, however, the reform schools were run as penal institutions.[44]

In an attempt to further the goal of reformation and to shed the image of a prison, some institutions experimented with a "cottage"-style living arrangement. Americans borrowed the idea from the *Rauhe Hause*, which the Germans developed in the 1830s (another example of the international exchange of correctional practices in the period). As the name suggests, the cottage system sought to reproduce a family setting. Massachusetts applied it to its farm school for boys in 1857.

The reform schools furthered the use of de facto indeterminate sentences that had begun with the houses of refuge. Wines and Dwight's survey revealed a variety of release procedures. The Connecticut Reform School discharged inmates either at the expiration of the sentence, "to friends," or "on parole of honor." Release in Illinois was equally discretionary: "on good conduct; being 21 years old; and sometimes . . . to the care of parents."[45]

In the absence of clear statutory guidelines, the reform schools operated in a legal twilight zone. Wines and Dwight specifically asked officials whether "the children committed to this institution [have] any right of protection against the decision of the functionaries who sent them there . . . ?" Several states replied that the writ of habeas corpus afforded some protection against arbitrary commitment. In Illinois the writ was used "not infrequently," and "about thirty boys have been discharged in this way within a year."[46] An 1870 decision by the Illinois Supreme Court challenged the existing state law that permitted commitment to the reform school without a trial. The court attacked "the uncontrolled discretion" of the board of guardians. This decision anticipated by nearly a century a legal attack upon the discretionary decision-making inherent in modern correctional practice.

The 1860s brought to an end the first period of criminal-justice institution-building. The police, the prison, and the first juvenile-justice agencies had appeared since the 1820s. The apparatus of social control was now far larger and more extensive than it had ever been; it was able to intervene in the lives of American citizens as never before. Although few persons realized it at the time, a genuine criminal-justice system was beginning to take shape.

The quality of justice administered by this emerging system, however, left much to be desired. The police were hopelessly corrupt and inefficient, providing little in the way of protection or service to the public. The prisons reformed no one and only inflicted more violent punishment than the system they were designed to replace. The houses of refuge, if less brutal, were no more successful in rehabilitating their inmates. The reformers who founded these institutions gave too little thought to the practical problems of administration. As a result the energy of a different generation of reformers in the last three decades of the nineteenth century was devoted not just to the problem of crime, but also to the problem of making the new criminal-justice institutions work.

4

COMPLETING THE
CORRECTIONAL SYSTEM

THE NEW PENOLOGY

Prison reform in the United States runs in cycles. Each cycle, extending over a period of several decades, has been characterized by the emergence of new ideas, a period of institution-building, and, finally, a process of stagnation, disillusionment, and decline. In the history of the American prison there have been three distinct periods of reform. The first began slowly in the 1780s, reached its peak in the 1820s and 1830s, and then died by the late 1850s. The second cycle began in 1870, gathered momentum slowly over the next thirty years, achieved fulfillment between 1900 and 1915, and then declined quickly. The third cycle began slowly in the 1930s, reached its peak in the late 1950s and early 1960s, and then collapsed suddenly after 1971.

Through this two-hundred-year history, the central thrust of prison reform has remained essentially the same. The concept of rehabilitation, of individualized correctional treatment, has energized each of the three great reform cycles. Each period has simply offered new ideas on how best to achieve this goal. The literature on prison reform is sadly monotonous: the same indictments of existing conditions, the same promises of a better and more effective form of correctional treatment. Yet, even the reforms have been depressingly similar. As Michel Foucault puts it, the prison has "always been offered as its own remedy."[1] The reformers tend to promise to do the same thing, only better.

The first cycle of prison reform came to an end in the late 1850s with the death of Louis Dwight and the consequent collapse of the Boston Prison Discipline Society. But faith in the reformative capacity of prison treatment died long before Dwight's death. There was clearly no evidence that incarceration rehabilitated any inmate, and even the staunchest advocates of prison treatment could not make a convincing argument. The prisons themselves had degenerated into custodial institutions, warehouses for the unwanted.

The 1867 *Report on the Prisons and Reformatories* by Enoch Wines and Theodore Dwight marked both an end and a beginning. A comprehensive survey of American prisons (although with a serious lack of coverage of southern states), the *Report* documented the failure of the system. Judged by the prisons' own standards, Wines and Dwight concluded that "there is not a prison system in the United States . . . which would not be found wanting."[2] The original concept of "prison discipline" was in total disarray: the prisons offered neither isolation nor meaningful secular or religious education, and their administration was dominated by ignorance, irrationality, the influence of party politics, and outright brutality.

In the midst of this sad state of affairs, however, Wines and Dwight identified the first stirrings of a new approach to penology in experiments with "conditional release" in Ireland, Australia, and America, notably in the Detroit House of Correction. The *new penology*, as it was called, was not really very new. It promised to make the prison work by more effectively individualizing correctional treatment. In short, it promised to do what a previous generation of prison reformers had earlier promised. Conditional release would eventually find institutional expression in the form of the indeterminate sentence and parole release. For Wines and Dwight, writing in 1867, the new ideas were still in an early and ill-defined state of development. Three years later, at the National Congress of Penitentiary and Reformatory Discipline, held in Cincinnati, they would crystallize as the new penology.

The Cincinnati Congress

The significance of the National Congress of Penitentiary and Reformatory Discipline in October 1870 cannot be overestimated. The ideas stated in its declaration of principles guided correctional thinking for the next hundred years. Writing in the 1950s, Harry Elmer Barnes and Negley Teeters could accurately say that the new penology "had its genesis in the heroic principles enunciated in 1870 in Cincinnati."[3] Conceived and organized by Enoch Wines, the congress drew 130 delegates from twenty-four states, Canada, and South America, the bulk of whom were prison officials. The published *Transactions*, included more than forty papers and resolutions on a wide variety of correctional topics.

The cornerstone of the new penology was the indeterminate sentence or "sentences limited only by satisfactory proof of reformation." According to the final declaration, "the prisoner's destiny should be placed, measurably, in his own hands; he must be put into circumstances where he will be able, through his own exertions, to continually better his own condition."[4]

The chief theoretician of the new penology was Zebulon R. Brockway, then superintendent of the Detroit House of Correction. Brockway's paper, "The Ideal of a True Prison System for a State," electrified the congress and influenced correctional thinking for decades. A careful reading of his paper reveals that the new penology was old wine in a new bottle. It reaffirmed the traditional goal of the prison: "The supreme aim of prison discipline is the reformation of criminals, not the infliction of vindictive suffering." Crime prevention remained the ultimate goal: "The central aim of a true prison system is the protection of society against crime." Moreover, religious instruction, secular education, and hard work ("industrial training") remained basic elements of prison discipline.[5]

But to make prison discipline effective, sentences would have to be indeterminate in length. "The remedy cannot be had," Brockway argued, "so long as a determinate sentence is imposed at the time of trial." With the indeterminate sentence, "all persons in a state, who are convicted of crimes or offenses before a competent court, shall be deemed wards of the state and shall be committed to the custody of the board of guardians, until, in their judgement, they may be returned to society with ordinary safety and in accord with their own highest welfare." The indeterminate sentence appeared to place complete responsibility upon the offender himself. As the declaration of principles put it, the inmate would be reformed "through his own exertions" or not at all. Like the initial concept of the prison fifty years before, the new penology rested on an environmental theory of human behavior, but it involved a more subtle manipulation of the inmate's environment.

Brockway proposed far more than a new sentencing structure. His paper also outlined a complete correctional *system*. The board of guardians would not only determine release dates for prisoners, but would also manage a state-police agency, primary schools "for the education of the children from the almshouses," juvenile reform schools and reformatories, and a variety of institutions for adult offenders. The inclusion of a police agency in this system indicates that it was a comprehensive approach to social control. The board of guardians would exercise law-enforcement, judicial, and correctional powers. It could determine who would be institutionalized, which institution they would be sent to, and for how long. Brockway's plan was the first tentative step toward a "systems" perspective in criminal justice.

Trends in Prison Reform

The Cincinnati congress inspired a new burst of prison reform. Brockway's paper and the declaration of principles provided a vision of a comprehensive approach to the treatment of convicted criminals. In practice, prison reform during the next three decades proceeded along several different lines. Although the development of the correctional system was chaotic and uncoordinated, several themes provide a unifying continuity.

The new penology was a refurbished attempt at rehabilitation through individualized treatment. The quest for individualization spurred three institutional developments: the emergence of alternatives to incarceration; the creation of institutions for specialized categories of offenders; and manipulation of sentence lengths and release procedures. The major alternative to incarceration was probation. Specialized penal institutions included women's prisons and reformatories for young male adults. Manipulation of sentence lengths and release procedures involved the indeterminate sentence and parole.

By the end of the century, the prison still remained at the center of the American punishment apparatus. It was surrounded, however, by a variety of institutions and processes designed to provide a wider range of treatment alternatives. It was, in short, a correctional "system."

None of these institutions or processes were entirely new in 1870. Most had appeared decades before, although under different names and often as makeshift solutions. The key elements of the new penology were almost always applied first to juveniles. The dominant trend of correctional reform through the latter part of the nineteenth century was the development of a coherent theory of treatment, which Brockway largely provided, and the gradual extension of new procedures to adult male felons.

PROBATION: OLD AND NEW

The history of probation has generally been told as the story of John Augustus, a Boston shoemaker who began functioning as a volunteer probation officer in 1841. Moved by a genuine sense of compassion for offenders, Augustus began to visit the criminal courts and take up the cause of particular individuals. He paid the fines for drunks who could not pay themselves, posted bail for indigent offenders, and helped many to find employment. Judges began to acknowledge Augustus's role as probation officer; thus, "when the defendant was later brought into court for sentence, Augustus would report on his progress toward reformation, and the judge would usually fine the convict one cent and costs, instead of committing him to an institution." Augustus claimed to have served some 1,152 men and 794 women in this manner by 1858.[6]

The colorful story of John Augustus has been told perhaps too often. By focusing on one individual, it diverts attention from the broader patterns of change in the administration of justice. Probation developed a common-law existence long before Augustus's time. The ancient practice of benefit of clergy, for example, allowed for the suspension of death sentences. "Judicial reprieve" permitted judges to temporarily delay imposition of sentence and to continue the delay upon evidence of good behavior. An 1836 Massachusetts law authorized security bonds for good behavior as an alternative sentence; the law only ratified practice that extended back many years. Prosecutors exercised a related form of discretion by "filing" or laying a case "on file." Although nominally only a temporary delay, it often became a permanent dismissal. Suspension of sentence existed in a legal twilight zone without statutory authorization. But this did not deter officials who for one reason or another wished to individualize justice and mitigate punishment.[7]

The significant aspect of John Augustus's work was *supervision*, a key ingredient in the modern form of probation. Simple Christian charity motivated Augustus, as it did so many other reformers. The practice of supervision evolved slowly, in many different ways. Some Massachusetts courts, for example, began placing youthful offenders under the supervision of law-enforcement officials as early as the 1830s. Edward H. Savage, then a captain with the Boston police, conducted "presentence investigations" following the mass arrest of prostitutes in 1858. In his memoirs, *Police Records and Recollections,* Savage describes how he interviewed the fifty-one women before trial and then, in court, asked the judge if it were "not inconsistent with the requirements of justice, to give all who were found guilty . . . a good smart sentence, with a suspension, to enable them to leave the city for their parents and home."[8]

Edward Savage resigned as chief of the Boston police in 1878 to become the first probation officer. The Massachusetts statute, the first in the country, authorized probation officers for Suffolk County (Boston) only. A second law in 1880 allowed other cities and towns in the state to hire probation officers if they chose. In 1891 Massachusetts created a statewide probation system and transferred the power of appointment from municipal officials to the courts. Missouri adopted probation in 1897, followed by Rhode Island (1899) and New Jersey and Vermont (1900).

The development of probation illustrates important dimensions of the process of change in the nineteenth century. First, probation laws provided statutory authority for a practice that was already well established. Second, supervision was justified in terms of the ideals of individualized treatment enunciated at the Cincinnati congress.

REFORMATORIES FOR WOMEN AND MEN

In their 1867 *Report*, Wines and Dwight condemned the practice of building huge fortress-like prisons. Institutions with eight hundred or nine hundred cells subverted the goal of individualized treatment. The proper alternative was to build a series of smaller institutions, with "the various classes of offenders being committed to prisons designed specially for their reception and treatment." They recommended four different types: prisons for women, young adult males, offenders employed (or being trained) in the same occupation, and for "the worst class of offenders."[9]

The Female Offender

From the time of John Howard, prison reformers complained about confinement of male and female offenders in the same institution. Although nominally kept in separate rooms or wings, the sexes frequently mingled. Reformers continually discovered instances of sexual debauchery in both jails and prisons. Wines and Dwight reported that New York maintained a facility for women at Sing Sing, but one which did not fully separate men from women. Most other states confined women to a separate "department" of the main prison. Massachusetts, on the other hand, committed all females offenders to county houses of correction.

The problem, as Wines and Dwight indicated, was the simple

fact that "there are not female convicts enough to warrant the erection and maintenance of prisons for them alone." Gradually, however, separate institutions began to appear. Indiana opened its women's reformatory in 1873; Massachusetts opened its women's reformatory four years later; and New York established its House of Refuge for Women in 1881.[10]

The Massachusetts Reformatory for Women had its origins in voluntary relief efforts during the Civil War. Hannah B. Chickering and Ellen Cheney Johnson, the latter the wife of a wealthy Boston merchant, served on the Sanitary Commission, which attempted to deal with the health and sanitation problems arising from the war. This work brought the problems of the female offender to their attention. In 1864 they helped establish the Temporary Asylum for Discharged Female Prisoners in Dedham, Massachusetts, and in 1869 they organized a conference on women offenders in Boston. The state first experimented by converting the Greenfield jail in 1870 and then authorized the women's reformatory, which opened in 1877. The idea of separate facilities for women was discussed at the 1870 Cincinnati congress. Opposition arose both from contractors who used female labor and from wardens who used women to do domestic work in their prisons.

Prison discipline had a special emphasis in the women's institutions. It meant instilling Victorian-era standards of sexual morality and training women in the duties of homemakers and mothers. Most of the inmates in the Massachusetts women's reformatory were convicted of drunkenness (456 out of a total of 519, according to the 1880 annual report), and the staff questioned the value of reformatory discipline for these offenders, who would serve only very short terms. Significantly, the state responded to this matter with a new law in 1879 extending the length of sentences. The law provided an indeterminate sentence of up to two years for second-offense drunkenness. Thus, the goal of rehabilitation led to longer prison terms. That same year the state also revived the practice of indenture and allowed women offenders to be placed in jobs as domestic servants. Two years later this early experiment with parole was broadened to a more general "conditional permit to be at liberty."[11]

Women's prisons, along with juvenile institutions, became a testing ground for the new penology. Prison reformers regarded women and children as good candidates for rehabilitation, probably because they were considered less "dangerous" or "hardened" than the adult male felon. The practice of conditional release, which had already been applied to the houses of refuge, was applied to the first women's prisons. Zebulon Brockway administered a conditional-release law that pertained only to female offenders in the Detroit House of Correction. Following Brockway's recommendation, the 1869 law provided for sentences of up to three years. In Detroit, as in Massachusetts, the goals of the new penology led to longer sentences. As a result offenders remained incarcerated or under some form of control for longer periods than before.

The Reformatory for Young Male Adults

In 1877 the Elmira reformatory was opened under the direction of Zebulon R. Brockway. Elmira stands with the Walnut Street Jail as one of the great landmarks in the history of American corrections. Its significance lies in the fact that it brought together two distinct developments: the creation of institutions for special classes of offenders, and the emergence of the new penology of indeterminate sentences and conditional release. Blake McKelvey observes in his history of the American prison that "all the best ideas of the day were woven into the plans for Elmira Reformatory."[12]

McKelvey points out that the reformatory, as a special institution for young adults, was a "mutation" that combined elements from a variety of existing institutions. Since 1825, the houses of refuge had confined juveniles. Meanwhile, some cities and counties had established houses of correction designed primarily for misdemeanants and in some cases women offenders. Thus, the house of correction was neither a jail nor a prison. The Detroit House of Correction, opened in 1861 under Brockway's direction, grew out of complaints about conditions in the local jail. Brockway immediately set out to offer what the jail did not: a correctional program of work and education.

New York took the first step toward creating a reformatory with an 1856 law committing male first offenders under the age of twenty-one to local jails or houses of correction, if they were available. The Detroit House of Correction was also designed to receive male first offenders under the age of twenty-one, but the state supreme court declared the law unconstitutional. The reformatory finally appeared as a distinct institution with the opening of the Elmira reformatory in 1877. The origins of Elmira, however, are interwoven with the development of both the indeterminate sentence and parole.

PAROLE AND THE INDETERMINATE SENTENCE

Conditional release—the decision to release an inmate from prison upon evidence of rehabilitation—was the basis of the new penology. This concept became an institutional reality in the form of the indeterminate sentence and release on parole. Although the two were closely related they developed independently in the decades following the 1870 Cincinnati congress. Some states adopted both, while others adopted one without the other. The situation is further complicated by the fact that the indeterminate sentence took many different forms, depending upon specific provisions for maximum and minimum sentences. As a general rule, however, both the indeterminate sentence and parole were applied first to young adults in reformatories and only later to adult felons.

The practice of early release from prison developed long before the 1870 Cincinnati congress. The history of the indeterminate sentence and parole can be traced back to the first years of the prison, and even further into the history of criminal justice. In this respect, it closely resembles the history of probation. Practice developed first in an ad hoc manner, often as an expedient solution to an unforeseen problem. The articulation of the new penology at Cincinnati represented the development of a coherent rationale. The laws creating the indeterminate sentence and parole simply formalized existing practice, clarifying and often relocating responsibility for decision-making.

Early release from prison had several antecedents. As we have seen, sentences to the houses of refuge were shortened through release under apprenticeship. The two most important techniques for shortening the sentences of adult felons were executive pardons and a variety of "good-time" or commutation laws.[13]

The pardoning power was excercised liberally during the nineteenth century. Wines and Dwight found that the incidence of pardon increased in proportion to the length of sentence. Between 1828 and 1866, 12.5 percent of all prisoners in Massachusetts received pardons. But the percentage increased from 20.5 percent for inmates with sentences of five to ten years, to 32 percent for those with sentences longer than ten years, and 50 percent for inmates sentenced to life imprisonment. In fact, "lifemen" in Massachusetts served an average of only seven and three-quarters years in prison.

Prison officials disagreed about the effect of pardons. The inspectors of the New York prisons reported in the 1850s that "the more liberal use of the pardoning power has created a desirable influence in the prisons, strengthening the hopes of the long sentenced, stimulating all to industry and obedience." In short, they believed it accomplished what subsequent generations hoped parole would achieve. Other officials took a different view. The warden of Pennsylvania's Western Penitentiary concluded that "nothing so much hinders the proper management and reformation of the prisoner, as his restless anxiety to obtain a pardon." Wines and Dwight argued that "It nullifies the certainty of punishment . . . the most potent element in the whole punitory system."[14]

The granting of pardons was inevitably arbitrary and capricious. One study called it "one of the most troublesome aspects of criminal administration" in antebellum Pennsylvania. The problem was not the number of pardons but the factors that influenced their use. A particularly severe controversy erupted in Pennsylvania over the 1841 *pretrial* pardon granted to the editors of a magazine accused of libeling Thaddeus Stevens, a prominent politician. This pardon became an issue in the state gubernatorial election later that year.[15]

Governors objected to the burden that the pardoning power placed on them. The Boston Prison Discipline Society noted the awkward situation faced by a governor confronted by a mother who "pleads in heart-broken accents, and with the moving eloquence of tears."[16] Prisoners with important political friends could also mount persistent efforts to secure a pardon. To alleviate the burden on the governor, Pennsylvania created a board of pardons in 1873, and many other states followed suit in the next few years. This represented another step in the bureaucratization of the administration of justice.

Pardons served a variety of purposes. They allowed persons with wealth or political connections to avoid punishment. At the same time, the pardoning power was a valuable form of patronage which politicians could use. On a broader scale, pardons allowed criminal-justice officials to systematically mitigate punishments. A characteristic feature of American criminal-justice history has been the subversion of the intent of the law. In practice, officials have never imposed the punishments advertised in the criminal codes. Several reasons account for this phenomenon. Discretionary leniency has been a device for individualizing justice. Also, administrative pressures encouraged leniency. Just as probation was cheaper and more convenient than incarceration, so early release helped to relieve the perennial problem of prison overcrowding. In its 1867 annual report, the Massachusetts Board of State Charities candidly admitted that "the prisons are crowded—conditional pardon would relieve them."[17] Parole and the indeterminate sentence served the same multiple objectives.

"Good-time" or commutation laws offered a second way to shorten prison terms. New York passed the first such law in 1817; it allowed prison officials to reduce the sentences of inmates serving more than five years by as much as 25 percent. Tennessee passed a similar law in 1833, followed by Ohio in 1856; by 1869 twenty-three states had some form of "good-time" law. Zebulon Brockway praised the commutation, (i.e., conditional-release) law that applied to the Detroit House of Correction. Reducing sentences by as much as three days per month was "most salutary in its effect upon the conduct of prisoners."[18] Good time also served multiple objectives. One of the most important was the maintenance of control over inmates. The power to grant or withhold good-time credit became a device for controlling inmate behavior. Ultimately, parole came to play a similar role.

English Origins

American penologists borrowed some of the theory and practice of conditional release from the English. An 1837 investigation by Parliament resulted in the development of the "ticket-of-leave" system. A convict sent to penal colonies in Australia began by working on a public-works chain gang. Upon evidence of good behavior he could be promoted through several "grades" and leased to private businessmen. Eventually, the convict could earn a conditional pardon and, with his ticket of leave, hire himself out as a free laborer. In time he could earn a full pardon.

Captain Alexander Maconochie is often regarded as the father of parole for his experiments at the penal colony on Norfolk Island, Northeast of Australia. When he became superintendent in 1840, Norfolk Island was a "turbulent, brutal hell," and regarded as the worst of England's penal colonies. Officials considered the two thousand inmates beyond all hope of reformation; they were mainly second and third offenders who had been rejected by the other penal colonies. Maconochie believed that these prisoners were capable of reformation and instituted the "mark" system. Under this arrangement the convict could progress through several grades and in due course earn a ticket of leave. Upon leaving Norfolk Island in 1844, Maconochie claimed great success for his system: "I found Norfolk Island a hell, but left it an orderly and well-regulated community."[19]

Conditional release next appeared in Ireland. Sir Walter Crofton, director of Irish Convict Prisons, adopted the essentials of Maconochie's system with slight modification. The convict began his term with a brief period of solitary confinement. Progression through five different classifications would culminate in a period of time in an "intermediate prison" or halfway house, and then eventual release with a ticket of leave. Because of Crofton's experiment, Americans often referred to parole as the *Irish System*.

Americans were well aware of these developments, for penology was an international community. Europeans came to study American prisons, and Americans attended a series of international conferences beginning with one in Frankfurt, Germany, in 1845. The Cincinnati congress of 1870 was also an international affair and featured a presentation of Crofton's system. Warden Gaylord Hubbell of Sing Sing had been to Ireland to study parole in 1866. At the Cincinnati congress he addressed the question of whether adults would respond to "reformatory discipline": "On this point I do not myself entertain the slightest doubt," he assured his audience; "and I am confirmed in my belief that they may be reformed."[20]

Brockway at Elmira

Zebulon Brockway led the campaign to make conditional release a formal part of American correctional practice. The Michigan commutation law applied only to female prostitutes in the Detroit House of Correction, and the Michigan legislature rejected his attempt in 1871 to extend the law to all inmates. Meanwhile, New York authorized the construction of a reformatory at Elmira in 1869. After many delays the Elmira reformatory opened in 1877 with Brockway as superintendent. Upon arriving in New York, Brockway drafted a bill calling for completely indeterminate sentences—that is, with no maximum term. He and the other advocates of the new penology argued that they should be allowed to maintain control over an offender indefinitely, until there was evidence of rehabilitation. The New York legislature balked at this radical proposal and passed a modified indeterminate sentence law in 1877 limiting sentences to "the maximum term provided by the law for the crime for which the prisoner was convicted and sentenced."[21]

Elmira was designed for males between the ages of sixteen and thirty who had been convicted of their first felony. Brockway served as superintendent until 1900 and established a reputation as the foremost authority on penology in the country. The Elmira program involved systematically grading inmate behavior. The law called for "a system of marks" under which "credit shall be earned by each prisoner" leading to increased privileges and ultimate release. Prisoners were to be "credited for good personal demeanor, diligence in labor and study and for results accomplished, and be charged for derelictions, negligences and offenses."[22] Brockway's reputation was based on his innovative educational and industrial programs. He employed college faculty, public-school teachers, attorneys, and clergy in a wide-ranging program of secular and religious instruction. At the same time, he developed prison industries and used them as a form of vocational education.

Despite Brockway's fame, the Elmira Reformatory was no more successful than other prisons. His memoirs, *Fifty Years of Prison Service* (1912), indicate that innumerable problems undermined his lofty goals. Upon becoming superintendent he found that "the prison structure was not completed; the required facilities were not at hand; the presence of so many prisoners from state prisons who were under definite sentence was an embarrassment; the building operations interfered; and a supposed need to produce income for current maintenance by utilizing the labor of prisoners also hindered."[23] In a chapter entitled "Difficult Prisoners," Brockway described a long history of breaches of discipline, near insurrections, and attempted escapes. Because there were nearly fifteen hundred inmates, the demands of custody prevailed over the ideal of individualized treatment.

The New Penology Spreads

The example of Elmira helped to spread both the indeterminate sentence and parole. The annual meetings of the National Prison Association and the National Conference of Charities and Corrections provided forums for Brockway and other advocates of the new penology. By the end of the century, eleven states had some form of the indeterminate sentence, although in some cases it applied only to the reformatory and not the prison. Another twenty states had some form of parole. Northern states were far more receptive to these innovations than southern ones, but no state adopted the completely indeterminate sentence (no maximum term) advocated by Brockway. The laws varied widely from state to state regarding provisions for maximum and minimum sentences. New York, for example, specified no minimum while Massachusetts required a minimum of two and a half years.[24]

Michigan provides an excellent case study of the slow and uncertain development of the indeterminate sentence and the manner in which it evolved out of earlier practices. Under the original Michigan constitution (1835), the governor had the "power to grant reprieves and pardons." The 1850 constitution expanded this power to allow "reprieves, commutations and pardons . . . upon such conditions and with such restrictions and limitations, as he may think proper, subject to regulations provided by law." Marvin Zalman points out that this represented "an embryonic parole system." Legislation in 1861 established the administrative machinery, but it was declared unconstitutional by the state supreme court in 1886. The court ruled that conditional pardon left the individual "half free and half slave" and therefore constituted a denial of due process of law.[25]

The Michigan legislature then passed an indeterminate-sentence law in 1889, providing for "general sentences" limited only by the statutory maximum. The law also included a parole system by which the prison board of supervisors could release prisoners at its discretion. The state supreme court, however, also found this law unconstitutional. Because the law transferred the governor's pardoning power to the prison board, the court ruled, it violated the concept of separation of powers. A constitutional amendment in 1902 finally resolved the legal questions surrounding the indeterminate sentence and parole in Michigan. The issues raised by the Michigan supreme court anticipated similar questions about the constitutional aspects of indeterminacy that appeared in the 1970s. The new penology rested upon an expansion of discretionary decision-making. Brockway and his followers, confident of their own ability to do justice, ignored many problems inherent in the idea of indeterminacy and expanded discretion.

The Habitual Criminal

Penal reformers were also uncertain about who would benefit from the reformative discipline of the indeterminate sentence and parole supervision. Delegates to the Cincinnati congress in 1870 debated whether it could be applied to adults at all.

Ambivalent feelings about the effectiveness of reformation were reflected in the emergence of "habitual-criminal" statutes, which paralleled the spread of the indeterminate sentence. Reformers pondered the problem of recidivism. Rollei Brinkerhoff told the National Prison Association in 1889 that recidivism rates for Sing Sing and Auburn prisons were 37 percent and 44 percent respectively. What should they do about the repeat offender? The advocates of the idea of rehabilitation voiced no objections to harsh treatment for the recidivist.

Louisiana passed the first habitual-criminal statute in 1870. The law enabled the judge to double or triple the prison term for second and third offenses; a fourth offense could result in life imprisonment. Ohio passed a similar law in 1884, and Massachusetts followed suit two years later. Reformers complained when these laws were not invoked. According to Brinkerhoff, "in Ohio the law has been largely nullified by the failure of prosecuting attorneys to indict habitual criminals as such." Prosecutorial discretion nullified the intent of the habitual-criminal laws.[26]

THE JUVENILE COURT

The creation of the juvenile court in 1899 brought to an end an entire era of criminal-justice institution-building. The juvenile court tied together a number of different developments within the administration of justice. Most obviously, it represented the creation of another specialized bureaucratic agency. At the same time, it marked the completion of the juvenile-justice subsystem. Finally, the juvenile court carried to its highest extreme the ideals of the new penology: individualized treatment, indeterminacy, and an expanded form of discretionary decision-making.

The 1899 Illinois law creating the Chicago juvenile court did not represent a radical departure. Instead, it marked the fulfillment of trends that had been clearly evident within the field of juvenile justice since 1825. As had been the case with respect to probation, the new law expanded and formalized existing practices. All of the juvenile-justice agencies, beginning with the house of refuge, had been committed to rehabilitation rather than punishment. The houses of refuge, moreover, sought to individualize treatment through conditional releases. The reformatory continued this practice.

The juvenile court reflected several motives. On the one hand, reformers deemed it necessary to segregate juvenile suspects from adult suspects at trial. The juvenile would be contaminated by contact with "hardened" adult criminals. On the other hand, reformers sought to formalize the discretionary decision-making by locating it in a special court. Massachusetts took the first hesitant step in 1870 when it provided for separate trials for young offenders. New York passed a similar law in 1892 (a Pennsylvania law was quickly declared unconstitutional). Massachusetts, meanwhile, created a state visiting agent to supervise all juveniles under jurisdiction of the state in 1869. In effect, the visiting agent was a juvenile probation and parole officer (adult probation was not authorized until 1878). Once again juvenile justice anticipated adult justice by many years.[27]

The primary impetus for the Chicago juvenile court came from the Chicago Women's Club. Organized in 1876 and active in a number of civic issues, the club began to take an interest in conditions in the Cook County Jail and the house of correction in the 1890s. It secured the appointment of a matron for women offenders and helped to supervise a school for boys in the jail. In 1895 Lucy L. Flower, a prominent member of the club, traveled to Massachusetts to study that state's system of juvenile probation. Upon returning she helped to draft legislation for a juvenile court. Because of its questionable constitutionality, this bill was never submitted to the legislature. But the women's club found powerful allies. A Cook County grand jury submitted a severe criticism of juvenile facilities in the county in 1898. The Chicago Bar Association, meanwhile, aided the club in drafting a new juvenile-court bill, which eventually became law on July 1, 1899.

The Chicago juvenile court incorporated the philosophy of *parens patriae*, that "the care, custody and discipline of a child shall approximate as nearly as may be that which should be given by its parents." The purpose of the court was "child-saving," the prevention of crime through early intervention. Court procedures, moreover, were to be as informal as possible. The object was to avoid placing the stigma of criminality upon the child. The juvenile-court judge was given broad discretion to individualize the disposition of each case as nearly as possible. The entire proceeding circumvented the formalities of criminal process with respect to arrest, arraignment, trial, confrontation with witnesses, introduction of evidence, etc. Supporters of the juvenile court saw it as a "helping" rather than a "punishing" agency.

In Denver, Colorado, Judge Ben B. Lindsey established a juvenile court through creative adaptation. The state did not have a juvenile-court law per se, but Judge Lindsey discoverd that an 1899 school law gave his county court jurisdiction over "juvenile disorderly" persons as well as anyone who was a "habitual truant" or engaged in "incorrigible, vicious or immoral" behavior. Although somewhat uneasy about stretching the law in this way, Judge Lindsey proceeded to operate a juvenile court in 1901. Instead of a formal trial, he talked with the children in his chambers. While the law gave him the power to sentence offenders to the reformatory, he generally suspended the sentence and used truant officers from the school system as probation officers. Lindsey subsequently became the most ardent advocate of the juvenile-court idea, traveling across the country urging other states to create similar institutions.

The End of An Era

The creation of the juvenile court brought to an end the era of criminal-justice institution-building. Not every state had adopted all of the new institutions by 1900 (although most would by 1915), but the basic framework of the modern-justice system was in place. No new institutions of significance appeared after 1900. In response to the profound changes that overtook American society between 1815 and 1900, a new apparatus of social control had developed. It was a complex network of specialized agencies, grouped into "subsystems" and designed to control crime, deviance, and disorder.

5

CRIME AND POLITICS IN
THE NINETEENTH CENTURY

IMPACT OF THE NEW APPARATUS

What effect did the new criminal-justice apparatus have on the administration of justice and the quality of American life? The institutional size of the apparatus expanded enormously between 1815 and 1900. By the end of the century, there was a vast range of agencies that had not existed before—police, the modern prison, juvenile institutions, community-based correctional programs. They were capable of exercising control over large numbers of American citizens. Did the quality of justice improve as a consequence? Or did it worsen?

These questions are central to an understanding of the history of American criminal justice. The traditional liberal interpretation is that the criminal-justice system has played a positive role in the maintenance of social control. The primary failure, according to the liberal view, has been the inability of the system to fulfill its ideals because of political interference, corruption, inefficiency, or a lack of adequate resources. Recently, Marxist criminologists have challenged this view. The Marxists argue that the criminal-justice apparatus plays an oppressive role in American society, serving the needs of the power elite by repressing the poor, the working class, and minority groups.[1]

Neither view adequately reflects the complex reality of the role of the criminal-justice system in American society. The Marxist view is only partly correct. The criminal-justice system has served the interests of those in power, and the poor and nonwhite minority groups have suffered the worst injustices at the hands of the system. But in the nineteenth century working-class and ethnic groups mobilized considerable political power and captured control of criminal-justice agencies. The wealthy elite, far from being all-powerful, bitterly complained about their inability to control the police and the lower courts. The cop on the beat might brutalize an unemployed worker, but he did so for his own reasons, not to protect the industrial capitalists.

The liberal view is also partly correct and partly wrong. The criminal-justice system did exercise an increasingly pervasive social control, both direct and indirect. The mere existence of the apparatus raised public expectations about how much order should prevail in society. Because there was a mechanism for dealing with disorder, the public came to think of it as something that could and should be eradicated. This revolution of rising expectations, a major part of the urbanization process, developed over a long period. It began slowly in the nineteenth century and continued to reach new heights in the twentieth. But the liberal view takes too uncritical a view of the criminal-justice system. Corruption and inefficiency were not the only problems. The new apparatus, as the Marxists contend, was a tool for suppressing and controlling unpopular individuals, groups, and ideas. And those in power did not hesitate to use the system unjustly.

Crime and Crime Rates

Did crime increase or decrease in the nineteenth century? Was there more or less disorder? Unfortunately, answers to these questions are not available. Much of the necessary data does not exist, while available records are extremely unreliable. The questions, moreover, may not be susceptible to precise measurement. What is acceptable behavior in one era may be unacceptable in another, and vice versa. As noted previously, we lack the "index of disorder" that would permit meaningful comparisons of long-term trends.

The concept of crime itself is problematic. The word refers to many different types of behavior and means different things to different people. Frequently, *crime* is a code word that expresses fear of social change. For Charles Loring Brace and his audience, "the Dangerous Classes" were the lower-class Irish immigrants in the urban slums.

Crimes against persons and property may have actually declined in the nineteenth century. This is the tentative conclusion of the few historians who have explored the available crime statistics. Theodore Ferdinand argues that "the aggregate crime rate in Boston has shown an almost uninterrupted decline from 1875–78 to the present era." Roger Lane, studying criminal violence in Massachusetts over a similar period, found that "serious crime in metropolitan Boston has declined sharply between the middle of the 19th century and the middle of the 20th." Samuel Warner, meanwhile, discoverd a sharp reduction in riot and disorder in Philadelphia during the same period.[2]

Did the quality of urban life improve even as the cities grew larger and larger? Lane and Warner believe that the process of urbanization exerted a civilizing effect. People gradually adjusted to urban living and, as time went on, developed higher expectations for the quality of life. Roger Lane has proposed that crime statistics may mean just the opposite of what they appear to indicate. Increased arrests for drunkenness and disorderly conduct may reflect a lowered tolerance for such conduct, not an increase in its incidence. A formal complaint of assault and battery is a more civilized response to a dispute than retaliatory violence.

Riots continued to plague the American city. The extent of rioting declined somewhat from its peak in the 1830s and 1840s, but the most important change was in the nature of the disorders. The riots of the pre-Civil War years were largely ethnic conflicts, pitting native-born Protestants against Irish-Catholic immigrants. After 1870 riots were more often industrial disputes.

The question of "deviant" behavior became even more complex as the nineteenth century progressed. Immigration brought to this country a rich variety of cultures, and each group attempted to preserve its own heritage by withdrawing as much as possible into a distinct subculture. Urban communities fragmented into distinct neighborhoods defined by class and ethnic identity. Every city had its own "Irish Quarter," "Little Italy," "Quality Hill" (where the wealthy elite lived), and so on.

As the cultural consensus broke down, the old Anglo-Saxon majority sought to impose its own definition of "Americanism." Alcohol became a touchstone of morality. The temperance movement began in earnest in the 1820s and remained a vital force in American politics for the next one hundred years, when it culminated in national prohibition. In the eyes of middle-class Anglo-Saxon moralists, German-Americans desecrated the Sabbath by drinking on Sunday (a practice the Germans found quite consistent with their Old World cultural patterns), and they firmly believed that Irish-Americans did nothing else but drink. Between the 1820s and the advent of national prohibition, the drinking issue dominated state and local politics. The opponents of drink tried to restrict the consumption of liquor or to ban it altogether.[3]

The political significance of the drinking question was also closely tied to the role of the saloon. Among the working-class communities in the cities, the saloon was a vital institution. More than just a place to get a drink and relax, it was the clubhouse of the political machine, where ward heelers met their constituents. The attack on drinking, therefore, was also an attack on the saloon (by the 1890s the major prohibition organization was the Anti-Saloon League) and the very fabric of working-class life and politics. The political machines fought back by simply nullifying the laws through their control of the police. The drinking question became inextricably tied up with issues of police corruption and the control of municipal government.

The controversy over drinking as a form of "deviance" represents a theme that runs through the entire history of American criminal justice. The attempt to maintain a cultural consensus in the colonial period, as we have seen, largely involved an effort to suppress religious unorthodoxy (the persecution of the Quakers, the Salem witchcraft hysteria). In contemporary society the question of "victimless crimes" involves broad questions of cultural values and lifestyle. The use of marijuana and other soft drugs, homosexuality, and other practices are viewed by many as "deviant" because they challenge the official morality. The American political tradition has been one in which questions of culture and morality are dealt with through the use of the criminal law.[4]

Roots of Organized Crime

The futile attempt to regulate morality laid the foundations for the modern phenomenon of organized crime. Despite the views of the middle-class moralists, there was a large demand for liquor (regardless of the day or hour), gambling, and prostitution. To meet this demand vice districts flourished in every major city. As we have already noted, this open lawbreaking was possible because of the corruption pervading all of municipal government. Corruption resisted every effort to stamp it out because it offered something for just about everyone. The "consumers" could have their liquor, gambling, and sex. Providing these services offered access to small-business careers for working-class entrepreneurs. The police and other municipal officials obtained handsome payoffs for ignoring illegal activity. And the trade-off between vice and nonenforcement provided a solid foundation for the political machines. Protest as they might, the middle-class moralists could not break this potent combination of mutual self-interest.

By contemporary standards the nineteenth-century vice districts represented a relatively *dis*organized form of criminal activity. Businesses were small and run by individual entrepreneurs. The business of providing illicit recreation, however, gradually followed the trend of legal ventures and became more highly organized. According to David R. Johnson, gambling syndicates appeared in the 1880s as vice entrepreneurs attempted to enlarge their profits and put their businesses on a more solid footing. The major turning point in the development of organized crime came somewhat later, in the 1920s. By outlawing alcoholic beverages altogether, prohibition simply enlarged the potential market and put a higher premium on a more businesslike approach to providing an illicit substance. But the origins of organized crime could be found in the vice districts of the nineteenth-century cities.[5]

ADMINISTERING JUSTICE

Continuities in Criminal Law and Procedure

While the institutional apparatus of apprehension and punishment was expanding during the nineteenth century, the substantive criminal law changed only slightly. The most important changes were subtle shifts in emphasis, and the dominant trend was a steady secularization of the law. We have seen that by the end of the colonial period, the law had lost much of its original concern with religious belief and behavior. Blasphemy, for example, was no longer regarded as a major crime. This is not to say that there was less concern with public morality. As the long conflict over alcoholic beverages suggests, concern over public morality simply shifted to concern over different types of behavior.

The secularization of the criminal law entailed a greater emphasis on crimes of a purely economic nature. As industrialization progressed and the ecomony became more complex, the number of laws increased dramatically. In Rhode Island the number of crimes increased from 50 to 128 between 1822 and 1872, while Indiana law specified more than 300 crimes by 1881. The criminal law remained a tool in the hands of those with political power, and as Lawrence Friedman suggests in this *History of American Law,* it played an increasingly important role as an administrative device for economic regulation. In most cases it was a latent threat, to be invoked only as a last resort.[6]

The regulatory effect of the law, of course, was not felt equally. In many areas the criminal law served the interests of industrial capitalists at the expense of workers and their unions. Initially, unionism was defined as a criminal conspiracy. But even after the 1842 *Commonwealth* v. *Hunt* decision, which rejected that concept, unions and union leaders felt the brunt of injunctions and other legal devices. At the same time, the law of vagrancy was used to control both the movement and behavior of the poor and the unemployed. Jerome Hall's classic study, *Theft, Law and Society*, although dealing primarily with earlier English law, identifies the changing role of the law in protecting the dominant economic interests.[7] In the United States, enforcement of vagrancy laws was a common response to the major depressions of the 1870s and 1890s.

Criminal procedure, the formal steps in the process by which the state prosecuted a suspect, also changed very little during the nineteenth century. The key elements of Anglo-American criminal procedure were well established by the colonial period. In 1936, the commemorate its fiftieth anniversary, the *Harvard Law Review* published a series of articles on developments in the various aspects of American law since 1886. The authors of the article on the administration of justice began by describing a murder case, following it from arrest through final disposition. The formal steps were familiar: arrest, grand-jury investigation, indictment, arraignment, trial (with assigned counsel), the admission of evidence, examination of witnesses, and a final verdict of not guilty. Then the authors revealed that the case had actually been tried in Massachusetts in 1873. The familiarity of the process was evidence of the relative "changelessness" of the criminal process.[8]

But subtle differences in emphasis did occur in criminal procedure, as they did in criminal law. The administration of justice became dominated with what Roscoe Pound later called the "hypertrophy of procedure," the preoccupation with the technical details of the process. Verdicts were frequently reversed for minor errors. A death sentence handed down by a North Carolina jury in 1801 was voided for a misspelling: ". . . in and upon the aforesaid left *brest* of him."[9]

Preoccupation with the technicalities of procedure was due in part to the increasingly important role played by the defense attorney. American practice differed from its English heritage by allowing the defense a much larger role in the criminal process. Meanwhile, the legal profession in nineteenth-century America became wildly democratic. One could easily enter the profession through an apprenticeship, by "reading law" with a practicing attorney. As a consequence the legal profession became an important avenue of upward mobility. Attorneys from immigrant and low-income backgrounds established themselves by serving the needs of people from similar backgrounds in the lower courts. The experienced criminal-defense lawyer, master of the intricate technicalities of criminal procedure, was one of the major resources that low-income groups could rely on in the face of the law.

The Amendment That Would Not Die

One of the most important consequences of the Civil War and Reconstruction period was the passage of the Fourteenth Amendment to the U.S. Constitution. Ratified in 1868, it specified that no state shall "deprive any person of life, liberty, or property, without due process of law; nor deny to any person within its jurisdiction the equal protection of the laws." The amendment was designed to protect the civil rights of the newly freed blacks in the South. Northern attitudes on the race question changed soon after the Reconstruction period, and the federal courts turned their backs on the question of civil rights for blacks. By the end of the nineteenth century, in fact, the Fourteenth Amendment was largely used to protect corporations from government regulation.

The original civil-rights purpose of the Fourteenth Amendment, however, "refused to die." After laying dormant for many decades it was rediscovered in the mid-twentieth century. It became a principal tool not only in the civil-rights movement of the 1950s and 1960s but also in the "due process" revolution in American criminal justice. Under the leadership of the U.S. Supreme Court in the 1950s and 1960s, the federal courts used the Fourteenth Amendment to examine the practices of state and local criminal-justice agencies and impose standards of constitutionality upon them. The Reconstruction-era Fourteenth Amendment proved to be a legacy of inestimable importance in the history of American criminal justice.[10]

The Jury as the Voice of the People

Juries played an important though declining role in the criminal process during the nineteenth century. The grand jury continued to serve many of the functions it had acquired in the colonial period. It was less important in its role of handling routine crimes and handing down indictments. Far more important was its role as an investigatory agency. In this respect the grand jury was a part of the administrative machinery of local government. It was a means by which one segment of the community could place a check upon official administrative agencies, by reviewing their work and publishing reports of wrongdoing or negligence. Thus, the grand jury still deserved its name as *the people's panel.*

Trial juries were an even more direct instrument of popular justice. The jury trial had not yet been completely displaced by plea bargaining. Not only did more cases go to trial, but juries still often ruled on both the facts of the case and the law itself, as they had done during the struggle for independence, when local juries served as bulwarks against British-controlled judges. This jury "lawlessness"—the right of the jury to judge both the facts and the law and to disregard the instructions of the judge— resulted in arbitrary, capricious, and often simply absurd decisions. A jury in South Carolina acquitted a defendant in 1827 despite his guilty plea. The jury foreman blandly explained that the defendant "has always been such a liar that we could not believe him." The jury became the direct voice of the community, expressing all of its irrationalities and prejudices. Jerome Frank described prejudice as "the thirteenth juror."[11]

The question of the proper role of the jury posed, in a direct fashion, the dilemma of "popular justice." The Jeffersonian view of an active and unchecked jury was solidly grounded in democratic principles. Alexis de Tocqueville observed that "the jury is pre-eminently a political institution; it should be regarded as one form of the sovereignty of the people." But the result was also the antithesis of consistency, one of the hallmarks of the rule of law. In 1835 the U.S. Supreme Court denied to the jury the right to judge the law in federal cases. Then, in a major review of the entire question in 1895, the Court greatly curbed the role of the jury in state proceedings as well. From its prominent place in the criminal process, the trial jury began its long slide into its limited contemporary role.

The Prosecutor and the Rise of Plea Bargaining

As the jury played a less important role in the criminal process, the prosecutor rose in prominence. Like the sheriff, the prosecutor was a major figure in county politics. Prosecutors went by a variety of names: county attorney, county prosecutor, state's attorney, district attorney. An 1867 survey revealed that in Massachusetts district attorneys were elected in each county and paid a fixed salary, while in Connecticut they were appointed by the judges of the superior court for two-year terms and paid through a system of fees. Prosecutors in New Jersey received $10 when the defendant entered a guilty plea, $15 when guilt was determined by jury trial, and nothing if the defendant was acquitted. One called it "a great stimulus to vigilance," while another complained that it "is bad, tempting to undue exertion to convict, and tempting to receive rewards from the defendants to favor them."[12]

Prosecutors were swamped by the rising load of criminal cases. In 1863 the lone Cuyahoga County, Ohio (Cleveland), prosecutor handled 60 indictments. By 1880 two prosecutors handled 187 indictments, and by 1900 three individuals handled 512 cases. The situation worsened in the next two decades. By 1920 there were six attorneys in the prosecutor's office but the number of cases had risen to 2,762.[13]

The historical origins of plea bargaining remain obscure. Historians have only begun to explore this aspect of the history of criminal justice. Fragmentary evidence, however, indicates that guilty pleas had become a major device for disposing of cases by the middle of the nineteenth century and were probably the dominant method by the end of the century. Milton Heuman found that in Connecticut between 1880 and 1910 only slightly more than 10 percent of criminal cases went to trial. Even more important, there was no significant difference between the busy courts in urban areas and the less busy courts in rural areas. The pressure of a heavy caseload, then, was not necessarily the primary factor in encouraging plea bargains. Then as now, plea bargains served a number of purposes. Even where the caseload was light, the bargain was a convenient means of settling cases where guilt was obvious.[14]

Surprisingly, the development of plea bargaining attracted little attention. Given the prominent role of the jury, particularly in the early part of the nineteenth century, one would expect that its gradual demise would cause some alarm. Enoch Wines and Theodore Dwight were among the few people to notice. In their 1867 survey of prisons, they appended a questionnaire investigating different aspects of the criminal process. Two questions dealt with plea bargaining. The respondent from Connecticut indicated that "more than one-half of those arraigned plead guilty," while in Kentucky "the proportion that plead guilty is small— say, one in twenty." Did prosecutor and defendant bargain over the charge or the sentence? The responses indicated varied patterns. In New Hampshire defendants pleaded "to the lowest grade of offense charged," while in Kentucky pleas were entered "with the view of inducing the jury to fix the shortest period of confinement."[15] Plea bargaining did not arouse great concern, however, until the 1920s.

The increased use of the negotiated plea—involving the gradual eclipse of the jury and an enlarged role for the prosecutor— was also part of the general trend toward bureaucratic specialization. The public played an increasingly less direct role in the administration of criminal justice as particular tasks were assumed by specialized bureaucracies. Viewed in long-range terms, the prosecutor replaced the jury just as the professional police replaced the citizen night watch. The replacement of the stocks, the pillory, and public floggings with the prison also reduced direct public involvement in punishment.

Courts and Politics

The basic structure of the American court system has remained virtually unchanged since the founding of the republic. The multilayered structure of trial and appellate courts prevailed at both the federal and state levels. The increased volume of business forced the few changes that did occur. At the federal level Congress established a circuit judge for each of the nine circuits in 1869; this judge handled cases along with the Supreme Court justice assigned to that circuit. In 1891 Congress established the circuit courts of appeal, completing the modern federal court system. The trend was toward specialized courts in the growing cities to handle the large volume of minor cases. Police courts or mayor's courts, as they were often called, tried the large number of drunk and disorderly cases that came to trial.

The county court was the workhorse of the criminal-justice system. And like the other major components of the system, the courts were thoroughly immersed in partisan politics and utterly corrupt. A valuable picture of the many roles of this pivotal institution emerges from Robert M. Ireland's study, *The County Courts in Antebellum Kentucky*. Justices of the peace, appointed by the governor, comprised the county courts. By 1848 Kentucky had a total of 1,550 JPs. The county court retained the multiple functions it had developed in the colonial era and exercised both judicial and executive functions. The Kentucky county courts, for example, administered the poor laws, collected taxes, and at one point even acquired the job of running ferries across rivers throughout the state. Criminal cases constituted only a small portion of the court's work.[16]

The political role of the county courts was based on the appointment process. In making appointments the governor deferred to the wishes of the local political establishment. The real power of the courts lay in their authority to appoint all other county officials, including the sheriff, county attorney, clerk, bailiff, and jailer. These other offices offered rich opportunities for corruption. The appointment process became so tainted that the job of sheriff and other appointments were literally put up for auction. A two-year term as sheriff of Fayette County, second largest in the state, cost about $2,000. In the smaller counties, a hopeful applicant expected to pay between $500 and $800. Incredibly, little attempt was made to keep the bribery a secret. The sale of offices and the general corruption in the Kentucky county courts indicate that the big cities had no monopoly on corruption. The situation in the rural areas was just as bad. The problem was not due to a few evil persons, or even to a faulty administrative structure. Rather, the heart of the problem was the American political system itself. In a democratic system the courts were open to popular influence. The people, speaking through the political machines, preferred corruption; it offered a little something for just about everyone.

Like the jury, the county courts were seen as an instrument of community sentiment. James Willard Hurst characterizes the JP as a "neighborhood court," one that would serve community interests (at least those of the powerful elite and the respectable majority). In the American federal system, the tradition of localism took firm root. Courts, sheriffs, and prosecutors served local interests, not necessarily some abstract concept of "the law." Americans viewed the law as a public utility, a device for getting things done, not as an institution that transcended immediate interests.[17] The demands of popular justice dictated a faith in how the law could further self-interest, not how it might serve the public interest.

Choosing Judges

The selection of judges was an issue of some controversy in the nineteenth century. A variety of methods prevailed, and states wrestled with the various alternatives. The basic struggle rested in the tension between the principles of appointment and election. The former, an elitist approach, seemed best to guarantee competence; the latter method conformed more strictly to the idea of democracy. At mid-century all judges in Massachusetts were appointed by the governor. Michigan stood at the opposite extreme; all judgeships became elective in 1851. Other states employed a variety of alternatives. In New Jersey justices of the peace were elected to five-year terms, common-pleas judges appointed by the legislature to five-year terms, and supreme-court judges appointed to six-year terms by the governor.[18]

The popular election of judges reached its peak during the nineteenth century. Between 1776 and 1831, 9.1 percent of all judges in the United States were chosen by election. Between 1832 and 1885, the figure rose to 73.3 percent.[19] This shift was but one part of the general trend toward democratization in the mid-nineteenth century, and many public offices became elective rather than appointive. The mayor of New York City, for example, became an elected official in 1832. The election of judges, however, eventually generated much discontent. Beginning in the latter years of the century, the tide turned and judgeships became more commonly selected by appointment.

In the final analysis the precise method of selection made little difference. Ireland's study of the Kentucky county courts, for example, clearly indicate that the appointment of JPs was dictated by the local political elite. Politics reigned supreme. The alternative of election or appointment meant, in practical terms, a question of which political faction would have the advantage.

"Rough Justice" in the Lower Courts

We have only a vague idea of what happened to most criminal cases during this period. In one of the few historical studies of the lower courts, Robert Percival and Lawrence Friedman paint a picture of the "rough justice" in the Oakland, California, police court between 1872 and 1910. Not everyone arrested faced further prosecution: nearly 10 percent were either released or returned to their parents or some institution. Most of the remaining defendants were released on their own recognizance. Bail was required in about 38 percent of the cases. Low bail ($20-$50) was set in more than half the cases involving morals and regulatory-ordinance violations, apparently in the belief that the expected forfeiture would constitute sufficient punishment. Relations between the judge, the prosecutor, and the police were informal and cooperative "with the judge frequently deferring to the prosecutor's bail recommendations."[20]

The courtroom itself, according to Percival and Friedman, was "a curious combination of legalism set amidst great informality." They found that "in the same court that entertained technical objections to the form of complaints, clucking chickens were introduced into evidence in theft cases. The same judge who presided over an endlessly technical voir dire once fined himself $50 for being drunk." By 1880–1881 the jury trial was a rare event in the Oakland police court. Only 30 percent of all cases were tried, and only 5 percent of those (28 out of 540) involved a jury. The criminal process was rather swift. The average time for all cases in 1880–1881 was 2.7 days, with crimes against property taking an average of five days and drunkenness cases less than half a day.[21]

ADMINISTERING INJUSTICE

The "rough justice" meted out by the criminal-justice system did not treat all Americans equally. The lower classes, especially the unemployed, the recent immigrant, the black or red American, and the alleged "deviant" suffered the worst abuses at the hands of the police, the courts, and the prisons. Yet, injustice was not terribly systematic either. The Marxist argument of continual, systematic, and thorough repression is not sustained by the evidence. In practice, the administration of justice was extremely arbitrary and capricious. Some suffered terrible abuses, while many others escaped the clutches of the system.

Capriciousness was most evident in the behavior of the police. According to the principles of Robert Peel, the police were a continual presence throughout society. But in reality the American police mounted a token presence at best. Patrol officers were spread too thin, and too often they were busy evading their responsibilities. There was nothing systematic about arrest patterns. Percival and Friedman characterize police operations in Oakland as a vast "trawling" operation. Many citizens were caught up in the net of arrest, but many others were ignored. The bulk of the arrests in every American city were for drunkenness or disorderly conduct (at least 60 percent and often as high as 80 percent of all arrests). The typical arrestee in Oakland was a thirty-three-year-old white male laborer "who drank too much on Saturday night, made a rumpus, and was swept along by the police."[22]

Arrest was not the only sanction available to the police officer. The "curbside justice" of the billy club was a common form of punishment for many citizens. According to Alexander "Clubber" Williams of the New York City Police Department, there was more law in his billy club than in the statute books. Police brutality was random and irrational. Officers did not wade through the streets systematically clubbing the poor. Violence was reserved for those who, for one reason or another, offended the sensibilities of an officer.[23]

The advent of the prison added a new dimension to the pattern of injustice. Colonial society had been more honest about corporal punishment, inflicting it openly. The prison moved corporal punishment behind walls and out of public view. The expansion of the correctional system through the nineteenth century resulted in a dramatic increase in the number of Americans incarcerated. Margaret Cahalan estimates that the number incarcerated per 100,000 in the population increased from 29.1 in 1850 to 115.2 thirty years later.[24]

The majority of the public tolerated the abuses of the system. As we have seen, both police and prison brutality were forms of "delegated vigilantism." The middle-class person undoubtedly felt that the victims "deserved" it. By the same token, the stigma of incarceration became a self-fulfilling label. Only a few prominent citizens protested the pervasive injustice. Governor John Peter Altgeld of Illinois spoke out against "our penal machinery and its victims." Writing in 1902, Clarence Darrow condemned "the machinery of justice" because it "simply takes a man into its hopper and grinds out a criminal at the end." But these were isolated voices of dissent. Politics offered the most effective protection against abuse. Individuals belonging to groups with some political power had avenues of redress, while members of politically powerless groups suffered the worst injustices.[25]

The Black American

The end of slavery changed the official legal status of most black Americans, but it did little to improve the quality of criminal justice they received. The racial bias that was built into the American legal system during the early colonial period remained. The laws of many southern states specified different punishments for black offenders. The widespread arbitrariness of discretionary decision-making brought unequal justice to blacks in both the North and South. The Reconstruction period ended with the triumph of Ku Klux Klan vigilantism. Blacks were denied political participation and reduced to economic servitude. Beginning in the 1890s, segregation became institutionalized. The disenfranchisement of black voters, achieved by statute, constitutional amendment, and terror, had a direct impact on the administration of criminal justice. It removed blacks from juries and eliminated any voice in the selection of criminal justice officials. The criminal justice system was one of the major instruments of white supremacy.[26]

Vigilante violence played a major part in the establishment of white supremacy. In the last sixteen years of the nineteenth century, there were a total of 2,500 recorded lynchings in the United States. Most of the victims were southern blacks (western states accounted for most of the rest). In 1900 alone more than 100 blacks were lynched. Lynch-mob participants hardly needed to fear prosecution with the machinery of justice firmly in white hands.

Under the system of white supremacy, four different standards of criminal justice evolved. Crimes by blacks against blacks were treated with indifference and inaction, while crimes by whites against blacks were hardly crimes at all. Crime by whites against whites were "normal" crimes, while crimes by blacks against whites could provoke the most vicious retribution. The majority of lynching victims were blacks accused of either the murder or rape of a white person. The lynch mob offered a swifter and more certain revenge than the official criminal-justice machinery.

Indian Justice

The legal status of American Indians was even more complicated than that of blacks. The individual Indian was caught in a maze of conflicting cultures and institutions. Traditional Indian culture maintained its distinct approach to crime and punishment. "Central to the concept of Indian law," writes Wilcomb Washburn, "was retributive justice." Kinship relations were the principal mechanisms of enforcement: "In the absence of complex formal legal machinery of the sort familiar to a European society, revenge or retribution was normally sought by the kin of the aggrieved party." This approach was not "lawless" by any means; rather, retribution was governed by a sophisticated web of tribal customs.[27]

White conquest shattered much of the traditional culture of the American Indian and imposed on it an alien legal system: the impersonal and bureaucratic formality of Anglo-American law. The existence of the Indian reservation made matters even more confusing. The tribal police were created in an attempt to control and assimilate the individual Indian. Jurisdiction over particular crimes depended upon the race of the victim and the offender, the crime itself, and where it occurred. As a result the offender might be subject to a federal, state, or tribal criminal-justice system. The problem of resolving this ambiguity continues to occupy the attention of constitutional scholars.

No matter which jurisdiction applied, however, the individual Indian did not fare well. State and federal criminal-justice systems were openly racist, dominated by whites who regarded the Indians as "savages," and tribal institutions were corrupted by the general condition of powerlessness and the more specific manipulation of opportunistic whites.

The Working Class

Members of the white working class suffered at the hands of the criminal-justice system as well. Individual workers, especially those who might drink to excess on occasion, were among the principal victims of police activity. The history of the American labor movement, meanwhile, is punctuated by incidents of police attacks on strikers. During both the 1877 railroad riots and the 1886 Haymarket Square incidents, the Chicago police ran amok, clubbing citizens indiscriminantly. And the chief of the Chicago police proudly defended his men's action in 1877. The machinery of justice punished the striker or union organizer rather than the employer or strikebreaker, regardless of who had committed what act.

Yet, the working class fought back with some success. Through the sheer weight of numbers, its members wielded considerable influence in local politics. This gave them influence over the police and the lower courts. Businessmen continually complained about the unreliability of the police, who were drawn from the working class and often identified with the interests of striking workers. Their effort to develop more dependable forms of law enforcement resulted in private police and such quasipublic agencies as the notorious Pennsylvania Coal and Iron Police. The militia was often as unreliable as the local police, and business interests encouraged the use of federal troops in labor disputes and the eventual development of the state police.

The working class also used its political influence to preserve the integrity of its lifestyle. The attack on the saloon by temperence advocates was a direct threat to the social and political culture of the working class. Through their control over the police and a systematic pattern of nonenforcement, the working class was able to subvert the laws designed to control the consumption of alcohol.

The American working class was not homogeneous, however. Ethnic identity fragmented it into a jumble of mutual hostilities. As a consequence, some groups fared better at the hands of the criminal-justice system than others. The Irish mastery of politics gave them influence over the police (hence the legend of the Irish cop) and the courts out of all proportion to other ethnic groups. Each group had to fight to win its share of political power. The system inflicted the worst abuses upon the most recently arrived ethnic group, the one that had no political power and was still regarded as alien or "foreign."

Vigilante Justice

For the most part, businessmen tolerated routine police corruption. The vice districts and the systematic payoffs did not threaten their economic interests. But in certain instances corruption so outraged the elite of the community that they felt compelled to take the law into their own hands and circumvent the official criminal-justice system altogether. The nineteenth century was the heyday of American vigilantism. Historian Richard M. Brown has documented 326 vigilante movements, most of them in this period.[28] Undoubtedly many more went unrecorded.

There were several sources of vigilantism. As we have already seen, people sometimes took the law into their own hands because the official agencies were too weak or simply did not exist. More often, however, vigilantism was a means by which the social and economic elite imposed their own standards of justice. The Ku Klux Klan was one of the most successful instances, but vigilantes purged their community of alleged "undesirables" in other areas of the country as well. The "white cappers," for example, threatened or whipped people deemed lazy and shiftless. Other victims included religious or political minority groups.

The San Francisco Vigilance Committee of 1856 was an example of vigilantism as a political movement. Business and commercial interests in San Francisco used it to destroy the local Democratic party machine, dominated by Irish-Catholics. The committee was organized when a reputed criminal with political connections was not convicted of a murder. Numbering between six thousand and eight thousand people, the committee took the law into its own hands: it arrested, tried, convicted, and executed four men and deported another twenty-eight from the city. The victims included many leaders of the local Democratic party. According to Brown, the vigilantes were primarily "concerned with local political and fiscal reform. They wished to capture control of the government from the dominant faction of Irish-Catholic Democrats." And in this they succeeded. Reborn as the People's party, the Vigilance Committee controlled city government for the next ten years.[29]

Vigilantism was popular justice with a vengeance. As Brown argues in his thorough study of the subject, vigilantes justified their actions in terms of democratic theory and the right of revolution. When government failed to serve their interests, they had a natural right to take action. Both the Klan in the South and the Vigilance Committee in San Francisco acted on the instinctive premise that they were defending the good of the community.

The lawlessness of these organized groups was only one manifestation of a general feature of American criminal justice in the period. The cop on the beat dispensed "curbside justice" confident that the "undesirables" deserved it. The prison guard also believed that the inmate merited the inhumane conditions and brutal treatment. In a similar though less vicious fashion, prosecutors, juries, and judges meted out justice on the basis of what they felt was proper. They justified this arbitrary style of justice in terms of the desires of the community. The pressures of this popular sense of justice were at odds with the ideals of consistency, equality, and fairness; that is, the rule of law.

III

REFORMING THE SYSTEM, 1900–THE PRESENT

6

PROGRESSIVISM AND CRIMINAL JUSTICE, 1900–1919

AN AGE OF REFORM

The spirit of reform swept American society in the first two decades of the twentieth century. *Progressivism,* as it was called, did not consist of a single unified movement. Rather, it was a mood that embraced many separate but parallel movements: antitrust, railroad regulation, the reform of municipal government, women's suffrage, the abolition of child labor, and many others. The mood of progressivism was a sense that American institutions had to be changed to adapt to the demands of a growing urban-industrial society.

Progressivism brought a renewed burst of reform to criminal justice. The era of Theodore Roosevelt and Woodrow Wilson also witnessed the birth of police professionalization, the rapid spread and development of correctional programs, an effort to raise standards in the legal profession, and a renewed campaign to abolish the death penalty. But even more important than these individual reforms, progressivism brought a new perspective to criminal justice. Experts increasingly thought in terms of a criminal-justice *system*. The various institutions, they recognized, had a common purpose. Reform was needed to streamline this system to make it more effective.

The reformers of the progressive era disagreed, however, about the exact purpose of the criminal-justice system. Their disagreement reflected the divided spirit of progressivism generally. One school of thought stressed *efficiency*. Theodore Roosevelt, for example, supported conservation because it would promote the more efficient use of natural resources. Various types of economic regulation were also intended to eliminate the costly and inefficient aspects of business competiton. The other school of thought emphasized *social justice* and sought to help the disadvantaged and to reduce the inequities of industrial society. At times the goals of efficiency and social justice coincided; at other times they conflicted. The result was a shifting set of political coalitions on specific issues.[1]

The same two perspectives applied to the question of criminal justice. One group of reformers desired to increase the efficiency of the system by improving its capacity to apprehend, convict, and either punish or correct criminals. Another group emphasized social justice. This could mean many things. For some it meant assuming a social-work orientation, of using the criminal-justice system to help rather than punish individuals.

The tension between these two perspectives on criminal justice is best described by Herbert Packer in his famous essay "Two Models of the Criminal Process." Packer's *crime-control model* emphasizes efficiency: the effective suppression of crime through a swift and certain criminal process. His *due-process model*, meanwhile, is a social-justice perspective, seeking to limit the powers of criminal-justice officials and protect individual liberties. It applies particularly to the rights of the powerless.[2]

The ebb and flow of criminal-justice reform through the twentieth century reflected the continuing tension between the efficiency-oriented crime-control perspective and the due-process-oriented social-justice perspective. Neither one ever gained complete dominance. But both shared a "systems" approach to the administration of criminal justice, and for both sides, the systems perspective fostered the nationalization of crime control. As crime became an increasingly important issue in American politics, the search for solutions led to greater involvement by groups with a national focus. National professional associations such as the American Bar Association and the International Association of Chiefs of Police were in the forefront of reform. Inevitably, the experts turned to the federal government as the agency with the greatest capacity to mobilize resources and effect change. The nationalization of crime control forms a major theme in twentieth-century criminal-justice history. The federal role began hesitantly in the progressive era, grew erratically over the next few decades, and finally reached its culmination in 1968 with the creation of the Law Enforcement Assistance Administration (LEAA).

Roscoe Pound's Call to Action

Roscoe Pound electrified the annual meeting of the American Bar Association in 1906 with his address "The Causes of Popular Dissatisfaction with the Administration of Justice." Pound was then in his mid-thirties, dean of the University of Nebraska Law School, and just beginning a career as one of the most brilliant and influential persons in the history of American law. Younger members of the bar found the 1906 speech a call to action; older members tried to have it suppressed.

Pound's address was a classic statement of progressive-era values. He indicted the American legal system as archaic and inadequate to the needs of a complex urban-industrial society. While he spoke primarily about the civil law, his remarks applied equally well to the administration of criminal justice. Pound embraced the efficiency perspective, maintaining that the legal system was ineffective in carrying out its obligation to suppress crime. The source of the problem, he argued, was the spirit of the common law itself. The Anglo-American legal tradition emphasized the individual—the individual plaintiff, suspect, witness, etc. Modern society, however, demanded a collective approach, an emphasis on broader social goals. Pound saw an irreconcilable "conflict between the individualist spirit of the common law and the collectivist spirit of the present age."[3]

One of the major consequences of the emphasis on the individual was the so-called *sporting theory of justice*. The legal process became a contest in which the main objective was to "beat the law" rather than arrive at the truth. The pursuit of victory permitted the use of any legal maneuver. With respect to criminal justice, Pound objected to the fact that defense attorneys could use technical procedural errors to gain acquittal for their clients. The criminal process, in short, was inefficient on two counts: too costly and time-consuming, and filled with loopholes that might benefit the criminal. (Pound and his followers developed many of the ideas that conservative "law-and-order" advocates would reiterate in the 1960s and 1970s.)

Despite this bleak picture, Pound saw reasons for optimism. He noted that many of the leading law schools and bar associations had become active advocates of change. The spirit of progressivism, he believed, would inspire an entire generation: "We may look forward confidently to deliverance from the sporting theory of justice, we may look forward to a near future when our courts will be swift and certain agents of justice, whose decisions will be acquiesced in and respected by all."[4]

An Age of Organizations

Pound's reference to the bar associations provides a clue to one of the central features of criminal-justice reform in the twentieth century. It was an age of organizations. Voluntary professional associations were the driving force for reform. The International Association of Chiefs of Police (IACP), first organized in 1893 and renamed in 1900, spearheaded the drive for police professionalization. The National Prison Association, an outgrowth of the 1870 Cincinnati congress, had been a focal point of innovation in corrections for several decades. The National Conference of Charities and Corrections, a social-work professional association, was also active in correctional reform. These organizations were joined by newer and more specialized groups such as the National Probation Association (1907). The American Institute of Criminal Law and Criminology emerged from a 1909 conference at Northwestern University Law School and began publishing the *Journal of Criminal Law and Criminology* in 1910. The American Judicature Society (1917) and the American Law Institute (1923) later joined the movement for law reform.[5]

In 1919 an important variation of the professional association appeared: the crime commission. The Chicago Crime Commission became a permanent watchdog agency; others, like the Cleveland Survey of Criminal Justice (1921-1922), were temporary groups that disbanded after delivering their final reports. These initial crime commissions established the model for later efforts, notably the Wickersham Commission (1929-1931) and the President's Commission on Law Enforcement and Administration of Justice (1965-1967).

The Politics of Reform

The professional associations adopted a posture of nonpartisanship, claiming to represent an objective, scientific point of view. They rejected the traditional approach to investigations which had been highly partisan, with one political faction seeking to embarrass its opponents. The scientific approach enlisted the newly important social sciences. As experts debated the effectiveness or fairness of the criminal-justice system, they turned to the social sciences for reliable data on police performance, judicial processing, and correctional programs.

The claim of nonpartisanship disguised latent political objectives, however. The values of efficiency and expertise served the interests of business and professional groups at the expense of the working class. In criminal justice, urban government, and other areas, progressive reform was an attack on "politics," on the corrupt political machine and the evil bosses who, reformers believed, perverted the democratic process. Politics should be cleansed so that the system could serve "the people." Progressives always claimed to speak for the people and the "public interest." With respect to criminal justice, reform meant eliminating the influence of the political machines over the police department, the county attorney's office, and the penal system. Agencies should be led by experts, not by political hacks, and staff should be selected on the basis of objective qualifications.[6]

The political machines served the interests of their working-class constituents. As we have seen, corruption was extremely functional in certain respects. Patronage appointments provided jobs for one's friends (which, in the context of American politics, meant specific class and ethnic groups). Control of the police department, the county attorney's office, and the lower courts meant that certain laws could be systematically unenforced. Protection of the vice districts also meant the protection of the saloon as a small business and a political center. The demand for efficieny, in the sense of both the enforcement of the laws and the selection of criminal-justice personnel, was a direct attack upon working-class interests. Not surprisingly, then, efficiency-oriented reform was supported by business and professional groups.[7]

The political struggle over control of the criminal-justice system, based on the class and ethnic-group divisions in American society, explained the rise of the professional associations and the crime commissions. From the standpoint of the reformers, the other side was already organized—in the political machine. The reform-oriented organizations were designed as a political counterweight.

The reform of the legal profession illustrated the political dimensions of reform in the progressive era. Roscoe Pound and others attacked the "unscrupulous" defense attorneys who used every possible loophole to gain acquittal. They also complained about the unqualified attorneys who became prosecutors and judges through their political contacts. In the name of "professional standards," the reformers set out to cleanse the bar. The elite of the legal profession waged all-out war on night schools and part-time legal study. The American Bar Association promulgated a canon of professional ethics in 1906, while state bar associations adopted restrictive admission requirements. As Jerold Auerbach argues in *Unequal Justice*, reform closed the door to persons from low-income groups. They were the ones who could only obtain legal training through night law schools, who were most severely hurt by the prohibition on advertising or solicitation in the new canon of ethics, and who were least likely to pass the new "fitness" tests for admission to the bar. The elitist reformers did little to disguise their hostility to recent immigrant groups, especially Jews and Italian-Americans. In short, "professionalism" served clearly defined political interests.[8]

The elite of the legal profession were not completely one-sided in their outlook. Some members were sensitive to the problems of the lower classes and figured prominently in social-justice-oriented reforms. In particular the public-defender movement, designed to provide legal counsel for indigents charged with crimes, enjoyed an important measure of support from well-to-do lawyers. The first public defender's office opened in Los Angeles County in 1914, and gradually the idea spread to other cities. The movement involved an odd coalition between organized labor, which actively promoted the idea in many cities, and elitist lawyers. Reginald Heber Smith, member of a prominent Boston law firm, was the most noted proponent of the concept. The Carnegie Foundation supported his report *Justice and the Poor*, a survey of the legal needs of the poor in both the civil and criminal areas of the law.[9]

THE BIRTH OF POLICE PROFESSIONALISM

Police reform took a new direction at the turn of the century. Previous efforts to improve the police had been local and overtly partisan. The Lexow Investigation of the New York City police (1894–1895) was typical: Republicans in the legislature sought to embarrass their opponents and gain control of the police department. These early reform efforts lacked an alternative vision of what policing should be.

The movement for police professionalization was national in scope. The reorganization of the IACP was a major turning point. Except for a national convention in 1871, law enforcement had lacked a professional association until the formation of the National Police Chief's Union in 1893. This organization languished until Richard Sylvester became president in 1901. Sylvester had already established a solid reputation as superintendent of the Washington, D.C., police. During his fifteen-year term as president of the IACP, he renamed and reorganized the association and invested it with the ideals of professionalism.[10]

The Bureau of Municipal Research, based in New York City, also contributed to the reform effort. Applying principles of scientific management, bureau staff members investigated more than seventeen police departments across the country. Their reports detailed the prevailing inefficiency and corruption and made specific recommendations for change. The bureau eventually became the National Institute of Public Administration. Staff member Bruce Smith conducted more than fifty investigations of police departments during a career that stretched from the progressive era to the 1950s.

Following Sylvester's pioneering work, August Vollmer emerged as the best-known spokesperson of police professionalization. Vollmer headed the Berkeley, California, police from 1905 to 1932. In his long career he conducted numerous investigations of other police departments, was the principal author of the 1931 Wickersham Commission *Report on Police*, and, as a tireless advocate of higher educational standards, initiated the first college-level training programs for police. Other important leaders of police reform included Arthur Woods, commissioner of the New York City police (1914–1918), Leonhard Fuld, author of the first textbook on *Police Administration*, and Raymond B. Fosdick, author of *American Police Systems*, a comprehensive survey of American policing.

Professionalism Defined

What did these reformers mean by police "professionalism"? They achieved a remarkable consensus, and their agenda for reform dominated thinking about police administration until the 1960s. The key to professionalization was elimination of the influence of politics. Over and over, Sylvester, Vollmer, and Fosdick hammered away at the need to "get the police out of politics and get politics out of the police." A professional police, they argued, was an efficient, nonpartisan agency committed to the highest standards of public service.

This concept of professionalism called for a number of specific reforms. First, police departments should be led by trained experts, selected on the basis of proven ability, not political favoritism. Second, police executives should be given a high degree of job security. They should be allowed to carry out their jobs without having to worry about being removed for political reasons. Third, the police department itself should be reorganized. Command should be centralized to allow the implementation of consistent policy in the pursuit of more efficient public service. Standards for personnel at all ranks should also be raised. Departments should require entrance examinations for applicants, formal instruction for recruits, and competitive examinations for promotions. Vollmer acquired his national reputation primarily for his recruitment of college students (the "college cops") in Berkeley.[11]

Professional policing also involved a redefinition of the police mission. The reformers agreed that a professional police were committed to public service, but they did not always agree on what that service included. Two definitions of the police mission emerged. One stressed efficient crime control. August Vollmer, for example, promoted scientific crime detection through the use of crime labs, the lie detector, and other devices. Fingerprinting also enjoyed wide popularity beginning in 1904. Vollmer also helped lead the way in putting patrol officers in automobiles. The patrol car offered the hope that the police could more effectively prevent crime by covering their assigned beats. A second definition of professional policing entailed a social-work model. The primary job of the police, according to this view, was to help individuals, often by diverting them out of the criminal-justice system. In his early years, Vollmer promoted this view as well, delivering speeches to the IACP on such subjects as "The Policeman as a Social Worker."[12]

The two models of the police role emerged during the progressive era and competed for dominance. Eventually, however, the crime-control model prevailed. By the 1930s it was clearly the dominant model of professional policing and remained so until challenged again in the 1970s.

Philadelphia: A Case Study

The reform of the Philadelphia police under Mayor Rudolph Blankenburg (1912–1916) offers a classic case study of professionalization in practice. For decades Philadelphia had had a notoriously corrupt city government. In *The Shame of the Cities,* Lincoln Steffens called it "the worst governed city in the country." The police were the key to the survival of the machine. According to Steffens they protected massive illegal voting and even physically attacked or arrested those who protested the fraud. Finally, after more than twelve years of battling the machine, a coalition of reformers elected Blankenburg mayor of Philadelphia in 1912.[13]

Mayor Blankenburg immediately set out to clean house in the police department. He started at the top by appointing George D. Porter as public safety director. Porter, in turn, forced the resignation of the police chief and appointed James Robinson in his place. Robinson promptly introduced military drills, added regular physical exercise, and, to enhance the image of the department, ordered new uniforms and organized a sixty-five-piece police band. Porter later claimed that "no city can show a police force more military in appearance or higher [*sic*] efficiency.[14]

The militarization of the police was one of the disturbing consequences of professionalization. Reformers in the progressive era were infatuated with the "military model" (Theodore Roosevelt, the former New York City police commissioner and hero of San Juan Hill, exemplified this aspect of progressivism). Although the American police had been originally created on the military model, police administration had been remarkably unmilitary. Police departments were decentralized and utterly lacking in internal discipline. The leaders of the professionalization movement took the military model as a technique to impose internal discipline and to project an image of efficiency. The short-run effect was beneficial—standards did improve—but the long-run consequences were tragic, as the American police acquired an overly militaristic character.

The Blankenburg administration raised personnel standards and reorganized patrol operations. Porter and Robinson introduced formal training for police officers by opening a school of instruction in 1913. For a textbook they prepared a new edition of the patrol officer's manual. The existing edition had not been revised since 1897, and only a few copies could be found. Chief

Robinson then replaced the old two-platoon patrol with a three-platoon system. This reduced by almost half the number of hours a partrol officer spent on duty. According to Robinson it not only improved morale and physical well being, but resulted in more efficient patrolling, yielding more arrests and a decrease in crime.

The hard-won accomplishments of the reformers enjoyed a precarious existence, however. Professionalization advanced very slowly, suffering frequent setbacks. The reformers had trouble staying in power. In Philadelphia subsequent administrations abolished many of the reforms of the Blankenburg administration. In New York City police commissioners came and went with great rapidity. Reformers such as Arthur Woods were followed by traditionalists who restored the old ways. Even some of the more significant accomplishments lacked substance. Formal training for recruits was one of the most important reforms. Yet, a 1913 investigation of the New York City police academy revealed that recruits took no notes, were required to pass no examinations, and automatically became patrol officers after sitting through their classes. By the end of the progressive era, police professionalism was still more an idea than a reality.

Cops as Social Workers

Some reformers saw the police as an instrument of social reform. Administrative efficiency was not enough; the police had an obligation to help uplift society. Moreover, they were ideally suited for this role because they were in direct contact with the problems of crime, delinquency, alcoholism, and prostitution. The police, in short, should function as social workers. August Vollmer described this role in his 1919 speech to the IACP on "predelinquency." The police had "far greater obligations than the mere apprehending and prosecuting of lawbreakers." Once a person had committed a crime, it was already too late. The police should try to prevent persons from entering lives of crime in the first place. Vollmer urged the police officer to intervene early: "If he would serve his community by reducing crime he must go up the stream a little further and dam it up at its source." The officer should work closely with schools and other social agencies to identify juveniles with educational or family problems.[15]

The social-work role for the police drew inspiration from other humanitarian and social-justice-oriented reforms of the progressive era. Many of the advocates of this role came from the social-work profession. And the annual meetings of the National Conference of Charities and Corrections frequently discussed police-related issues. The social-work role also contributed to another important aspect of police professionalization: the development of functional specialities. Police departments began to create specialized units devoted to juveniles and vice. This was part of a more general trend toward specialization. Units devoted to traffic, training, and records also began to appear. Thus, the professionalized police department became a large and complex bureaucracy.

To implement the social-work role, a number of police departments hired women officers. This was a radical innovation in American policing. Some departments had employed women as matrons to supervise women in the jails and lockups as early as the 1840s, and the practice became widespread in most of the larger cities by the 1880s. But no department granted women powers of arrest or put them on patrol.

The first woman police officer in the United States was Lola Baldwin, hired by the Portland, Oregon, police in 1905. She was assigned to "child-protection" work during a world's fair in the city that summer. A number of civic leaders were concerned about the welfare of children during the fair, fearing that it might offer too many temptations. Baldwin was assigned the task of supervising a group of volunteer social workers who would try to "protect" children from potential evils. The experiment proved satisfactory to those involved, and Lola Baldwin was then given a permanent assignment with the department.[16]

An organized policewomen's movement emerged in 1910. Its leader was Alice Stebbins Wells of the Los Angeles police department. In addition to her juvenile work with the department, Wells undertook a heavy speaking schedule, carrying the message of the policewoman's role across the country. In 1914 she addressed the IACP, assuring the chiefs that women officers would not take the place of men. The following year she organized the International Association of Policewomen and became its president. Her efforts were quite successful. By 1916 as many as 40 departments employed policewomen, and by 1925 the number had risen to 145.

Policewomen were limited to the specialized duty of juvenile work. The leaders of the policewomen's movement, moreover, stressed the idea that policewomen would project a helping image. They would not wear uniforms, would not patrol regular beats, and would not arrest adults. Spokeswomen emphasized the traditional child-caring role of the woman. According to Mary Hamilton, the first policewoman in New York City, "the position of a woman in a police department is not unlike that of a mother in a home. Just as the mother smooths out the rough places, looks after the children and gives a timely word of warning, advice or encouragement, so the policewoman fulfills her duty." The policewoman was assigned to patrol places of amusement, looking for children who appeared to be lost or on the verge of a predelinquent act. Hamilton expressed the moralistic outlook of the policewomen's movement, warning that "danger lurks in parks, playgrounds, beaches, piers and baths unless there is someone to watch over these pleasure haunts experienced in recognizing a devastating evil, however well disguised."[17]

Policewomen were instructed to take "endangered" children into protective custody. Thus, their role was similar to that of the juvenile court. Both represented a substantial expansion of the power of the state to intervene in people's lives, even though a crime might not have been committed. This intervention was justified in terms of the duty of the state to eliminate social ills. The good intentions of progressivism brought an increase in state coercion. Like juvenile-court officials, policewomen were granted enormous discretion in carrying out their duties.

A double standard prevailed in terms of personnel requirements for policewomen. Most of the first women officers had previously been involved in some form of social work, and they generally had some college education and often graduate training as well. The International Association of Policewomen recommended both college training and prior social-work experience as a prerequisite for all policewomen. This contrasted sharply wih prevailing standards for male officers, few of whom had even a high-school education.

The policewomen's movement illustrated both the hopes and the frustrations of police reform. The movement generated enormous excitement and spread rapidly until the mid-1920s. Then it stagnated, and policewomen's work became increasingly relegated to a minor role. Mary Hamilton complained that her office was little more than a place for "miscellaneous complaints." By the late 1920s and 1930s, the crime-fighter model of policing moved to the forefront. The high ideals of the social-work model dissipated as juvenile work and other social-work-oriented functions became routine, bureaucratized tasks.

In addition to delinquency prevention, some police departments experimented with programs designed to rehabilitate adult offenders. The most notable experiments occurred in Cleveland under Police Chief Fred Kohler. His two most important programs were the Sunrise Court and the Golden Rule.[18]

The Sunrise Court was an early form of *diversion* although Kohler did not use this terminology. He introduced it in 1905 as a way of releasing "at an early hour all honest working people." Persons arrested and detained overnight were released early in the morning so they could return home, wash, and go to their jobs. Kohler expressed great concern about the impact of the criminal process on individuals who were guilty of nothing more than drunkenness or some other petty offense. A full criminal proceeding would disrupt the person's job and family life and might result in a criminal record. Thus, Kohler devised a technique that allowed such persons to obtain an early release in exchange for a de facto admission of guilt. The individual signed a form stating, "Having been arrested for —— I hereby admit my guilt of the violation charged me. . . ."[19]

The Golden Rule policy, which Kohler introduced in 1908, carried the concept of diversion even further. It consisted of instructions to police officers on the proper handling of certain situations. Kohler directed officers to release juveniles to the custody of their parents rather than put them in jail. Also, officers should use their "kindly efforts" to mediate domestic disputes rather than settle them by arrest. Finally, Kohler ordered the de facto decriminalization of minor offenses. He advised that "some men fail through some unfortunate circumstances and are not criminal at heart, and should be treated accordingly, in which case the best results might be accomplished with a well-applied reprimand." In short, drunks were to be diverted out of the system with a simple warning.[20]

The Golden Rule policy took effect in Cleveland on January 1, 1908. The results were dramatic. Arrests fell by two thirds. Enthusiastically describing his program to the IACP, Kohler pointed out that arrests for 1908 totaled only 10,085, compared with 30,418 for the year before. He claimed that it saved the city of Cleveland more than $100,000 and allowed the police to concentrate on the more serious crimes. Moreover, thousands of individuals were spared the indignity of arrest, incarceration, and trial. It was both a more efficient and more humane approach to law enforcement. Detroit, Toledo, and other cities followed Cleveland's lead. In Detroit the Golden Rule policy also resulted in a sharp reduction in the number of arrests. Mayor "Golden Rule" Jones of Toledo went even further and took billy clubs away from police officers. Temperance leaders in Los Angeles, meanwhile, staffed the Sunrise Court as volunteers, providing hot coffee and antidrinking lectures.

Kohler's innovations reflected the popularity of the rehabilitative ideal during the progressive era. The Sunrise Court and the Golden Rule rested on the belief that the police, through the proper strategy of intervention, could help to steer individuals away from lives of crime. Delegates to the IACP conventions debated Kohler's ideas. These discussions reflected the intellectual vitality of the early years of the police professionalization movement. The Sunrise Court and the Golden Rule, however, focused attention on the question of discretion. The Sunrise Court transferred an enormous amount of discretionary power to the police chief. Critics pointed out the potential for the arbitrary application of the waiver and the possible misuse of the forms that accumulated in the police chief's desk. The Golden Rule, on the other hand, was a step in the direction of providing guided discretion. It offered clear guidelines for handling specific situations. Kohler was ahead of his time; police administrators for the most part evaded rather than confronted the issue of discretion.

Prostitution

Police chiefs also became involved in the national crusade to eliminate prostitution. Under the system of police corruption that developed in the nineteenth century, prostitution flourished in the vice districts. Major cities had as many as two hundred recognized houses of prostitution. In Chicago it was big business. According to the Chicago Vice Commission, the city contained over five thousand working prostitutes and the revenue exceeded $15 million annually. Beginning around 1907 a national crusade to eradicate the "social evil," as it was called, emerged. This movement united reformers from many different groups: social workers, feminists, moralists, and others. The campaign reached its peak in 1912–1913 when thirty-nine cities officially "closed" their vice districts. Tolerated prostitution virtually disappeared during World War I, when the campaign to keep American soldiers "fit to fight" intensified the antiprostitution drive.[21]

The police participated in a vigorous debate over the question of prostitution. The debate reflected different strategies of law enforcement. Traditionally, the police had tolerated or even welcomed official vice districts. The police, after all, were controlled by politicians who often had a direct financial stake there. Police chiefs also found it convenient to concentrate the bulk of illegal activity in one section of town. Finally, many chiefs accepted the idea that it was wiser to control illegal activities which could not be eliminated.

At the 1907 meeting of the IACP, Fred Kohler outlined the alternative policies which police departments could adopt. They were: "First, official toleration; second, attempted suppression by crusade; and third, police repression." He considered the first to be indecent and the second impossible. Consequently, he recommended the third alternative. His concept of "police repression" involved a program of systematic harassment, including vigorous enforcement of municipal ordinances, especially building codes, and stationing police officers outside of known vice dens to intimidate patrons. Other chiefs joined in the debate. Their ranks included advocates of complete suppression, official toleration, and various compromise positions.[22]

For all practical purposes, World War I settled the prostitution question. The war effort gave renewed vigor to the antivice crusade, largely because of the felt need to eliminate venereal disease. The federal government joined the crusade by virtue of the Military Conscription Act. This law creating the draft authorized the President to ban prostitution near military bases. Secretary of War Newton D. Baker appointed Raymond B. Fosdick to head the Commission on Training Camp Activities. By the end of 1917, Fosdick announced that "every red light district in the United States had been closed." As the author of *European Police Systems* (1914) and *American Police Systems* (1920), Fosdick was one of the leading authorities on police administration. Both books were sponsored by the American Social Hygiene Association, an organization funded by John D. Rockefeller, Jr., that led the crusade against prostitution. Fosdick's career illustrates the close connection between police reform and other social reforms in the progressive era.[23]

New Forms of Law Enforcement

During the wartime crusade against prostitution, the federal government virtually took control of the Philadelphia police department. The U.S. Navy had been protesting the continued toleration of open prostitution, and the secretary of the Navy finally dispatched a lieutenant colonel to Philadelphia to oversee a cleanup campaign. While the newspapers carried headlines declaring "Federal Control of the Police in Philadelphia," the superintendent of police was forced out and the vice district effectively closed. Local officials denied that the Navy was running the police department, but federal pressure made the crucial difference.[24]

Although it was only a minor incident, the Navy's intervention in Philadelphia was symptomatic of a larger and more important trend: the nationalization of crime control. During the progressive era, various social problems were defined as issues of national importance. The crusade against prostitution was an excellent example: vice was too important to be left to local authorities, and federal action was imperative. The creation of the Bureau of Investigation (renamed the Federal Bureau of Investigation in 1935) within the Department of Justice in 1908 was a significant first step toward a stronger federal role in law enforcement.

President Theodore Roosevelt initially asked Congress to create a federal detective force in 1907. Up to that time, federal agencies had contracted with private detective firms for investigative services. This aroused some controversy, primarily because of the notorious reputation of the Pinkerton firm. Congress, however, opposed Roosevelt's idea. Two congressmen had recently been prosecuted for fraud, and the legislators were afraid to grant the executive branch even greater investigative powers. Instead, Congress moved to curb the powers of the Justice Department, passing a law forbidding it from borrowing detectives from the secret service of other federal agencies.[25]

Congressional opposition did not stop President Roosevelt. When Congress adjourned, he simply created a Bureau of Investigation by executive order. A bitter political battle then followed as Roosevelt's congressional opponents attacked the new agency. The fact that Attorney General Charles Bonaparte was a descendant of Napoleon stimulated fears that this new detective force would become a secret police. The first years of the bureau only confirmed these fears. The staff was caught opening the mail of Senator Benjamin Tillman, one of its most vocal opponents. Roosevelt himself offered the unconvincing argument that the package had come open "accidentally."

The initial illegal activities of the bureau foreshadowed more systematic abuses of power under the regime of J. Edgar Hoover years later, and the first two decades of its history were marked primarily by scandal. It acquired a specific law-enforcement mandate in 1910 with the Mann Act. Making it a crime to transport a female across state lines for immoral purposes, the Mann Act was another example of federal intervention in the criminal-justice area. The Bureau of Investigation, however, proceeded to use the law in a political vendetta against a U.S. Senator. It was also deeply involved in the gross violations of civil liberties during the Red Scare of 1919–1920. The bureau remained a relatively small but scandal-ridden agency until the appointment of J. Edgar Hoover as director in 1924. Under his leadership it later emerged as the dominant voice in American law enforcement.

The second new form of law enforcement to appear in the progressive era was the state police. Pennsylvania created its State Constabulary in 1905. A highly centralized, mobile, and quasi-military agency, the constabulary had general law-enforcement powers and was designed to supplement the inadequate law enforcement in rural areas. In practice, however, the Pennsylvania State Constabulary acted most often in labor disputes. Organized labor felt that it consistently sided with management and denounced the state troopers as the "American cossacks." Other states, however, gradually created state police of their own, although not all of them followed the Pennsylvania model. The authority of some was restricted to traffic control, and few of the new police forces were as militaristic as the Pennsylvania Constabulary.[26]

Like the Bureau of Investigation, state police agencies reflected the rising importance of the crime issue. At both the federal and state levels, public concern about crime led to the creation of new and more centralized law-enforcement agencies. Both the bureau and the state police embodied the progressive-era values of social control through expanded government powers.

CORRECTIONS: FULFILLMENT AND CRISIS

The progressive era brought to fruition the second cycle of American prison reform. The ideas and institutions of the "new penology" which had been articulated in 1870 achieved fulfillment with dramatic suddenness. In 1900 probation, parole, the indeterminate sentence, and the juvenile court each existed in only a handful of states. They were still widely regarded as novel but untested ideas. By 1915, however, these institutions were the norm. At the same time, reformers launched a new round of attacks upon the prison itself, exposing scandalous conditions and experimenting with new concepts of prison administration and correctional treatment. Prison reform drew much of its energy and idealism from the broader currents of the progressive era.

The Eighth International Prison Congress, held in Washington D.C., in 1910, marked the high point of correctional reform. The congress lent additional prestige to ideas that were already enjoying rising popularity, but the meeting also dramatized the divergence between American and European thinking on penology. The American representatives were thoroughly committed to the idea of rehabilitation through individualized treatment. This was not a new idea, of course; it was implicit in the creation of the prison almost a century earlier and had been made more explicit by Zebulon Brockway at the 1870 congress. The excitement of progressive-era activities arose from the belief that the institutional means of achieving this goal were at hand. The Europeans, however, were far more pessimistic on the question of rehabilitation. Delegates to the congress vigorously debated the question of which offenders the indeterminate sentence should be applied to, and the congress finally approved a resolution indicating that it be applied to young offenders and moral degenerates only. Nevertheless, American correctional thinkers remained firmly committed to the belief that adult felons were susceptible to reformation.[27]

The skepticism of the Europeans could be attributed in part to the influence of new ideas about the determinants of crime. Modern criminology, the scientific study of the causes of crime, originated in Europe in the latter half of the nineteenth century. The "father" of modern criminology was an Italian physician, Cesare Lombroso. His original theories have long since been discredited, but as one criminologist points out, they "proved so challenging that they gave an unprecedented impetus to the study of the offender."[28] The attempt to prove or disprove Lombroso sparked the birth of an entire discipline.

Lombroso first published *L'Uomo Delinquente* (Criminal Man) in 1876. As it attracted notice and generated controversy, Lombroso published revised and expanded versions. The fifth and final edition in 1896 contained 1,903 pages, compared with the 252 pages of the original edition. In brief, Lombroso argued that criminals were born, not made. Influenced by Darwin's theories of evolution, he believed that criminals could be identified through certain physical features ("atavisms") characteristic of primitive or subhuman beings. Lombroso arrived at this theory through the study of patients in Italian mental institutions, and his methodology was one of the main points raised by his critics. Two other Italian thinkers, Enrico Ferri and Raffaele Garofalo, adopted the essentials of Lombrosian theory and expanded on the social and legal implications. Lombroso's theory was fatalistic in important respects. Since the criminal was born, not made, there was little hope of rehabilitation.

More congenial to the optimistic tenor of American corrections was an alternative school of thought that emerged in response to Lombroso. A sociological explanation of criminal behavior was first suggested by Friedrich Engels, colleague of Karl Marx, in *The Condition of the Working Class* (1844). Engels and Marx, however, were only indirectly concerned with the problem of crime. A more thorough statement of the sociological theory of crime came from Gabriel Tarde, a French social scientist who published scathing attacks on Lombroso in 1886 and 1890. Another French scholar, Emile Durkheim, further explored the influence of social structure upon criminal behavior. In *Division of Labor* (1893) and *Suicide* (1897), Durkeim developed the concept of *anomie*, the absence of rules and norms to guide human behavior, as an explanation for crime.

The pioneering work in the development of modern criminology took place in Europe, and Americans made no significant contributions until the 1920s and 1930s. Nonetheless, the Americans were deeply influenced by the emergence of the social sciences.

The National Conference of Charities and Corrections sponsored sociological discussions of crime beginning in 1894, and in 1910 the *Journal of Criminal Law and Criminology* became a vehicle for research in the field of criminology.

Prison and Jail Conditions

The reformers unleashed a new wave of exposes of prison and jail conditions. Most of these accounts followed the model of John Howard's *The State of the Prisons*. Typical of the genre was Joseph Fishman's *Crucibles of Crime*, an indictment of local jails. As inspector of prisons for the Justice Department, Fishman had visited over fifteen hundred jails. The jail, he concluded, was nothing more than "a debauch of dirt, disease and degeneracy." Conditions in the Auburn County (N.Y.) jail were typical. The jail itself had been built in 1847, and prisoners were confined for up to twelve hours a day in cells (8'x4'x7') with no light whatsoever. On weekends they remained locked in these cells from noon on Saturday until 7:30 Monday morning. During the week prisoners would spend half of the day sitting idle in the large day room. Fishman calculated that in the course of one year, a person would spend 5,536 hours in a dark cell and 3,380 hours sitting on a bench in the day room doing nothing. The fee system encouraged corruption and scandalous conditions. In Pennsylvania the jailer received 50¢ per day for each prisoner and was allowed to keep whatever was not spent for food. Fishman found another situation where the jailer received 75¢ per prisoner, contracted with a cook for meals at 13¢ per prisoner, and pocketed the rest. With an average of seventy-five to one hundred inmates, the jailer realized a profit of $50 to $75 a day. In the Kentucky jails, inmates themselves exercised internal discipline through "kangaroo courts." While virtually all of the jails segregated male and female inmates, only 10 percent provided matrons for supervising women prisoners.[29]

Conditions in the prisons were little better. A special commission appointed by Governor Sulzer to investigate the prisons in New York State reported that "the worst features of the prison management cannot be discussed in any public document." Sing Sing prison was "so many square feet of hell." The problems were the age-old ones of all jails and prisons: overcrowding, lack of adequate sanitation and ventilation, and brutality between staff and inmates and among inmates themselves. Conditions in the Kansas state penitentiary were exposed in a unique fashion. The Kansas prison housed prisoners from Oklahoma, which had no institution of its own. Kate Barnard, commissioner of charities for Oklahoma, visited the Kansas prison in the guise of a private citizen. There she found the 575 Oklahoma prisoners (13 of them women) at work in the prison coal mine. Prisoners who failed to dig their quota of three cars of coal per day were punished even further. She found one seventeen-year-old, who had been able to mine only two carloads, chained to the wall of the prison. Other punishments included a form of water torture and "the crib," where inmates were thrown with hands and feet tied and drawn together at the back. In addition to the value of the prisoners' labor, the state of Kansas received 48¢ a day for keeping Oklahoma's prisoners and paid about 10¢ a day for meals. After revealing her official position, Kate Barnard protested the treatment of Oklahoma prisoners and eventually secured their removal and an end to the arrangement.[30]

New Directions in Prison Reform

The exposés of prison conditions aroused public opinion. Shock and indignation, however, were a result of public ignorance about prison conditions. The conditions themselves had existed for a long time. The cycle of prison reform involved a fluctuation between long periods of public indifference and brief outbursts of indignation and reform activity. The problem, of course, was what to do about the prisons. Obviously, only new facilities and adequate staffing could end overcrowding and lack of sanitation, and this solution required more money to be spent. Public officals, unsurprisingly, preferred to avoid the fiscal implications of this approach. Even when new facilities were constructed, they too become overcrowded almost immediately.

The progressive era saw a number of different experiments intended to make the prison a more effective instrument of rehabilitation and a more humane institution. Three particular reforms illustrate the variety of activities during the period.

From the very beginning, the prison had been designed to rehabilitate the individual offender. Wines and Dwight declared the "individualization" of treatment the supreme goal in their 1867 *Report on the Prisons*. Yet, as they and most other candid observers realized, the prisons subjected all inmates to a standard daily regimen. The advocates of rehabilitation deplored not only the widespread brutality but also the impersonal lockstep of the daily routine, which precluded any possibility of individualized treatment.

The emergence of the social and behavioral sciences in the late nineteenth and early twentieth centuries offered the prospect of a new era in correctional treatment. Much of the energy of prison reform in the progressive era, as exemplified in the international prison congress of 1910, arose from the exciting prospect of being able, for the first time, to individualize treatment. The disciplines of psychology and sociology would make it possible to diagnose the offender and his or her circumstances and then prescribe a properly individualized treatment. The so-called "medical model" had always been implicit in the prison; the social and behavioral sciences seemed to make its application a reality.

A report of the Illinois state prison at Joliet pointed out that "under existing conditions at the State Penitentiary all convicts are treated alike . . . [and] the occupation selected for each depends more upon the needs of the different departments of the prison than upon the requirements of the individual convict." But a new system devised by a psychologist and psychiatrist hired as consultants allowed (1) "the study of each convict when received and during detention with adequate records, and (2) the provision of means for separately housing and properly employing the different types of persons." The report emphasized that the new approach was "not a matter of humanitarianism, but strictly one of economy." The protection of society demanded that potential recidivists not be released early under the indeterminate sentence.[31]

One of the most notable experiments in developing a system of diagnosis and classification occurred at the New York Women's Reformatory at Bedford. Dr. Katherine B. Davis became director of the reformatory in 1900 and, according to one account, "proceeded to make it the most active penal experiment station in America." In 1909 and 1910 she encouraged psychologists to conduct studies of the inmates at Bedford. As a result she received a foundation grant to add a woman psychologist to her staff. John D. Rockefeller, Jr., was impressed with a pamphlet written by Dr. Davis and created the Bureau of Social Hygiene in 1910 with her as director. The bureau established a Laboratory of Social Hygiene at Bedford and developed a formal arrangement for the study and classification of inmates. In 1916 the bureau opened a psychopathic hospital in conjunction with the reformatory.[32]

Although Dr. Davis's experiment achieved wide publicity, it was short-lived. A decline set in soon after her departure in 1914, and the programming of the institution was seriously disrupted by a public investigation in 1916. By 1919 both the laboratory and the hospital were closed, and a riot in 1920 followed by the trial of institution officials for mismanagement delivered the final blow.

The goal of individualized treatment through diagnosis and classification, however, survived and eventually became part of the official ideology of American corrections. The initial experiments during the progressive era set the tone for a long process of development in subsequent decades. Nonetheless, this dream foundered on the rocks of institutional reality, as had earlier prison reforms. Correctional goals continued to be undermined by the age-old problems of overcrowding and a preoccupation with custody. Moreover, most prisons lacked the staff to conduct adequate diagnoses and were unable to offer any meaningful individualization of treatment. Despite the rhetoric and the trappings of modern social science, the prison remained a warehouse for society's rejects.

Thomas Mott Osborne's brief adventure at Sing Sing penitentiary represented perhaps the most idealistic of all the progressive-era attempts to reform the prison. A retired businessman and former mayor of Auburn, New York (1903–1905), Osborne chaired the New York State Commission on Prison Reform in 1913. To learn about prison conditions firsthand he entered Sing Sing voluntarily and spent one week there as inmate "Tom Brown." In his account of the experience, *Within Prison Walls,* Osborne reported that he was accepted into the prison community and treated by the inmates as one of their own. This sense of trust and community gave birth to the idea of the Mutual Welfare League.[33]

The Mutual Welfare League was an experiment in inmate self-governance. The only way to genuinely rehabilitate offenders, to build self-reliance, and to run a humane institution, Osborne argued, was to give inmates responsibility for their own affairs. Osborne began to speak and write about this idea as soon as he left Sing Sing. In February 1914 he was invited to organize a Good Conduct League at Auburn penitentiary. As members of the league, inmates would elect their own officers and enforce their own standards of discipline. Serious infractions could involve expulsion from the league and loss of privileges.

Osborne's greatest test came later that year. Troubles at Sing Sing brought about the removal of the warden, and Osborne took his place on December 1, 1914. A week later he launched a daring experiment in converting the entire prison to the Mutual Welfare League idea. Considering Sing Sing's reputation as one of the roughest prisons, turning the entire discipline over to the inmates took courage. Only a few months before, prisoners had rioted and set fire to one of the shops. Osborne's predecessor had carried a pistol for his own protection. Addressing 250 workers in the knitting shop, Osborne told them, "Boys, I understand that you are the worst behaved bunch in the whole prison—and I'm going to put a stop to it! I'm going to dismiss your guards . . . and you'll have to choose your own delegates from among yourselves, to preserve order."[34]

To the surprise of almost everyone, the Mutual Welfare League seemed to work. Osborne argued that it even improved the efficiency and profitability of prison industries. Gross sales of products produced by inmates increased from $318,733 in 1913–1914 to $354,327 the next year. Discipline also improved, as the gruesome medical statistics suggested. With an average prison population of 1,466 in 1913–1914, 363 inmates had been treated for wounds (one wonders how "typical" Osborne's week as "Tom Brown" had been). But with the Mutual Welfare League the next year, and an average population of 1,616, only 155 were treated for wounds. Previously, inmates had taken their meals in absolute silence, with sixty guards watching for even the slightest turn of the head. Under Osborne's system, the prisoners ate "pleasantly and sociably together" with no guards present at all.

But Osborne's experiment was not to last. Disciplinary problems continued and, under the glare of national publicity that Osborne himself had helped to generate, even minor problems became sensational news. An investigation by state officials resulted. Even though he was cleared of all charges of mismanagement, Osborne resigned in disgust. The concept of "prison democracy" went into the dustbin along with other idealistic experiments in prison reform. But despite its failure, the Mutual Welfare League addressed itself to an important issue in prison administration: the inmate subculture. Academic sociologists did not "discover" the subculture until many years later. But it seems evident that a distinct set of group norms developed early in the history of the prison and played an important role in its day-to-day operation. Osborne's plan at least had the virtue of recognizing the reality of the subculture and attempting to transform it into a positive rather than a negative force.

The question of prison industries attracted much of the attention of the muckrakers and prison reformers during the progressive era. Abuses connected with the use of inmate labor continued to be one the most unsavory aspects of the American prison system. Subtle but important changes in the administration of prison industries had begun in the late nineteenth century, when the convict-lease system slowly passed from the scene. Southern states replaced it with the state-use system, but putting prisoners to work on vast plantations where they raised crops for state use, or on roads and other public works, did little to improve their lot.

The southern chain gang became the new symbol of barbaric penology. Prisoners were shackled together, and the leg irons cut into the flesh. At night they were chained to their bunks to prevent escape. Those who complained were frequently whipped and placed in iron collars in their bunks at night. In the prison farms of Texas, Louisiana, and Arkansas, prisoners were routinely murdered and buried in unmarked graves.[35]

The state-use system replaced the contract-labor system as the prevalent form of prison industries in the North and Midwest. New York converted to state use in 1897. The shift was due in part to the growing strength of the American labor movement. Samuel Gompers, president of the AFL, denounced contract labor as "a menace to free labor and to convicts." Organized labor fully supported the idea of prison work, provided that inmates work by hand, for no more than eight hours a day, producing goods for use in state or charitable institutions.[36]

By 1914–1915 the so-called *good-roads* movement attracted attention as a solution to the prison labor question. The plan called for employing prisoners in the construction and improvement of public highways. According to its advocates, it was healthy outdoors work which did not compete directly with free labor. Colorado, Washington, and other states outside the South made extensive use of convict labor on highways. "Good roads and good men" became the slogan of the plan's advocates, notably the American Highway Association. Self-interest explained the support of the new highway lobby, which saw convict labor as a cheap and convenient solution to the growing need for decent highways.[37]

The good-roads movement proved to be only a temporary solution to the question of prison labor. The abuses of the southern chain gangs gave road work a bad image. Organized labor argued that it did take jobs from free workers, while others raised questions about the overall efficiency of prisoners in construction work. In the end the good-roads movement was but another chapter in the long and sorry history of prison labor: a marriage of convenience between the rhetoric of rehabilitation and the self-interest of public officials and private industry.

Probation, Parole, the Juvenile Court, and the Indeterminate Sentence

In the first decade and a half of the new century, probation, parole, the indeterminate sentence, and the juvenile court were ideas whose time had come. The concept of individualized justice seemed to fulfill the highest ideals of progressivism. The adoption of these new institutions came in a flood. Twelve states adopted probation for juveniles between 1900 and 1905. Eleven more states joined the list by 1911. Adult probation arrived with equal suddenness a few years later, with six states adopting it in 1909 and then seven states in a final flurry of activity in 1915. The year 1915 brought the period of expansion to an end. By then, forty-six states had juvenile courts, thirty-four had parole and adult probation, and thirty-one had the indeterminate sentence. The rapidity with which so many states adopted these new institutions testifies to the intensity of reform spirit during the period.

A few innovative programs also appeared during the flood tide of progressivism. The Sunrise Court and the Golden Rule policy developed by Chief Kohler of the Cleveland police, although technically located in the law enforcement area, should be seen as correctional programs. Both reflected the philosophy of rehabilitation through individualized treatment. They foreshadowed the more elaborate diversion programs of the 1960s. The development of juvenile units and the use of women police officers also represented the aims of correctional programs. In short, the rehabilitative ideal was so strong that it pervaded even the area of law enforcement.

The year 1913 is generally given as the birthdate of *work release,* a program designed to permit the prison inmate to reenter society gradually by being released daily to work at a regular job. The Wisconsin Huber Law authorized judges to impose conditional sentences in the case of certain misdemeanors, allowing the offender to work while serving a short jail term. This idea was not completely new in 1913, however. It was essentially a modification of the old practice of releasing juveniles and in some cases women offenders under apprenticeship arrangements. The Wisconsin law took the hesitant step of applying it to male misdemeanants. No other state copied the idea, and the concept of work release languished for four decades. It gained great popularity after North Carolina adopted it in 1957.[38]

Several factors account for the decline in activity after 1915. An overwhelming majority of states simply completed building their correctional networks. The majority of the holdouts were in the South, an area that had traditionally resisted correctional innovation. Also, the advent of World War I sapped the strength of progressive reform in all areas of American life. Finally, as Blake McKelvey suggests, the field of American corrections entered a period of uncertainty and drift after 1910.[39]

The crisis in corrections was not simply the lack of new ideas. It was more the confrontation with difficult and mundane problems of administration. In one sense the history of American corrections was repeating itself. Nearly a century earlier the creation of the prison, far from solving the problem of crime, only introduced a new and more difficult set of problems: how to manage the institution. Probation, parole, the indeterminate sentence, and the juvenile court were exciting ideas, and this excitement spurred the enormous activity of the 1900–1915 period. But once these new institutions were established, correctional officials faced the problems of administering them.

Probation illustrated the many issues involved in correctional administration. Who should receive probation? Authorities generally agreed that juveniles, first offenders, and those guilty of minor offenses were the prime candidates. But even these broad categories provided precious little guidance. Furthermore, what mechanism existed to monitor or control the judicial decision to grant probation? As a form of correctional treatment, probation was based on the idea of effective supervision. Who then should serve as probation officers? A survey by the U.S. Children's Bureau in 1918 found that only 1,071 of the 2,391 courts had full-time, paid officers, while 337 used irregularly employed officers. Another 42 courts relied on truant officers from the schools, 43 used police officers, and 58 depended on volunteers. Also in question was the nature of supervision. What should it consist of? And supervision raised the issue of caseload size and the supervision of the probation officers themselves.[40]

Answers to these and related administrative issues were necessary if probation was to be more than a slogan. The response came in the form of a self-conscious professionalization movement. The National Probation Association was organized in 1907, and the U.S. Children's Bureau also undertook a number of activities related to the development of standards for juvenile justice. (The role of the Children's Bureau had important long-term significance: it marked the advent of a more direct role for the federal government in the administration of criminal justice. This involvement would grow slowly over the next few decades until finally becoming a major factor in the late 1960s.)

The legal status of probation at the federal level received a traumatic shock with the 1916 "Killits" case (*In re U.S.*). The U.S. Supreme Court, drawing a distinction between suspension of sentence and supervised probation, ruled that probation was not sanctioned by the common law. In the absence of a federal statute authorizing judges to grant probation, the ruling threw a cloud over the status of several thousand persons then on probation from various federal courts. To resolve the immediate crisis, President Wilson granted pardons to some five thousands probationers. Agitation began immediately for a federal probation law, but one was not passed until 1925.[41]

The indeterminate sentence and parole introduced a set of administrative questions similar to those raised by probation. Who should be granted parole? How soon? On what basis? By whom? Under what conditions? And so on. The advocates of parole had to defend the concept against charges that society was being threatened by the early release of dangerous criminals. Replies to these allegations revealed a disturbing trend toward longer prison terms. In a forcefully argued editorial in the *Journal of Criminal Law and Criminology*, Robert H. Gault claimed that 80 percent of those on parole "made good," and only 5 percent committed new crimes while under supervision. "There is no evidence that society is endangered thus far through unwarranted parole of habitual criminals," he concluded. The indeterminate sentence, however, resulted in longer prison terms. The average time served by Illinois prisoners under the old sentencing laws was one year, seven months, and eleven days. Under the indeterminate sentence, the average increased to two years, ten months, and eight days. Moreover, the increase was most pronounced for second and third offenders. Second offenders at Joliet state prison served an average of two years and twenty-seven days under the old system and slightly more than four years under the new system. The terms of third offenders increased from an average of two and a half years to six years.[42]

These figures dramatized the ambiguity in correctional reform that had been evident in Zebulon Brockway's initial ideas. The advocates of the new penology saw it as both a more scientific and humanitarian response: scientific in the sense that officials could fashion a punishment that fit the offender, and humanitarian in that this individualized justice would serve the offender who genuinely reformed (and thus could earn early release). But the effect was to lengthen actual prison terms; and since the prisons offered little to facilitate rehabilitation, this meant an increase in the sum total of punishment. The indeterminate sentence greatly expanded the amount of discretion exercised by both judges and parole boards. Ungoverned by standards or mechanisms for review, the American approach to criminal sentences in the twentieth century became, in the words of Marvin Frankel, "law without order."[43]

Capital Punishment Under Attack

Anti–capital-punishment sentiment reawakened during the progressive era, drawing upon the humanitarian ethos of the period. The intensity of the campaign matched that of the pre-Civil War movement. Activity was strongest at the state level, for the movement lacked the focus of a strong national organization or prominent national leader. The effort to abolish the death penalty was also a striking illustration of the rise and sudden collapse of criminal-justice reform during the progressive era. It arose slowly in the 1890s, achieved considerable success between 1911 and 1917, and then suffered a stunning reversal in the next two years. The capital-punishment issue was a barometer of public attitudes toward the crime problem.

After some early failures in Massachusetts, Pennsylvania, New Jersey, Illinois, Ohio, and the U.S. Congress, the movement achieved its first success in 1907 when Kansas abolished the death penalty. Actually, no one had been executed in Kansas since passage of a "Maine Law" (requiring a one-year delay on executions) in 1872. In the next ten years six other states joined the abolitionist ranks: Minnesota (1911), Washington (1913), South Dakota and Oregon (1914), Arizona (1916), and Missouri (1917). Meanwhile, abolition bills passed one house of the legislature in six other states. Not since the 1840s and early 1850s had there been such widespread feeling against the death penalty. Other states approached near abolition by greatly restricting use of the death penalty. North Dakota retained it only for murder committed by a prisoner serving a life sentence, and Tennessee abolished it for all crimes except rape.[44]

The success of the movement was short-lived. By 1920 Washington, Oregon, Arizona, and Missouri restored the death penalty. Why the great success of abolitionism between 1907 and 1917 and the sudden reversal in the next two years? The fate of the anti-capital-punishment movement provides insight into the changing mood of the country and its impact upon attitudes toward crime and criminal justice—an impact that was felt for the next two decades.

Events in Missouri provided a microcosm of national trends. The Missouri legislature abolished the death penalty in the spring of 1917, but restored it again in 1919. The murder of two police officers immediately prior to abolition had greatly agitated the law-enforcement community. They led the fight for restoration and succeeded in getting a bill through the state senate. The bill might have died in the house of representatives had it not been for two more sensational events. In June 1919 a mob lynched a man sentenced to life imprisonment for murdering a sheriff and the sheriff's son. Then one police officer was killed and another wounded during a St. Louis bank robbery. The legislature was meeting in special session that year to ratify the women's suffrage amendment. Newspapers in Missouri popularized the idea of a massive national crime wave, and the legislature restored the death penalty for murder, treason, rape, kidnapping, and certain forms of perjury and train robbery.

Oregon voters restored the death penalty by popular referendum in 1920 after having abolished it in 1914. Actually, abolition succeeded by the narrowest of margins: 157 votes out of more than 200,000. Antiradical hysteria contributed significantly to the 1920 restoration. The radical Industrial Workers of the World (IWW) had been especially active in the Northwest and had suffered official repression and popular vigilantism. Oregon's governors fed the popular fears. Governor Withycombe warned in 1919 that the state needed a law against treason. His successor declared that "a wave of crime has swept over the country" and recommended restoration of the death penalty. In a referendum the voters restored it by a comfortable 17,000-vote margin.

The sudden shift in public sentiment over the death penalty was only one manifestation of a more pervasive change in attitudes. The idealism and optimism of the progressive era faded during the war years, and a series of crises in 1919 heightened fears of a breakdown in law and order. The next two decades were characterized by a more conservative approach to crime and punishment. The accomplishments of the progressive era, however, were significant. Concepts of police professionalism and correctional treatment had been defined and tested, and these ideas would not change substantially for the next half-century. The progressive era also left a powerful legacy in the various professional associations, which continued to be the major forces for change.

7

THE CRIME CONTROL DECADES, 1919–1940

Crime control became a steadily more prominent issue in national politics during the decades of the 1920s and 1930s. For the first time, presidents of the United States felt it necessary to speak and act on the crime problem. Shortly after taking office in 1929, Herbert Hoover appointed a national crime commission to study and make recommendations about the administration of criminal justice. By the 1930s two federal agencies, the FBI and the U.S. Bureau of Prisons, had become leaders in their respective fields, exemplifying the growing nationalization of crime control.

The expanded role of the federal government, like the return to the death penalty, was an indication of widespread public concern about crime and crime control. Attitudes hardened during the twenties and thirties. The progressive commitment to rehabilitation gave way to a "get-tough" attitude toward crime and criminals. The crises of 1919, gangland violence associated with prohibition in the 1920s, and a number of sensational crimes in the early 1930s all reinforced the concept of a "crime wave."

The short-term panics about crime waves reinforced long-term trends in the administration of criminal justice. The fear of crime fostered a demand for greater efficiency in apprehending, convicting, and punishing criminals. This in turn encouraged a "systems" perspective toward criminal justice. Experts increasingly raised questions about both the effectiveness of the various subsystems (law enforcement, the courts, corrections) and the extent to which they interacted in an efficient manner. The efficiency perspective became a steadily more important theme in criminal-justice reform.

1919: YEAR OF CRISIS

The year 1919 was an exceptionally anxious period in American life. World War I effected social changes and unleashed passions that erupted in a number of distinct crises that year. Although these events were separate phenomena, they merged in the public mind to create a national hysteria. The news media were filled with scare stories about rising crime and the break-down of law and order. Three events in particular encouraged the development of a hard-line public attitude toward the administration of criminal justice.

The Red Scare

The Red Scare of 1919–1920 involved the suppression of radical and left-wing political groups by the federal government, state agencies, and vigilante groups. The episode stands as one of the worst chapters in the history of the violation of civil liberties in America. Members of radical groups, notably the IWW, were arrested en masse and even deported; the records of the IWW were seized and burned; and numerous other Americans guilty of no crime suffered harassment and arrest. The entire affair poisoned the atmosphere of American politics, leaving a cloud of suspicion over alleged "aliens and dissenters."[1]

The Red Scare had its origins during World War I. Opposition to American involvement was extremely widespread, notably among German-Americans and left-wing groups such as the American Socialist party and the IWW. Wartime passions unleashed a flood of hatred directed against foreigners, particularly Germans, in which German communities were attacked by mobs, the teaching of German virtually disappeared from the public schools, and hamburgers were renamed "liberty burgers." The federal government moved to suppress antiwar political groups. President Wilson's postmaster general banned Socialist party publications from the mail, while the Justice Department prosecuted and sent to prison party leader Eugene V. Debs.

The end of the war did not halt the attacks on foreigners and political dissidents. The Red Scare reached its climax with the "Palmer Raids" in January 1920. Attorney General A. Mitchell Palmer, a man with political ambitions, authorized a series of raids on January 2nd and 6th that resulted in more than five thousand arrests in thirty-three cities. More than five hundred of those arrested were later deported. The Bureau of Investigation, and an obscure bureaucrat named J. Edgar Hoover, played an important role in setting the stage for the Palmer Raids by developing lists of alleged subversives and fostering the idea that it was "un-American" to hold certain ideas or belong to certain organizations. Hoover, of course, went on to become director of the bureau in 1924 and authorized a long series of illegal activities in the name of anticommunism from the 1930s through the 1970s.

The involvement of the Bureau of Investigation in the Red Scare represented the most ominous aspect of the nationalization of crime control. Dissent was equated with disloyalty; in effect the government criminalized certain political beliefs and associations. Federal sedition laws and "criminal syndicalism" statutes in many states became convenient tools for the repression of left-wing leaders and groups. Fear of radicalism had always been a part of American culture, but attacks on radicals had usually been carried out by local vigilante groups. Beginning in the World War I years, political repression became part of the federal criminal-justice machinery.

THE BIRTH OF THE ACLU

The Red Scare did not go unanswered. Even conservatives and moderate liberals were outraged by the abuses committed by government agencies. Out of the struggle to defend the victims of repression grew the American Civil Liberties Union. Initially, opponents of World War I organized the American League for the Limitation of Armaments in 1914. The league was soon renamed the American Union Against Militarism (AUAM). Roger Baldwin, a social worker from a comfortable middle-class background, organized a subgroup to defend conscientious objectors who had refused military conscription. Conservative members of the AUAM opposed this activity and, in a compromise settlement, Baldwin's work was relocated in a separate group called the Civil Liberties Bureau. It became the National Civil Liberties Bureau in 1917 and then the American Civil Liberties Union (ACLU) in 1920.[2]

The ACLU, a professional association committed to defending individual rights as defined in the U.S. Constitution, developed into an important force for change in American criminal justice. Its very existence represented a historic shift in the administration of justice. Individual rights had been consistently violated throughout American history, but there had never been an organized effort to protect individuals against the abuses of vigilante groups or official agencies. The ACLU championed the abstract principles of constitutionalism as a check upon the passions of "popular justice." The ACLU was part of an important long-term shift in thinking within the American legal profession. Gradually, the Bill of Rights became nationalized along with crime control. By the 1960s state and local criminal-justice agencies were held accountable to national standards as defined in the Bill of Rights and interpreted by the U.S. Supreme Court.

Racism and Riots

Racial violence swept the country during the "long hot summer" of 1919. There were at least twenty serious disturbances that year, including major riots in Chicago, Omaha, Knoxville, and Washington, D.C. This was the climax of twenty years of steadily worsening race relations in both the North and South. An epidemic of lynchings (an average of more than one hundred per year) accompanied the advent of institutionalized segregation in the South, but race relations were little better in the North. The New York City race riot of 1900 set the pattern for interracial violence over the next two decades. Rumors of an alleged assault by blacks unleashed an orgy of white aggression. White New Yorkers ran through the streets beating any blacks they found, even pulling persons from streetcars. The police not only ignored white violence, but took part in the attacks themselves.[3]

The 1919 Chicago riot, the worst single disorder, illustrated both the causes and the consequences of urban racial violence. Wartime prosperity accelerated the "great migration," the movement of black Americans from the rural South to the urban North. Blacks and whites competed for jobs, housing, and the use of recreational areas. The Chicago riot erupted on a Lake Michigan beach when a black youth crossed the unofficial color line that divided the white and black swimming areas. Whites threw rocks and killed him. A general melee broke out on the beach, and before long the entire city was engulfed in riot.

The pattern of rioting (in Chicago and other cities) involved white aggression and black retaliation. Gangs of whites swept into the ghetto to kill and burn. Blacks passing through white areas on their way to jobs were also attacked. Although the governor mobilized the state militia on the fourth day of rioting, lawlessness prevailed for more than a week. When it was over thirty-eight persons were dead (twenty-three black, fifteen white) and more than five hundred were injured. Arson, meanwhile, left more than a thousand black Chicagoans homeless.[4]

The riots in Chicago and elsewhere produced another phenomenon of twentieth-century politics: the riot commission. A committee of the U.S. Congress examined the 1917 riot in East St. Louis, Illinois, while the Chicago Commission on Race Relations studied the Chicago riot. These reports revealed serious misconduct by the police. The racist actions of the police took three specific forms. Discriminatory law enforcement contributed to racial tensions leading up to the outbreak of violence. During the riot police largely ignored white violence (thereby persuading blacks that their only hope lay in retaliatory violence) and arrested blacks in disproportionate numbers. Finally, police officers often became active rioters themselves.[5]

Despite the overwhelming evidence of police racism, nothing was done to improve police-community relations in the aftermath of the riots. Police chiefs attending the annual conventions of the IACP completely ignored the issue of race relations, and the recommendations of the Chicago Commission on Race Relations

fell on deaf ears. In his 1920 book *American Police Systems,*
Raymond Fosdick mentioned only the problem of "negro criminality." Several factors explain this response. Most police chiefs
and other public officials shared the racism that pervaded America
in those years. Only a small number of people were actively
committed to the idea of racial equality and integration. Police
reformers were preoccupied with other issues, one of which was
the establishment of police training programs. Special training in
race relations was virtually unthinkable in an era when most
police departments offered no formal training of any sort.

Another reason for the lack of response was the curious fact that
race riots virtually disappeared after the 1919 orgy of violence.
Historians have identified only two significant incidents between
1919 and 1943: the 1921 Tulsa and 1935 Harlem riots. Why did the
riots cease? Violence can be seen as a response to the initial phase
of a major social change. Just as the riots of the 1830s were a
consequence of the first wave of immigration from Europe, so the
riots of 1900–1919 were a result of the "great migration" of blacks
to the cities. Patterns of accommodation were then established.
The urban ghetto represented an institutionalized form of racial
segregation. Whites tolerated the black presence in the city as
long as segregation confined them to certain jobs and neighborhoods.

The riots of the 1900–1919 period were a clear warning signal
of problems ahead for the administration of criminal justice. The
inner-city poor had always suffered the worst abuses at the hands
of the system. As blacks replaced European immigrants as the
major group in the cities, the problems of justice (police conduct,
disparities in sentencing) became inseparable from the questions
of race and racism. Even though rioting disappeared during the
twenties and thirties, the race problem remained. It erupted again
in the early 1940s and then became *the* dominant issue in the
administration of criminal justice during the 1960s.

The Boston Police Strike

The strike by the Boston police in September 1919 is perhaps the
most famous event in the history of American policing. Coming

in the midst of nationwide racial turmoil, the Red Scare, and bitter strikes in other major industries, it galvanized public fears of a breakdown in law and order. President Woodrow Wilson called it a "crime against civilization," and Massachusetts governor Calvin Coolidge built his own national political reputation on the basis of his statement that "there is no right to strike against the public safety by anybody, anywhere, at any time."

The immediate cause of the strike was the inflation produced by the wartime economy. The cost of living doubled between 1915 and 1920, while salaries for the police and most other public employees remained the same. In addition to the basic necessities of life, Boston police officers had to purchase their own uniforms, and price of these doubled during the war. Police officers also felt bitter and alienated because their status had dropped relative to that of other working people. During the nineteenth century, police salaries had far exceeded the earnings of factory workers and skilled craftsmen. But as unionism spread among these other occupations, the police lost their traditional advantage.[6]

Police unionism was also a long-term consequence of the professionalization movement. In their effort to make policing a profession, reformers sought to promote the idea of police work as a lifelong career. Cincinnati, one of the first police departments to professionalize, began to experience difficulties with its pension fund in the late 1890s as more officers remained on the force until retirement. The more police officers expected to make a career of policing, the more interested they became in organizing professional associations of their own. Fraternal organizations sprang up in the middle of the nineteenth century, but they became a more potent factor in the 1890s. The New York Patrolman's Benevolent Association, for example, began lobbying for salary increases and other benefits.

Unfortunately, the leaders of the police professionalization movement did not respond to the changing attitudes of rank-and-file officers. Most of the reformers were contemptuous of the rank and file. The average officer, they believed, was an unqualified and untrained political appointee. Raymond Fosdick spoke for most of the reformers when he argued that police departments needed strong executives who had a free hand to hire and fire.

Significantly, Fosdick and his colleagues objected to civil service which, they felt, protected the incompetent officers. In short, the reformers failed to perceive that career police officers would inevitably seek to have some effective voice in police affairs.

Prounion sentiment among the police spread rapidly across the country in 1917. It was a spontaneous, grass-roots movement, for police officers were impressed by the gains made by unions in the private sector. The movement caught organized labor off guard. The American Federation of Labor had serious reservations about attempting to organize the police. In June 1919, however, grass-roots pressure forced the AFL to change its position. It endorsed unionism and in the next two months issued charters to thirty-three of the sixty-five locals that applied for recognition.

The Boston police were not the first to strike. Cincinnati police officers walked off the job in a brief three-day strike in September 1918. Although no formal union existed, officers demanded that their maximum salaries be increased from $1,260 to $1,500 a year. The strike was a remarkable event. For two full days the city was policed by only 48 nonstriking officers and a 600-person volunteer force. Even more remarkable, law and order prevailed despite a massive selective-service parade of some 25,000 people in downtown Cincinnati. The city had a large German-American population, and anti-German passions had flared across the county. On the third day the striking police returned to their jobs; several weeks later they gained a salary increase.

Events took a very different turn in Boston. The officers' fraternal group, the Boston Social Club, began seeking a $200 a year raise in late 1917. After negotiations produced nothing for a year and a half, the club voted to become a union and affiliate with the AFL. The question of affiliation became the principal obstacle to a settlement. Police Commissioner Edwin U. Curtis, an arrogant and inflexible person, ordered his officers to disaffiliate. When they refused Curtis took disciplinary action against the leaders of the Boston Social Club. The firing of nineteen officers precipitated the strike.[7]

On Tuesday afternoon, September 9, 1919, a total of 1,117 police officers walked off their jobs, leaving only 427 officers available for duty. Disorder erupted in the city. In addition to looting and vandalism, citizens attacked both striking and non-striking officers. Prominent members of the community, including many from Harvard University, organized a volunteer force to help preserve order. After much confusion and delay, Governor Coolidge mobilized the state militia, which took control of the city by Thursday afternoon. Compared with the recent race riots, the disorders were rather limited. But newspapers across the country painted a lurid and exaggerated picture of "anarchy" in Boston.

Public opinion turned against the police, and the strike soon collapsed. All the striking officers were fired and replaced by new recruits. Meanwhile, police unionism in other cities quickly subsided, and by 1920 the movement was completely dead. The Boston police strike discredited police unionism for decades. As a result American police officers acquired no effective voice in police administration. Instead, they retreated to their fraternal associations, such as the Fraternal Order of Police (FOP), which avoided any overt political activity. The defeat of police unionism fostered the development of a distinct *police subculture*.[8] Without a mechanism for expressing legitimate grievances, the alienation and anger of police officers expressed itself in terms of suspicion and hostility toward the public. Police executives, however, found their hand strengthened. The management style of American policing became steadily more authoritarian in the decades that followed.

THE ERA OF THE CRIME COMMISSION

The crime commission became the principal instrument of criminal-justice reform in the 1920s. It was a logical outgrowth of progressivism, but also another manifestation of the crime-wave scare of the period. Essentially, a crime commission was a professional association that mobilized the talents of experts from different fields (or different geographic areas) and focused their energies on a specific set of problems. Commission reports were then used to arouse public opinion and win support for specific recommendations. The various commissions also reflected the crime-control perspective that dominated thinking in the 1920s. They emphasized improving the efficiency with which the criminal-justice system apprehended, convicted, and punished offenders.

Crime commissions took many forms. The first one established, the Chicago Crime Commission, was a private agency funded by local businessmen which adopted the role of a permanent watchdog over the local criminal-justice system. The Chicago Crime Commission grew out of a spectacular daytime payroll robbery in downtown Chicago in 1917. Local businessmen became alarmed at the thought that the machinery of justice was not adequate to protect their interests. They founded the commission, which began its work in January 1919. The commission published a monthly *Bulletin* reporting on local developments. "Modern Crime," it declared, "like modern business, is tending toward centralization, organization and commercialization." Because "our criminals apply business methods, it was necessary to bring business-like efficiency to the administration of justice."[9]

Other crime commissions took different approaches. The Cleveland Survey of Criminal Justice was an agency that delivered its final report and disbanded. Numerous crime commissions were created as public agencies. In many states, for example, the legislature established a temporary commission for the purpose of revising the criminal code. Crime commissions also appeared at the national level. Business groups sponsored the National Crime Commission in 1925 and modeled it after the Chicago Crime Commission. President Herbert Hoover then created the National Commission on Law Observance and Enforcement in 1929, following the model of the Cleveland survey.

Criminal Justice in Cleveland

The Cleveland Survey of Criminal Justice was the single most important crime commission. It established the model of examining a complete criminal-justice system and was copied by numerous state and federal crime commissions. The co-directors of the

Cleveland survey were two of the most significant figures in the history of American law: Roscoe Pound and Felix Frankfurter. Their influence contributed to the impressive scholarly weight of the final report. Like the Chicago Crime Commission, the Cleveland survey was prompted by a single highly publicized event. In early 1920 a local judge was implicated in a particularly sordid crime. This incident galvanized discontent with the quality of justice in the city, and the Cleveland Bar Association, the mayor, and a group of scholars at Western Reserve University joined in a call for a thorough examination of the local criminal-justice system. The Cleveland Foundation, a local philanthropy, provided funding, and a staff of thirty-five persons began work in early 1921.[10]

The final seven-hundred-page report, *Criminal Justice in Cleveland,* published in 1922, represented the best thinking on the subject to be found in the country. The section on the police, for example, was written by Raymond B. Fosdick, author of *American Police Systems*. Reginald Heber Smith, a prominent Boston attorney, author of *Justice and the Poor* and a principal advocate of legal-aid and public-defender systems, examined the criminal courts. Statistical work was handled by C. E. Gehlke, who subsequently did similar work with the Missouri and Illinois crime commissions.

The final chapter of the report, "Criminal Justice and the American city," represented a summation of the efficiency perspective on crime control. In it Roscoe Pound developed ideas he had set forth in his famous 1906 address. The administration of justice, he concluded, had nearly collapsed and was not able to perform its basic task of punishing criminals and preventing crime. The problem was threefold: "men, machinery, and environment." The administration of justice demanded better qualified personnel, changes in the structure of agencies to remove obstacles to speedy justice, and, finally, eliminating the corrupting influence of the political environment.

The most notable feature of the report was the section on the courts. In addition to analyzing the structure and personnel of the court system, the survey traced the flow of criminal cases. It found that about 60 percent of the felony cases initiated in 1919 were either dismissed or reduced to lower charges. Moreover, only one third of the cases that did reach a final judgment came to trial; the remainder were settled by guilty pleas. The Cleveland survey, in short, discovered plea bargaining. Actually, it discovered not only plea bargaining but the entire process of discretionary decision-making, involving the police, the lower courts, grand juries, and the prosecutor.

On this issue the Cleveland survey broke new ground in thinking about the administration of criminal justice. Previously, attention had been focused on the various components of the criminal-justice system, but these parts had been viewed as discrete units. By starting from the premise of improving efficiency and then looking at the flow of criminal cases, the survey conceptualized the criminal process *as a system*. It raised for the first time the question of inputs and outputs. This approach to the subject would dominate official thinking about the administration of criminal justice for the next half-century.

The Missouri and Illinois Surveys

Following publication of *Criminal Justice in Cleveland* in 1922, groups in other states copied the survey's approach. The work of two of the most important crime commissions of the period was summed up in *The Missouri Crime Survey* (1926) and *The Illinois Crime Survey* (1929). The Illinois and Missouri commissions originated with their respective state bar associations, were funded by business interests, and retained social scientists in the actual research. As studies of criminal justice at the state level, they had a broader perspective than the Cleveland survey. Both the Missouri and Illinois reports examined law enforcement in rural areas and the operations of state correctional programs. The Illinois survey also included a lengthy and valuable study of organized crime in Chicago.[11]

By examining state correctional programs, the Missouri and Illinois crime surveys carried one step further the conceptual approach of the Cleveland report. They examined not only the "mortality" of cases from arrest to trial, but also the outcomes of court disposition. They defined "success" in terms of imposing punishment and concluded that the system had failed. In his summary of the Missouri data, Raymond Moley found "an almost incredible contrast between cases begun and punishments decreed and a still more startling contrast between crimes committed and punishments administered. In St. Louis, for example, only one robber was punished for every twenty-five robberies committed." Large numbers of cases were dismissed without prosecution, and most convictions were the reslt of guilty pleas. Moley concluded that " the practice of a criminal profession is not unduly hazardous," for the risk of punishment seemed very low.[12]

The Missouri and Illinois crime surveys reflected the disillusionment with the philosophy of rehabilitation and the institution of parole. According to Moley the Missouri data suggested that parole was "a mere method of turning criminals loose without any reference to the fundamental principle upon which parole rests," namely rehabilitation. Of 254 criminals sent to prison from St. Louis, 40 were never incarcerated at all, and 100 of the remaining 214 obtained their release within a year and a half. Moley viewed this as an "astonishing breakdown of the whole system of punishment for crime in this state."[13] Similar findings emerged from the *Illinois Crime Survey*. Public disappointment was reflected in the decline in the relative proportion of convicts released on parole during the 1920s which followed the peak reached in 1917–1921.

The Wickersham Commission

The crime-commission phenomenon reached its culmination in 1929, when President Herbert Hoover appointed the National Commission on Law Observance and Enforcement, popularly known as the *Wickersham Commission* after its chairperson, former Attorney General George Wickersham. The fourteen reports published in 1931 represented the first comprehensive survey of American criminal justice at the national level.

Hoover had several reasons for establishing a national crime commission. An engineer by training, he believed in solving social problems by applying expert intelligence to them. For example, he also appointed a Commission on Recent Social Trends which examined virtually every phase of American life in its 1933 report. Public concern about the crime problem reached new heights in the late twenties. Highly publicized gangland murders in Chicago dramatized the general problem of lawlessness associated with prohibition. Prohibition also created a political problem for Hoover as the Republican party was split between "wets" and "drys." He hoped that the Wickersham Commission would recommend an effective compromise.

Although a landmark in the history of American criminal justice, the fourteen volumes published by the Wickersham Commission in 1931 had only a modest immediate impact. The Great Depression struck the economy in late 1929, and by 1931 the question of economic recovery dominated public attention. The commission also disappointed Hoover by failing to resolve the prohibition issue. While it documented pervasive nonenforcement of prohibition laws, the report opposed repeal of the Eighteenth Amendment.

One of the Wickersham Commission reports attracted virtually all the publicity. Report eleven, *Lawlessness in Law Enforcement,* created a national sensation with its revelations about the "third degree" and other abuses of authority by the police. It defined the third degree as "the inflicting of pain, physical or mental, to extract confessions or statements." Physical brutality was "extensively practiced" in police departments across the country. The commission documented cases where the police had suspended criminal suspects by their ankles out of second-story windows and subjected them to beatings and even sexual indignities in an effort to extract confessions. The Detroit police took suspects "around the loop," moving from one station house to another to isolate them from family, friends, and legal counsel. The chief of the Buffalo, New York, police expressed open contempt for guarantees of individual rights in the U.S. Constitution.[14]

The Wickersham Commission revelations had a profound impact on the police. The report reflected a widespread concern about police conduct and was accompanied by publication of a popular version entitled *Our Lawless Police* (1931) and by numerous magazine and newspaper articles. This represented a historic shift in public attitudes toward the police. The informed and articulate public was no longer willing to tolerate the misconduct that had been a part of American policing for so long. Publicity surrounding the third degree also gave a strong boost to police professionalization. Reform-minded police chiefs could now rely on a reservoir of public support for their efforts to improve their departments. Police misconduct remained a problem (surfacing again as a controversial issue in the 1960s), but the 1930s were a watershed. Brutality and abuse of authority became steadily less and less common.

The remaining volumes of the Wickersham Commission reports were a mixed bag. The best summarized the most advanced thinking on their respective subjects. Volume fourteen, *The Police*, was a concise statement of August Vollmer's views on police professionalism. Restating an agenda that had not changed in over twenty years, he called for the elimination of political interference, the use of experienced administrators with secure tenure, and higher qualifications for police officers. Report four, *Prosecution*, continued to explore the phenomenon of plea bargaining and the decline of the jury trial. Other volumes had such titles as *Criminal Statistics, Crime and the Foreign Born,* and *The Cost of Crime.* The commission refused to release a report on the controversial Mooney-Billings case, involving the repression of labor-union activists on the West Coast.

The Revival of Rehabilitation

Two volumes issued by the Wickersham Commission signaled the beginnings of a revival of the commitment to rehabilitation. The mood of the 1920s had not been hospitable to the idea of correctional treatment, as the somber conclusions of the Missouri and Illinois crime surveys testified. Yet beneath the surface of this public disillusionment, a new generation of correctional leaders was emerging. The late 1920s marked the stirrings of the third great cycle in American correctional reform, one that would build slowly and reach its peak in the mid-1960s.

Volume nine of the Wickersham Commission report, entitled *Penal Institutions, Probation and Parole,* unequivocally endorsed the concept of individualized correctional treatment: "Individualization is the root of adequate penal treatment." Casting aside the doubts expressed by previous crime commissions, it declared that parole was "the best means yet devised" for releasing persons from prison. In effect, the report was a restatement and elaboration of the ideas expressed by Zebulon Brockway at the Cincinnati congress. It admitted the failure of the prison ("the present prison system is antiquated and inefficient") and placed its hopes in noninstitutional forms of treatment, namely probation and parole.[15]

The report marked the coming of age of a new generation of penal administrators. Psychologist F. Lovell Bixby, following up on ideas first tested during the progressive era, developed an elaborate program of diagnosis and classification for the New Jersey prison system. Sanford Bates, meanwhile, earned a national reputation during his nine years as commissioner of corrections in Massachusetts. He too employed psychiatrists to examine incoming prisoners. In 1929 President Hoover hired Bates to become director of the new U.S. Bureau of Prisons. Bates in turn recruited some of the most talented persons in American corrections as his assistants. Under Bates's direction, the Bureau of Prisons assumed an important role in American corrections, setting the standard by which state programs would be judged.[16]

New Vistas in Criminology

The revival of rehabilitation derived much of its energy from new theoretical perspectives on criminal behavior. American criminology came into its own in the 1920s. Until then Americans had borrowed from the work done by European thinkers. By the end of World War I, American social and behavioral scientists began to make important orginal contributions of their own. The body of literature grew steadily during the twenties, and the Wickersham Commission summarized this development with a two-part report called *The Causes of Crime.*[17]

Two distinct though interrelated schools of thought emerged in American criminology. One emphasized the sociological factors surrounding criminal activity, while the other stressed the psychology of the offender. Despite different points of emphasis, the two merged. In the words of Dr. Bernard Glueck, who directed a pioneering psychiatric clinic at Sing Sing, "the criminal act, in every instance, is the resultant of the interaction between a particularly constituted personality and a particular environment." Both the sociological and psychological approaches rejected the more deterministic theories emanating from Europe, including both the genetic theories of Lombroso and the class-conflict theories of Marx, Engels, and their followers.[18]

The Wickersham Commission report gave an unequivocal endorsement to the sociological perspective on criminal behavior. In an extensive review of the literature, Morris Ploscowe concluded that "the soundest data on crime causation seem to have been contributed by the literature which has studied the criminal in terms of the demoralizing social influences which have acted upon him."[19] To give further support to this perspective, the Wickersham Commission devoted the entire second part of the report on the causes of crime to Clifford R. Shaw and Henry D. McKay's "Social Factors in Juvenile Delinquency."

Shaw and McKay were associated with the University of Chicago Department of Sociology, which generated the most original contributions to the study of crime. Members of this group explored the connection between delinquency and the problems of poverty, inadequate housing, broken homes, and the cultural-adjustment difficulties of second-generation Americans—all of which were concentrated most intensively in the slums of the inner city. Important early work on the social context of criminality was also done by social workers in the progressive era. Sophonisba Breckenridge and Edith Abbott in *The Delinquent*

Child and the Home (1912) found that 76.1 percent of the delinquent boys and 89 percent of the delinquent girls in Chicago came from homes that were either "poor" or "very poor."

Various environmental influences also reinforced tendencies toward criminal behavior. In his study *The Gang* (1921), Frederick Thrasher pointed out that while ganglike groups existed in all communities, they acquired a pathological character in the slum environment: "The definition of the situation for the gang boy must emanate largely from the disorderly life of the economic, moral and cultural frontiers of which gangland is a manifestation. The problem of gang morality, therefore, may be stated largely in terms of the patterns which prevail in the immediate social environment." Ploscowe, summarizing the work of others, argued "crime and juvenile delinquency, if not approved, are at least apt to be tolerated by a substantial portion of the adult population" in the "delinquency areas."[20] Clifford Shaw, author of *Delinquency Areas,* also suggested that penal institutions only reinforced antisocial attitudes. In *The Jack-Roller: A Delinquent Boy's Own Story* (1930), he reported that the inmate subculture celebrated criminal activity.

While the Chicago sociologists investigated the criminogenic facets of the urban environment, Sheldon and Eleanor Glueck of Harvard University made a major contribution toward the possible application of social-science data to the administration of correctional programs. In *500 Criminal Careers* (1930), the Gluecks conducted a follow-up study of 510 men released from the Massachusetts reformatory between 1911 and 1922. They reached the shocking conclusion that "almost four-fifths of our group were found to have committed criminal acts during the post-parole period." This recidivism rate of nearly 80 percent devastated the optimistic claims of success made by correctional administrators. In fact, it lent persuasive support to the public fears that correctional programs did not work.[21]

The Gluecks were not deterred by their gloomy statistics. To the contrary, their research suggested that probation and parole could be made to work through the proper application of the scientific method. *500 Criminal Careers* consisted of detailed examinations of the various factors in the lives of these men: their family, personal, and social backgrounds, criminal experience, conduct within the reformatory, and parole and postparole histories. Sifting this data for significant patterns, the Gluecks argued that "it was possible to construct prognostic instruments for the use of judges and administrative agencies concerned with the scientific administration of criminal justice."[22] In short, it would be possible to predict which individuals were more likely to "succeed" on parole. Decisions could then be made scientifically, rather than on an uninformed and arbitrary basis.

Roscoe Pound endorsed the Gluecks' view, contributing an entire chapter titled "Predictability in the Administration of Criminal Justice" to *500 Criminal Careers*. He pointed out the historical significance of the concept of prediction. The American approach to criminal justice had shifted from the idea of making the punishment fit the crime (which he characterized as a "futile, cast-iron" approach) to making the punishment ("penal treatment") fit the criminal. The individualization of treatment was at the heart of the whole idea of rehabilitation. Yet, it raised two problems. First, many people feared that correctional programs simply turned dangerous ciminals loose in society. Second, it threatened the liberty of the individual offender "by committing too much to the discretion of administrative officers." Public safety and individual liberty both demanded a more rational basis for decision-making.[23]

The research of the Gluecks, Thrasher, Shaw, and other criminologists underpinned the new burst of energy in correctional reform. A scientifically valid explanation of the causes of crime offered the prospect of a rational and effective basis for treatment programs. The continued development of the social sciences seemed to hold the key to fulfilling the age-old dream of individual treatment. The discipline of criminology responded to the interests of the practitioners. Theoretical criminology focused its attention on the search for the root causes of individual criminal behavior.

ORGANIZED CRIME: MYTHS AND REALITIES

The popular image of the 1920s, the so-called "roaring twenties," has always been one of prosperity, prohibition, jazz, a revolution in morals (led by the "flaming youth"), national folk heroes such as Babe Ruth and Charles Lindbergh, and the gangland violence of Al Capone and the St. Valentine's Day massacre. Although these images present a terribly one-sided view of the decade, they do contain important elements of truth. They also suggest some of the significant changes that occurred in American criminality, expecially the development of "organized" crime. The myths that surround organized crime convey only a part of the reality of this aspect of American life.

The intimate connection between vice, crime, and political corruption was nothing new. We have seen that vice districts arose and flourished in virtually every American city during the nineteenth century. Despite what the laws might say, a substantial number of people wanted gambling, prostitution, and alcohol at any time of day. The systematic corruption of municipal officials, especially the police and judges of the lower courts, protected the vice districts. But the vice business, like other businesses of the day, was relatively small-scale. The significant phenomenon of the twenties was that vice, the provision of illegal goods and services, became *big* business. The emergence of organized crime involved the adoption of big-business techniques: consolidation, rational organization, and the elimination of competition.

The key to the transformation of the vice business was the Eighteenth Amendment to the U.S. Constitution, the "noble experiment" in national prohibition. Supported by enabling legislation, the Volstead Act, prohibition went into effect on January 16, 1920. The Anti-Saloon League had promised the day before that "a new nation will be born." They were very wrong. Not only did the experiment in prohibition fail to end the consumption of alcoholic beverages, but it generated a number of unfortunate consequences. Prohibition was simply impossible to enforce. The federal goverment put only slightly more than three thousand agents in the field, state governments contributed little additional help, and municipal police forces, already steeped in a long tradition of corruption, adapted easily to the new order.[24]

With the demand for alcohol unabated and the risk of punishment rather low, prohibition opened up an enormously profitable field of endeavor. It was the special genius of Johnny Torrio, the most prominent figure in Chicago's vice business, to recognize that profits could be increased through oligopoly. Torrio drove smaller competitors out of business (through bombing or murder) and established agreements for the orderly division of territories with other large operators. It was the classic style of American big business. Torrio assumed his leadership in Chicago in 1920 upon the death of James Colosimo in the same year that prohibition went into effect.[25]

The Torrio arrangement rested upon a corrupt relationship with the Chicago police and the rest of city government. The mayoral administration of William ("Big Bill") Thompson between 1919 and 1923 happily complied. The system broke down with the election of Mayor William Dever in 1923. Promising to clean up the city, Dever ordered his police chief to crack down on the bootlegging industry. This set off the famous "beer wars." With Torrio's power challenged by the authorities, smaller operators decided to carve out a larger portion of the business for themselves. The result was violent competition for control of the Chicago bootlegging industry. Chicago criminals murdered an estimated 215 of their colleagues between 1923 and 1926, while the police killed another 160 suspected gangsters.

Al Capone assumed control of the Torrio organization in 1925, after Torrio suffered both a short jail term and a nearly fatal gunshot wound. Far more ruthless than his predecessor, Capone established complete dominance of the Chicago crime syndicates by 1929. The Capone organization murdered one major competitor, Hymie Weiss, leader of the North Side organization, and then brought the gangland wars to a brutal climax with the famous St. Valentine's Day "massacre." The reelection of the corrupt "Big Bill" Thompson as mayor in 1927 helped to restore order to the crime business.

Crime was incredibly lucrative. A federal agent estimated in 1927 that the Capone organization controlled annual revenues of $60 million from bootlegging, $25 million from gambling, $10 million from miscellaneous vice services, and another $10 million from the "rackets," involving the control of labor unions and the extortion of money from businesses. Two events testified to the "organized" character of criminal activity in Chicago. Capone went to federal prison in 1931 for income-tax evasion, and then prohibition was repealed in 1933. Yet, the crime syndicates continued to flourish. In effect they were like modern corporations, large bureaucracies that could survive the loss of a top leader and adapt to changing business conditions.

The Gangster as Popular Hero

The myth of organized crime was almost as powerful a force as the reality. The American public became fascinated with the evil doings of the crime syndicates. While the newspapers chronicled the violent gangland wars, Hollywood transformed the gangster into a national folk hero. A rash of gangster films appeared in the early 1930s, with Edward G. Robinson as "Little Caesar" (1930), James Cagney as "The Public Enemy" (1931), and Paul Muni as "Scarface" (1932). Hollywood script writers created a rough and fast-paced style of conversation that captured the public imagination. The image of the amoral gangster created such a vivid impression that professional comedians were still imitating the Robinson and Cagney roles four decades later.[26]

The gangster as hero was only one part of a general phenomenon of the late 1920s and early 1930s. Radio and the movies emerged as genuine mass media in the 1920s, exerting a powerful influence on public attitudes. They transformed both real and fictional persons into larger-than-life creations. Hollywood stars became models of dress, language, and behavior for the common person. The exploits of Babe Ruth, Charles Lindbergh, and others were also inflated to near mythic proportions. The film gangster was simply another of these national heroes, in this case an antihero.

A reaction to the image of criminals as heroes set in almost immediately, at least in some circles. Sensitive to accusations that it made crime glamorous, Hollywood adopted the Breen Code in 1934. Among other things the code dictated that films demonstrate the point that crime does not pay. Both the FBI and the IACP persuaded Hollywood to produce law-and-order-oriented films. The public fascination with crime and criminals remained, providing an endless source of material for the movies, radio ("Gangbusters," "The FBI in Peace and War"), the popular novel, and eventually television ("Dragnet," "Perry Mason," and a host of "cop" shows).

The mass media played a complex role in simultaneously reflecting and manipulating public attitudes. These attitudes were themselves a curious mixture of love and hate. The enormous success of *The Godfather* in the 1970s, first as a novel and then as two films, testified to the continuing fascination with organized crime. The media deepened the myth of the "Mafia" to the point where it was difficult to tell where reality ended and the myth began. The public image of the police, meanwhile, was shaped in a profound but unfortunate manner by television cop shows, beginning with "Dragnet." The image of the outlaw reappeared in the slightly different form of the rebel as hero in the 1950s.

LAW AND ORDER IN THE 1930s

The New Crime Wave

Despite the publicity about a national crime wave in the 1920s, the actual level of serious crime increased only slightly. Surveying the available data in *Recent Social Trends* (1933), criminologists Edwin Sutherland and C. E. Gehlke found "no evidence here of a 'crime wave,' but only a slowly rising level."[27] But in the early 1930s, a series of sensational crimes stirred public hysteria about crime to new heights. The 1932 kidnap-murder of the infant son of Charles and Anne Lindbergh was a major news event. A kidnapping scare swept the country, resulting in a number of harsh antikidnapping laws. At the same time, the exploits of John Dillinger, Ma Barker, Alvin "Creepy" Karpis, and Bonnie and Clyde generated even more publicity than the gangland violence of the twenties.

J. Edgar Hoover played a major role in creating the hysteria of the 1930s. He skillfully manipulated the media and transformed a group of otherwise ordinary criminals into national "public enemies." Bureau publicity always emphasized the prominent role of its agents, and Hoover in particular. Dillinger became the most famous criminal in the history of the bureau (the official version of the case conveniently ignored the repeated bungling by bureau agents in their pursuit of him).[28]

Hoover was a new breed of bureaucrat, the first to understand the key role of the mass media in shaping public attitudes. Genuinely disturbed about Hollywood's glamorization of criminals, he set out to create an alternative role model: the cop as hero; the FBI agent as a fearless, professional, and relentlessly efficient law-enforcement officer. Heroes, of course, need to do battle against great enemies. So Hoover inflated the reputation of the Dillingers to make bureau exploits all the more impressive. In addition to shaping public attitudes, Hoover used the media to serve his own ends. By exaggerating the threat of crime and posing as the last bulwark of law and order, he was able to expand the size and role of his agency. He became the master of public relations, cultivating his image and using it for political advantage.

The New Federal Role

The crime scare of the early thirties provoked both the White House and the Congress into action. In the wake of the Lindbergh tragedy, Congress rushed through the "Lindbergh Law," making kidnapping a federal offense. Two years later Congress passed a series of laws expanding the scope of federal jurisdiction over criminal activity. It added new provisions to the Lindbergh

Law and enacted the Fugitive Felon Law, which made it a crime to cross state lines to avoid prosecution. The Interstate Theft Act expanded federal jurisdiction over the interstate transportation of stolen merchandise, while the National Firearms Act was a tentative but very weak first step in the direction of federal gun control. Later in 1934 Roosevelt's attorney general, Homer Cummings, convened a national conference on crime.[29]

The depression only heightened public fears of a breakdown in law and order. The economic collapse stimulated a revival of socialism and communism, which in turn frightened conservatives. But both moderates and conservatives were disturbed by the growing militancy of the American labor movement, particularly as shown by the sit-down strikes in the automobile industry. The marijuana scare of the mid-thirties was also evidence of public anxieties. Harry Anslinger of the Bureau of Narcotics, following the example of fellow bureaucrat Hoover, mounted a publicity blitz about the threat of "reefer madness." One result was the Marijuana Tax Act of 1937, establishing harsh penalties for the possession and sale of marijuana.

The Transformation of the FBI

The FBI represented the most significant expansion of federal criminal-justice activities. Under Hoover's direction the bureau experienced a dramatic transformation in the early 1930s. By the end of the decade, Hoover had carved out a role as the nation's "top cop," and FBI procedures were regarded as the very essence of police professionalism. The change was especially remarkable in light of Hoover's first years in charge. Attorney General Harlan Fiske Stone appointed him director of the scandal-ridden bureau in 1924. Although implicated in the abuses of the Red Scare, Hoover in 1924 appeared to be little more than a cautious and faceless bureaucrat. Ironically, even the American Civil Liberties Union supported his appointment. In the next ten years Hoover quietly managed the bureau, reducing the scope of its operations and raising its personnel standards.[30]

The first important change came in 1930, when the bureau won the responsibility for administering the new Uniform Crime Reports (UCR) system. As the first national crime-records system, the UCR was a landmark event in the history of American criminal justice. Various individuals and organizations had agitated for such a system since the late nineteenth century. The IACP attempted to maintain a national crime-records system in the late 1890s but lacked the necessary funds and expertise. Different state agencies and the U.S. Census Bureau maintained statistics on criminal sentences and prison populations from the mid-nineteenth century onward. In 1911, however, prison reformer Louis N. Robinson declared all the existing statistics to be worthless.

The systems perspective that emerged in the 1920s increased the need for accurate criminal statistics. They were necessary, the experts argued, to measure the effectiveness of both law enforcement and correctional programs. Finally, the IACP launched a new campaign in 1927. A collaborative effort drew experts from many different groups: the IACP itself, the Bureau of Investigation, professional social workers, and the Rockefeller Foundation, which provided funding for the project. Most of the work was done by Bruce Smith, staff member of the National Institute of Public Administration and one of the leading experts on police administration.[31]

The UCR system, in which the FBI served as a central clearing house for reports of "crimes known to the police" submitted by local law-enforcement agencies, had serious flaws. These included its failure to deal with unreported crime, the lack of any auditing procedure to determine accuracy of figures, and the inefficiency of records maintained by most police departments, including instances of willful falsification for political reasons. Moreover, the system focused attention on seven felonies (which became the so-called index crimes) to the exclusion of other offenses. Thus, it presented a distorted picture of criminal activity. Despite its flaws, it remained unchallenged as the authoritative measure of criminality for the next four decades.

The FBI and Police Professionalism

As custodian of the UCR system, the FBI enhanced its status considerably in relation to local police departments. Henceforth, they reported to Washington, and the bureau had the privilege of announcing the annual crime index. The effect was subtle but important. For leadership in law enforcement, the message said, look to Washington. Hoover also established the bureau as the paragon of professionalism. The result was a reorientation of the idea of policing, emphasizing tough and efficient crime-fighting. The social-service aspects of the police role fell into eclipse. Hoover's authoritarian and quasimilitary style of administration shaped American law enforcement for decades to come.

The professional law-enforcement officer, according to the bureau, was highly trained. The FBI set the standard for law-enforcement training in two ways. It offered an intensive curriculum for its own agents, and it began to train officers from local departments in its National Police Academy. The idea of a national police school or institute of criminology had been suggested at the 1934 Attorney General's Conference on Crime, but the FBI seized upon the concept and made it its own. The National Police Academy began operation in July 1935. By virtue of training local officers in intensive courses, the bureau gained another degree of status vis-à-vis the local police.

The bureau also put a great deal of emphasis on scientific crime detection. In 1932 it opened its crime laboratory for the examination of hair and blood specimens, firearms, and other evidence from crime scenes. The aura of modern science became an important dimension of the growing image of the FBI as an efficient crime-fighter. Even more important was the fascination with fingerprints. The fingerprint method of identification had arrived in the United States in 1904 and quickly replaced other systems. But until the 1930s, it still filled only a minor role in the law-enforcement repertoire. Hoover, with a genuine fetish for fingerprints, changed all that. He won a fight to control federal fingerprint files in 1930 and then embarked on a campaign to collect as many prints as possible. Starting with slightly more than 800,000 sets of prints, the bureau built up a collection that numbered more than 159,000,000 by 1974, with 3,000 new sets arriving daily.

Nothing better illustrated the crime-control mood of the country in the mid-thirties than the brief flirtation with universal finger-printing. Hoover, August Vollmer, and other prominent figures advocated fingerprinting every American citizen. In 1935–1936 a national campaign was launched to secure, voluntarily, every-one's prints. (American law-enforcement officials had long been impressed with national identification systems used in Europe.) Hoover once again turned to the media. Prominent citizens such as John D. Rockefeller, Jr., Walt Disney, and even President Roosevelt publicly submitted their prints to the FBI's Civil Identi-fication Division. Meanwhile, local officials embarked on simi-lar campaigns in a number of cities. Nearly half the population of Berkeley, California, for example, submitted to voluntary finger-printing. Fortunately, the universal fingerprinting campaign proved to be a fad and disappeared within two years. But the FBI continued its relentless collection of prints in Washington.[32]

Another disturbing aspect of FBI-style professionalism was the stress on firearms. The bureau put great emphasis on marksman-ship in the National Police Academy curriculum (it even offered training in firing machine guns from moving patrol cars). Grad-ually, the handgun became the symbol of the American police officer. This represented a historic shift in American policing, for weapons had received very little emphasis in the early history of the police. The sudden cult of the gun in the 1930s was part of a pervasive upsurge in domestic violence. Homicide rates reached a peak in the mid-thirties, as did the number of civilians shot and killed by the police. The Chicago police killed sixty-two "crimi-nals" in 1931, forty-eight in 1932, and fifty-five in 1933. The figures then began a gradual decline. Police departments also stocked up on other weapons. Chemical manufacturers found the police a lucrative market for tear gas and other crowd-control devices. In short, for the first time in their history the American police fully embraced a military mentality, complete with the ideology of a "war" on crime and the weaponry to carry it out.

The FBI further contributed to the miltarization of American law enforcement through the example of Hoover's administrative style. Hoover established a rigid authoritarian regime. He won exemption of bureau special agents from federal civil-service regulations, thereby gaining a free hand to hire, fire, promote, and demote as he pleased. Stories of Hoover's arbitrary and capricious personnel practices became a fundamental aspect of the bureau's image. In this respect, however, he simply fulfilled the goal of police professionalism as it had been defined by Fosdick and Vollmer years before. Strong executive leadership, they had argued, was the way to upgrade the police.

Hoover tood a cynical attitude toward the U.S. Constitution. In a series of speeches and articles in the FBI *Law Enforcement Bulletin,* he counseled against brutal, "third-degree" tactics. Coerced confessions risked bad publicity and possible loss of the case on appeal. Thus, the professional approach was both constitutional and more effective. In the wake of the Wickersham Commission revelations about police brutality, Hoover's approach earned him wide popularity. His actions, however, did not match his rhetoric. By the late 1930s, he launched the bureau on a systematic campaign of illegal actions against alleged subversives.[33]

The Hidden Revolution in Police Work

As Hoover refashioned the image of law enforcement, American police work was undergoing a quiet but radical change of its own. Tragically, the two developments were moving in opposite directions. While the police role was redefined toward crimefighting, day-to-day police work increasingly involved miscellaneous services to the public. Few people noticed this hidden revolution. Not until the 1960s, when a major racial crisis forced a complete reexamination of the police, did experts discover that the image and reality of policing had radically diverged.

Modern technology made the revolution in police work possible. The primary agent of change was the automobile, although

the telephone and the two-way radio played important supporting roles. The automobile affected policing in several different
ways. By fostering the growth of suburbs and the physical expansion of the city, it enormously increased the area to be patrolled.
At the same time, criminals themselves took to the automobile
and became more mobile. Of necessity then, the police slowly
converted from foot patrol to automobile patrol. The allocation
of patrol cars became the primary issue in police administration.
O. W. Wilson, pupil of August Vollmer, established a national
reputation on the basis of his pioneering work in managing
automobile patrol. Increased efficiency in patrol "coverage" was
important for two reasons: to keep up with the expansion of the
cities, and because the depression limited the growth of police
departments.

The automobile had a curious effect on police contacts with
civilians. On the one hand, the patrol car removed the officer
from the street and eliminated a great deal of routine police-
civilian contact. At the same time, it brought the police into an
adversarial relationship with new segments of the population.
Previously, the middle and upper classes had had little contact
with the police. In the age of the automobile, however, the traffic
laws governed every driver, regardless of social class. Minor traffic
offenses became the source of a strong undercurrent of conflict
between the police and the public.

The communications revolution altered police work in yet a
different direction. The telephone and the two-way radio permitted the rapid mobilization of police service. For the first time the
citizen could pick up the phone and summon the police, for
whatever reason. The more progressive departments vigorously
advertised the availability of assistance, and as a result the public
gradually called upon the police for a wider range of services. By
the 1960s noncriminal matters consumed as much as 80 percent of
police time. During the same period, police supervisors found
that the new communications technology facilitated monitoring
the whereabouts of patrol officers. Command and control became
far tighter and more centralized than ever before in the history of

the American police. The communications revolution of course did not occur overnight. It was a gradual process that began in the 1920s and was completed by the late 1950s.[34]

While day-to-day police work increasingly involved noncriminal activities, the crime-fighter image continued to grow. The advent of the UCR in 1930 contributed to this development. Simply because it was the only available set of statistics (and no one thought to devise a different one), it became the standard measure of police work. "Success" in policing was defined by the fluctuations of the official crime rate and the percentage of crimes cleared. This drew attention even further away from the noncriminal, social-service aspects of policing.

The National-Security Issue

In 1934 President Roosevelt took the fateful step of asking the FBI to investigate the activities of various German-American groups in the country. Hitler's Nazis had taken control of Germany in 1933, and the President was concerned about possible attempts to influence American foreign policy. This request contributed to an ominous trend in American criminal justice. As during the World War I–era Red Scare, the government in effect made it a crime to hold certain political beliefs or belong to certain organizations. Protection of "national security" justified an intrusion into the First Amendment rights of Americans. The intelligence agencies, particularly the FBI, proceeded to abuse their authority. The harassment of political dissidents became a permanent feature of the federal bureaucracy.[35]

Hoover wasted no time in capitalizing on this new opportunity to expand the size and jurisdiction of his agency. In 1936 the bureau received a mandate to investigate all forms of alleged subversion. Three years later Roosevelt authorized it to coordinate all antiespionage and counterintelligence efforts. The FBI gained an enormous amount of power and status in the process. Other federal agencies, including the State Department, were required to report to it. In 1940 Congress passed the Smith Act, which made it a crime to advocate the overthrow of the government by force or violence. The law gave the antisubversion campaign legal justification.

The formal authority granted the FBI by the President and Congress constituted only one part of its expanded role. Far more important were covert and often illegal activities of FBI agents against political groups. The full story of abuses of authority did not start to come into the open until the 1970s, in the wake of the Watergate scandal, but beginning in the mid-thirties, Hoover played a double game. Some activities were undertaken at the specific request of presidents and attorneys general. Others, however, he secretly ordered on his own without informing his superiors.

Once again, Hoover skillfully manipulated the media to achieve his ends. The "spy," "subversive," or "un-American" replaced the bank robber as the chief bogeyman in FBI publicity. The advent of World War II in 1939 and United States involvement in 1941 created an atmosphere receptive to the idea that threats to America were omnipresent. The Smith Act was directed at all forms of totalitarianism, whether Fascist or Communist, and during the war Nazism was the principal enemy. But immediately after the war, communism quickly moved to the top of the list. The FBI played a major role in both manipulating public fears of communism and harassing left-wing individuals and organizations.

By the late 1930s, Hoover was virtually above criticism. He had so successfully cultivated a reputation as the uncorruptible "top cop" that no president dared remove him. Hoover also began to act completely independently of the attorney general, his nominal superior. By the 1940s, as he wrapped himself in the mantle of Americanism, criticism of Hoover became tantamount to disloyalty itself. He purged all internal critics in the bureau, and his clever handling of the media enabled him to isolate and silence external critics. Before long he did not have to worry about criticism from politicians either. The bureau's "intelligence-gathering" activities collected abundant material on the misdeeds, major and minor, of public officials, including presidents of the

United States. Hoover's administration confirmed the worst fears of the bureau's original critics in 1908. It indeed had become a secret police, spying on the public and flouting the law.

The illegal activities of the FBI represented a new twist in the long history of American vigilantism. Through the nineteenth century, the intimidation of "undesirables" was the work of private groups, mainly the vigilance committee or lynch mob. Popular violence declined in the twentieth century, replaced by the subtler form of institutionalized vigilantism of the intelligence agencies. The new style of vigilantism was perhaps even more insidious because it was largely covert, supported by an enormous bureaucratic apparatus, and justified in the name of "national security."

8

CONFLICTING TRENDS IN CRIMINAL JUSTICE, 1940–1960

Conflicting trends beset the administration of criminal justice during the 1940s and 1950s. Substantial improvements occurred in both law enforcement and corrections. Police professionalization continued to make steady advances. A new generation of police chiefs emerged, sure of their goals and confident of their abilities. Those in the field of corrections continued their quest to make individualized treatment a reality. In short, the capacity of both law enforcement and correctional institutions to fulfill their own goals appeared enormously strengthened by the late 1950s. The police could boast of an impressive array of new technology, particularly patrol cars and sophisticated communications systems. Correctional leaders could point to additional specialized treatment facilities and programs.

The progress made in law enforcement and corrections, however, was rendered increasingly irrelevant by the new problems that arose. As criminal-justice agencies approached fulfillment of goals defined decades earlier, they confronted a new set of demands and expectations. In retrospect, one can see the gradual development of problems that would explode into a national crisis in the 1960s. The new expectations could be defined in terms of race and justice. The continuing movement of black Americans to the large cities of the North and West brought first the police and then the prisons into direct confrontation with the problems of the black ghetto. The administration of criminal justice increasingly became intertwined with the larger issue of racism. But the question of racial justice was only one part of a more pervasive set of new demands. The 1950s witnessed the initial groundswell of the *due-process revolution,* the demand that criminal-justice institutions conform to constitutional standards of equal justice under law.

In brief, the decades of the forties and fifties witnessed a heightening of the latent tension between the crime-control and due-process perspectives, a tension that had been latent since the turn of the century. The increased efficiency of criminal-justice agencies confronted new demands for due process.

THE IMPACT OF WORLD WAR II

The United States entered World War II in December 1941, following the attack on Pearl Harbor. The total commitment of American energies to the war effort affected criminal justice in three important ways. With regard to two problems, the war years resembled the previous world war experience. The social and economic dislocations wrought by the war effort produced renewed racial disorder and a second outburst of police labor-union activity.

Riots and Response

Racial violence flared once again in American cities in 1943. Detroit, New York, and Los Angeles experienced serious disorders, while violence was narrowly averted in the nation's capital and other cities. Once again the police were on the front line of the conflict, but this time the official response to the crisis was completely different. The riots of 1943 gave rise to an effort to improve relations between the police and minority-group communities. The fact that many concerned police officials were active in the movement testified to the great strides that had been made in police professionalism since 1919.

The riots of 1943 were the result of several changes in American race relations brought on by World War II. Wartime production stimulated the migration of both blacks and whites to the industrial cities of the North, Midwest, and West Coast. Detroit, for example, gained 440,000 white and 50,000 new black residents between 1940 and 1943. As had been the case during World War I, blacks and whites competed for jobs, housing, schools, public transportation, and recreation areas.[1]

The ideology of race relations changed even more dramatically than demography. During the late thirties and early forties, black leaders escalated their demands for equality. They promoted the idea of the "Double V," victory over tyranny aboard and the defeat of racism at home. Why should blacks fight for the freedom of others, they asked, when they did not enjoy freedom in their own country? Black leaders proposed a "March on Washington" in 1943 to demand equal employment opportunities. The display of militancy worked. President Roosevelt issued an executive order requiring equal employment, and the march on Washington was canceled.

Meanwhile, the attitudes of whites began to change. The Nazi persecution of the Jews caused many Americans, for the first time, to confront the reality of racism at home. American propaganda during the war stressed racial and ethnic egalitarianism. Publication of Gunnar Myrdal's classic study of racism, *An American Dilemma* (1944), was an important benchmark in the growing commitment to racial equality and integration. During the war years, the modern civil-rights movement was born.[2]

Racial conflict began to escalate in 1941. Much of it involved black servicemen who found themselves in segregated armed forces and who encountered discrimination in the communities surrounding southern military bases. At the same time, problems began to develop in the northern cities. The Detroit police, for example, documented a steady increase in racial incidents involving the integration of schools and a public-housing project.

Major violence finally erupted in 1943. The worst riot occurred in Detroit, and like the 1919 Chicago riot, it took place at a public-recreation area on a hot summer afternoon. For two days chaos engulfed the entire city, eventually leaving thirty-four people dead and more than $2 million worth of property destroyed. A riot in the Harlem district of New York City resulted in more property destruction ($5 million), but no deaths. Meanwhile, in Los Angeles the so-called "Zoot Suit" riot involved a three-way clash between the Mexican-American community, white servicemen, and the Los Angeles police. Violence was narrowly averted in Washington, D.C.

Although the riots of 1943 resembled those of 1919 in terms of both causes and patterns of violence, the postriot response was completely different. A broad coalition of public officials and civic leaders quickly emerged and began to take steps to improve race relations. The Mayor's Commission on Unity in New York City was typical of similar organizations that appeared in dozens of cities. The war effort spurred much of this concern about race relations. As Alfred McClung Lee and Norman Humphrey point out in their study of the Detroit riot, the violence disrupted production in the vital defense plants, costing more than a million man-hours of production time. Other civic leaders worried that the Nazis would exploit the racial conflict to undermine American unity.

These concerns produced the modern police–community-relations movement. Police behavior in the 1943 riots had been as bad as in those of 1919. Thurgood Marshall of the NAACP referred to the Detroit police as a "gestapo." They had been guilty of discriminatory conduct before the riot and excessive violence toward blacks during the disturbances, and it was believed that police actions had helped to escalate rather than defuse racial conflict. The police-community-relations movement advocated training for police officers, improved contact between police departments and minority-group leaders and improved riot-control tactics.

A number of enlightened police chiefs joined with experts from other fields to develop training programs. Joseph Kluchesky, chief of the Milwaukee police, addressed the IACP on the problem and conducted race-relations training for a number of police departments. The Boston police department hired Harvard psychologist Gordon Allport for a training program. The International City Management Association published *The Police and Minority Groups,* written by Joseph Weckler and Theo Hall. This brief manual became the basic text on police-community relations for the next twenty years. Meanwhile, the Chicago Park District published a more elaborate text, also entitled *The Police and Minority Groups,* written by University of Chicago sociologist Joseph H. Lohman. Thus, the movement brought police chiefs, academicians, and other professionals into a broad-based coalition. There was now a small cadre of enlightened and self-styled "professional" police chiefs who were sensitive to broad social problems and willing to embark on innovative programs to deal with them.[3]

California gave the police–community-relations movement the strongest official support. Governor Earl Warren, in office less than a year, responded swiftly to the crisis. He sponsored an official report on race relations and civil disturbances, written in cooperation with the California Peace Officers' Association. In 1946 the state attorney general's office published *A Guide to Race Relations for Peace Officers* which covered race relations, riot-control techniques, and the legal aspects of equal justice. The state revised and republished the *Guide* in 1952 and 1958 as part of a continuing commitment to police-community relations. The direct involvement of the California Peace Officers' Association (the professional association of the state chiefs of police) was an index of the high level of professionalism throughout the state.[4]

Violent racial disturbances disappeared after 1943, just as they had after the 1919 outburst, but police–community-relations programs became an established part of American police administration. Weckler and Hall's manual was incorporated into the International City Management Association's text, *Municipal Police Administration.* Valuable support came from private foundations, religious groups, and universities. The Rockefeller Foundation sponsored the Southern Police Institute at the University of Louisville in 1950, while the National Conference of Christians and Jews co-sponsored an annual conference on police-community relations with Michigan State University from 1955 until 1970.[5]

Unfortunately, the rapidly changing context of American race relations outpaced these pioneering efforts. Metropolitan areas became steadily segregated into a heavily black inner city and virtually all-white suburbs. The recruitment of black police officers lagged far behind the growth of black communities. Urban police work became dominated by the tensions between white police officers and the black ghettos. The riots of 1943 were a foreshadowing of even worse racial conflict in the mid-1960s.

Police Unions Again

The war imposed a severe manpower crisis on law enforcement, one that produced a second upsurge in police unionism between 1944 and 1946. During the depression, with millions of people out of work, jobs as police officers were highly prized. They offered considerable protection against layoffs (some departments did cut back), and salaries actually improved relative to other jobs as the cost of living dropped. An abundance of qualified applicants coincided with slow but steady progress in personnel practices. Departments raised entry-level requirements, and a number of the more progressive ones began to experiment with psychological screening. The New York City police department in particular gained a generation of officers with college degrees.

The recruitment situation changed almost overnight. The Kansas City police department had five thousand applications on file in 1940; two years later it had none and was twenty officers short of its authorized strength. Military service and booming wartime prosperity drained off qualified applicants. The IACP estimated that American police departments suffered an overall 11 percent reduction in strength between 1940 and 1942. And between 1942 and 1945, according to the International City Management Association, the average number of officers per thousand residents (in cities with ten thousand or more people) fell from 1.72 to 1.33.

O.W. Wilson and other leaders worried about the long-term effect of the war on personnel standards. Many departments lowered their standards with regard to age and health in an attempt to fill vacancies, and some training programs were abandoned because of tight budgets. In short, the war threatened to wipe out many of the improvements that the professionalization movement had fought for over the previous twenty years.[6]

Rank-and-file police officers were more concerned about their salaries. Despite wartime wage and price controls, inflation eroded the relative position of police salaries, wiping out the gains made in the 1930s. Full employment and the spread of unionism in the major industries gave an additional boost to blue-collar wages. In response to their deteriorating situation, the police in 1943 again turned to unionism. The American Federation of State, County and Municipal Employees (AFSCME) was in the best position to capitalize on the rising discontent, for it had begun to organize police in the late 1930s. By the end of 1944, AFSCME had chartered thirty-nine all-police locals, while thirty-four more locals included some police along with other employees. By 1946 there were forty-nine viable AFSCME police locals and a number of Fraternal Order of Police (FOP) locals converted to unions.

The revival of unionism provoked concerted opposition from chiefs of police, elected officials, and, most important, the courts. The IACP was itself much better organized and responded to the challenge with an official bulletin entitled "Police Unions" in September 1944. In it the chiefs pointed to the violence surrounding the Boston police strike. The ideology of professionalism became a weapon against unionism. Union membership and the resulting ties to the labor movement, the chiefs argued, would compromise the loyalties of police officers. The "professional" officer should be completely impartial in all disputes.[7]

The new police unions enjoyed brief success in some cities. The Los Angeles police organized a local in 1943 and won a pay increase the next year, but the union collapsed in the face of strong opposition from city hall in 1946. A threat to dismiss all union members also killed an incipient Chicago police union. The unions suffered their worst defeats in the courts. The two most important decisions involved the Detroit and Jackson, Mississippi, police departments. In both cases the courts upheld the right of city officials to fire officers for union activity. These decisions broke the back of the union movement. By 1947 the IACP could identify only ten major cities with police unions, and within a year unionism had disappeared almost entirely.[8]

The brief struggle over unionism in the mid-1940s reinforced trends in American police administration. The defeat of the unions further strengthened the hand of police administrators, and they emerged from the war years more self-confident than ever. Police professionalism advanced during the late forties and fifties under the leadership of a new generation of police chiefs—William Parker in Los Angeles, Wyman Vernon in Oakland, California, and O.W. Wilson, first of Wichita, and later of the University of California School of Criminology. Their approach to leadership only reinforced the authoritarian and quasimilitary style of American police administration.

JUVENILE DELINQUENCY:
THE NEW CRIME SCARE

The war years also stimulated concern about the problem of juvenile delinquency and generated an antidelinquency effort that continued into the early 1960s. Criminologists noted a significant increase in commitments to juvenile institutions between 1941 and 1942, along with other evidence of greater delinquency: the disruption of families through military service for the husband and employment for the mother, the potential for easy money in wartime black markets, and so on. Other criminologists cited figures showing not only that juvenile arrests reached a peak in 1945 but also that the average age of the delinquent had dropped from nineteen to seventeen years. And even after the war, the problem continued. FBI Director Hoover announced with alarm that juvenile arrests in the first nine months of 1947 were 27 percent higher than the year before.[9]

The statements of Hoover, and others reflected national anxiety about the problem of youthful crime. Delinquency in fact became the new crime scare of the 1940s and 1950s. Concern about maintaining domestic tranquility during the war stimulated these fears, but they continued through the next two decades. The result was a national crusade against delinquency, a broad coalition that united the efforts of juvenile-justice practitioners and social workers with those of the federal government, private foundations, and academic criminologists. The work of this group shaped the theory and practice of delinquency control until well into the 1960s and had a significant impact on both the antipoverty programs of the mid-1960s and the report of President Johnson's crime commission.

The delinquency scare was not the figment of someone's imagination. Important changes were transforming the role and status of young people throughout the country. One could perceive the emergence of a distinct "youth culture." *New York Times* reporter Harrison Salisbury captured the flavor of both the new behavior patterns of the young and the anxieties of the older generation in his book *The Shook-Up Generation*. Salisbury adapted the title from a hit song by Elvis Presley, himself the symbol of the generational revolt. Actually, public fears about youthful lawlessness focused on two distinct phenomena: lower-class gang violence and middle-class deviance. The movies *Blackboard Jungle* and *Rebel Without a Cause* dramatized each of them in the popular mind. The media shaped attitudes and behavior, as well as reflecting them. James Dean in *Rebel Without a Cause* and Marlon Brando in *The Wild One* defined the terms of youthful alienation and restlessness.[10]

The federal government played a significant role in leading the search for solutions to the delinquency problem. Federal agencies had been heavily involved in the area of juvenile justice since Theodore Roosevelt's White House Conference on Child Welfare in 1909, which resulted in the creation of the U.S. Children's Bureau in 1912. The bureau worked closely with other groups involved in juvenile justice. In cooperation with the National Probation and Parole Association, it developed and published a

Standard Juvenile Court Act in 1925. Beginning in 1927 it published an annual summary of juvenile court statistics. The 1909 conference also led to regular White House conferences every ten years (1919, 1930, 1940, and 1950). The World War II delinquency scare stimulated a special National Conference on Prevention and Control of Juvenile Delinquency in 1946, and the National Mental Health Act that year mandated the Mental Hygiene Division of the Public Health Service to undertake research into the problems of delinquency.

Long before the creation of LEAA, then, the federal government was deeply involved in assisting state and local agencies in the administration of justice, although these activities were largely confined to the area of juvenile problems. The sentimental appeal of "saving" children from lives of crime overcame fears of federal control which blocked government involvement in other areas of criminal justice. The delinquency-related activities from 1909 onward demonstrated the potential range of federal programs. National conferences helped to dramatize the problem and arouse public opinion. They also brought together experts from different fields and geographic areas, thereby aiding professional development. Finally, federal agencies commanded the resources to collect systematic data and sponsor research. Federal juvenile-justice activities, in short, provided a model for developments in the LEAA era.

The national preoccupation with delinquency, supported by continuing federal involvement, stimulated academic research on the subject. A number of important theoretical works on crime and delinquency appeared in the late 1940s and 1950s. This scholarly work had substantial impact upon public policy, shaping the programs of the late 1950s and early 1960s. Building upon the earlier work of the Chicago school of sociology, criminologists focused on the social pathology of the urban slum. Albert K. Cohen advanced the concept of a *delinquent subculture* which reinforced antisocial behavior. Walter B. Miller argued that certain aspects of lower-class culture—the felt need to be "tough," to appear "smart," and to seek "excitement"—helped generate gangs and gang violence. Because of publicity surrounding gang violence, the gang received considerable attention from the criminologists. Not all "gangs" were the same, however, and criminologists drew a distinction between the purely social gang, the "delinquent" gang, and the violence-prone gang.[11]

The dominant trend in criminological theory focused on problems in the American social structure. Cohen stressed the idea that delinquents shared the dominant values of American society but simply had no legitimate way to fulfill them. David Matza and Gresham Sykes maintained that the delinquent had to "neutralize" internalized values (guilt, responsibility, etc.) in order to commit illegal acts. Delinquent behavior was shaped by the social environment, and the offender learned how to act in a delinquent manner. For the idea that criminal and delinquent behavior was *learned,* criminologists were indebted to the theory of *differential association* developed by Edwin Sutherland. Not all juveniles, of course, learned the same things. It appeared that some were more likely to become delinquent than others.[12] Richard Cloward and Lloyd Ohlin united Sutherland's theory of learned behavior with the work of the Chicago school by arguing that there were "differential opportunity structures." That is, juveniles in the slums had fewer opportunities to realize their legitimate aspirations and more opportunities to learn how to be delinquent.

Cloward and Ohlin's theory, published as *Delinquency and Opportunity* in 1960, had an enormous impact on social policy. It clearly suggested that something had to be done to improve the opportunities available to lower-class youth. This in turn meant improving the quality of the schools, providing specific types of job training, stimulating the economy to provide more jobs (during the 1950s there had been a series of economic recessions) and, finally, eliminating racial discrimination.[13] This last point linked the antidelinquency crusade with the emerging civil-rights movement. The steady growth of the black ghettos in the 1950s meant that the issues of crime and delinquency were increasingly inseparable from the problem of race relations.

A consensus emerged among government officials, academicians, and the private foundations. Taking office in 1961, President John F. Kennedy quickly created the President's Committee on Juvenile Delinquency and Youth Crime. By appointing his brother, Attorney General Robert Kennedy, as chairman the President clearly indicated that this was a high-priority item. At the same time, the private foundations sponsored innovative approaches to delinquency prevention. The Ford Foundation funded the Mobilization for Youth (MFY) in New York City, which attempted to implement the concepts of Cloward and Ohlin. These developments finally culminated in President Johnson's "war on poverty." The various programs of the Office of Economic Opportunity, beginning in 1964 (especially the Job Corps and job-training programs), were designed to decrease the opportunities for illegal behavior and increase the opportunities for fulfilling legitimate aspirations.

Criminologists and policy-makers had more difficulty dealing with middle-class deviance during the 1950s. The emergence of a distinct youth culture was the result of both the "baby-boom" and affluence: suddenly there were a large number of kids with a lot of money to spend. And they spent that money on records, movies, and other items that catered specifically to their interests. The growing economic autonomy of youth paralleled a decline in authoritarian patterns of family discipline, at least within the middle class. The cultural heroes of middle-class youth tended to be figures who expressed a rejection of polite society, such as James Dean, Marlon Brando, Elvis Presley, and innumerable other rock-and-roll stars. Yet no expert could devise an official policy that would overcome a sense of alienation from everything that was official and programmatic. The middle-class deviance of the 1950s would emerge as the counterculture of the 1960s.

ORGANIZED CRIME: THE MYTH GROWS

The second crime scare of the postwar period involved organized crime. The public mind in the mid-1940s seemed particularly susceptible to panic over a wide variety of alleged threats to the national security. J. Edgar Hoover's publicity apparatus sounded a persistent theme: the nation was in imminent danger from Com-

munists and criminals. Fear of subversion led to the anti-commu-
nist witch hunt of the cold war. More restrained voices emphasized
the problem of juvenile delinquency, and still others warned that
the country was in the grip of a "national crime syndicate." The
media continued to feed the public's seemingly insatiable appetite
for lurid information about organized crime. As a result, the myth
of the so-called Mafia became inflated out of all proportion to the
reality of organized illegal activity.

Public fears were not totally groundless. In the mid-forties,
organized crime was alive and prospering. Repeal of prohibition
in 1933 simply forced local crime syndicates to diversify into other
activities, of which gambling became the most important source of
revenue. The crime syndicates attached themselves to a growth
industry. Horse-racing grew in popularity during the late 1930s,
but the real turning point came with the return of prosperity.
First during the wartime economic boom and then even more so
during the affluent postwar years, gambling became a major
leisure-time activity. Americans had more money to spend and,
with the shortening of the work week, they had more time to
spend it. By the late 1940s, the press and politicians began to
notice the pervasiveness of gambling.[14]

As gambling expanded and became more of a national enterprise
(especially with off-track betting), the crime syndicates expanded
accordingly and attempted to centralize their operations. The
control of news was crucial, and by the late 1930s Moses Annen-
burg, who had purchased the General News Bureau from a Chicago gambler, had a near monopoly on racing publications,
"scratch" sheets, and other news vital to bookmaking. The crime
scare of the mid-forties was stimulated in part by fights between the
various crime syndicates to control the wire services.

Organized crime was a reality. The "syndicates" consisted of
individuals engaged in the systematic provision of gambling
services and other illegal activities. The popular novel and film
The Godfather contained an essential ingredient of truth in por-
traying such crime as a business organized around a tightly knit
family. The idea of a monolithic national crime syndicate, however, was more myth than reality. Many factors contributed to the

popularity of the Mafia myth, especially the public's eagerness to believe in alien conspiracies. Congress helped to popularize the myth as well. Senator Estes Kefauver of Tennessee, looking for an issue that might win him the 1952 Democratic nomination for Vice-President, seized upon the organized-crime issue in early 1950. After much senatorial maneuvering, he gained control of a special investigating committee. The Kefauver Committee conducted widely publicized hearings in Washington and other cities and issued a report declaring unequivocally that a national crime syndicate in fact existed. Later, another special committee headed by Senator John McClellan generated even more sensational publicity with its investigations into corruption and racketeering within organized labor.

Despite the publicity, the attack on organized crime was remarkably feeble. Local law-enforcement officials were too often enmeshed in the web of corruption spun by the syndicates. Even those officials who had the will lacked the manpower and sophisticated skills to investigate a complex and often multistate business enterprise. It was exceedingly difficult to gather information since the code of silence prevailed, and those who talked could expect to find their lives in danger.

The FBI was logically the agency best equipped to attack organized crime. Yet, it did virtually nothing. For reasons that are not entirely clear, Hoover chose to ignore organized crime and continue his emphasis on bank robbers and Communists. Perhaps organized crime was too formidable a foe. This touched off a long and bitter struggle within the Justice Department. One faction urged a vigorous attack on organized crime, while Hoover marshaled his support in Congress against it. The attorney general established an Organized Crime and Racketeering Section in 1954 and, four years later, created a Special Group on Organized Crime with regional offices across the country. This move was provoked in part by the highly publicized meeting of about seventy-five organized-crime leaders in the small town of Appalachin, New York. Critics of the FBI argued that the bureau had almost completely ignored organized crime. The bureau in fact refused to cooperate with the new Justice Department units until 1960. The

Justice Department effort expanded enormously in 1961 under Attorney General Robert Kennedy, who had developed a special interest in racketeering as staff counsel for Senator McClellan's investigating committee in the 1950s.[15]

CALIFORNIA'S LEADERSHIP IN
LAW ENFORCEMENT AND CORRECTIONS

California made the greatest advances in both law enforcement and corrections through the 1940s and 1950s. Its police departments were the most professional, while the state correctional system was the largest, most elaborate, and most heavily committed to individualized treatment. In other states reformers and progressive administrators looked to California for a model they might follow. It is not entirely clear how one state managed to establish such a clear lead. Many factors contributed. In policing, the legacy of August Vollmer and his disciples was a decisive factor. California's leadership in corrections owed much to the governorship of Earl Warren (1942-1953), who vigorously promoted prison reform.

Police Professionalism: California-Style

Because he succeeded in institutionalizing reform, Vollmer's influence extended far beyond his own immediate activities. He developed the first college-level police training programs, thereby giving police reform an institutional base within higher education. He also cultivated a cadre of disciples who carried on the work of professionalization, either as police chiefs or academicians.

Vollmer discovered the value of higher education in 1908 when he asked a University of California scientist to examine some evidence in an alleged suicide case. He then began to use university faculty as a regular part of the training program for the Berkeley police. In 1916 he developed the first formal academic law-enforcement program. This was the forerunner of the School of Criminology on the Berkeley campus and the grandfather of all college criminal-justice programs. Vollmer also recruited university students and graduates for the Berkeley police. At a time when most departments offered no training at all and when most police officers lacked even a high-school diploma, Vollmer's "college cops" attracted enormous publicity.[16]

College-level police programs began to flourish in the late 1920s and early 1930s. Vollmer helped to develop the first four-year program at San Jose State in 1931, and in 1932 he expanded the Berkeley criminology program. Some of the leading universities in the country experimented with criminal-justice research and teaching. The University of Chicago, already a leader in criminology and various aspects of public administration, hired Vollmer as a visiting professor of police administration in 1929. Meanwhile, Northwestern University launched what became the Traffic Institute in 1933 and Michigan State College (later university) began its law-enforcement program in 1935. Law-enforcement training at the college level, however, took root most firmly in California.

August Vollmer's disciples, the best of his "college cops," included such persons as George Brereton, John D. Holstrom, V. A. Leonard, and O. W. Wilson. They all went on to establish reputations of their own as administrators, educators, and writers. Without any question, O. W. Wilson was the legitimate heir to Vollmer's role as the leading voice of police professionalism.

Wilson first attracted attention while chief of the Wichita, Kansas, police between 1928 and 1939. He assumed control of a corrupt department with an unsavory reputation for brutality and proceeded to quickly clean house. In the first year alone, he either fired or forced the resignation of 20 percent of the force, launched an in-service training program, and published the "Square Deal Code," a statement of principles that subsequently became the IACP law-enforcement code of ethics. Later he expanded the training program, which involved a working relationship with the Kansas League of Municipalities and the University of Wichita. He also initiated a three-week pre-service training program and what may have been the first police cadet program in the country.[17]

These accomplishments represented the implementation of Vollmer's principles. Wilson established his own reputation in the area of administration through the application of rational planning to the management of a police department. He developed a comprehensive personnel policy and revised the criminal-records system (and in an act of independence challenged the validity of the M.O. [*modus operandi*] technique developed by Vollmer and copied by many other departments). But Wilson's particular area of expertise was the allocation of motorized patrol. He became the principal advocate of allocating patrol cars on a scientific basis to increase coverage. He eliminated foot patrol as much as possible, transferred officers from desk jobs to patrol, and argued vigorously in favor of staffing patrol cars with one rather than two officers. This approach had enormous appeal in the 1930s as police departments felt the financial constraints of the depression and tried to do more with fewer resources. In the long run, Wilson helped accelerate the growing emphasis on motorized patrol. The new gospel of police administration became crime prevention through patrol-car "presence."

Despite his accomplishments, not everyone in Wichita liked Wilson. His enforcement of vice laws offended powerful interests, and in 1939 he resigned under pressure. Although painful, this move allowed him to further solidify his national reputation. In 1938 he had written a text on police administration for the International City Management Association. *Municipal Police Administration* appeared in book form in 1943 and became the standard text on the subject (the eighth edition appeared in 1977). Leaving Wichita, he worked with the Public Administration Service in Chicago and wrote an authoritative manual on patrol car allocation. In mid-1939 he became professor of police administration at the University of California. Except for a brief period of service during the war, he remained there until 1960. In addition to building the School of Criminology, which offered the first doctor of criminology degree, Wilson wrote *Police Adminis-*

tration (1950). This book and his previous one together became the "bible" of modern police management. By the late 1950s, Wilson was acknowledged to be the leading expert on the subject. When Mayor Richard Daley of Chicago faced a major scandal in the Chicago police department in 1960, he called upon O. W. Wilson to assume the job of superintendent and reform the department.[18]

From his office as dean of the School of Criminology in the 1950s, Wilson shared the limelight with another prominent California law-enforcement official: William Parker, chief of the Los Angeles police. The two men represented different dimensions of police professionalism. Wilson was well known and respected within law-enforcement circles as the exponent of modern management techniques. Parker was better known to the public at large as the embodiment of a tough law-and-order approach to crime prevention. In many respects, Parker was the J. Edgar Hoover of municipal policing. He adopted Hoover's ruthlessly authoritarian administrative style and mastered the art of public relations. The popular "Dragnet" TV show popularized the image of the Los Angeles police as relentlessly efficient crime-fighters.

When Parker assumed control of the Los Angeles police in 1950, the department had a long reputation as one of the most corrupt in the country (Vollmer had left in frustration after a one-year stint as chief in 1923–1924). Parker immediately proceeded to clean house by establishing the most authoritarian and militaristic administration in the country. Even minor breaches of internal regulations could bring severe disciplinary action. The military ethos of professionalism in Los Angeles served two purposes. First, it gave officers a clearly defined sense of purpose: that they were engaged in an unending "war on crime." Second, it supported the rigid internal discipline. Even the department's harshest critics admitted that Parker had eliminated corruption.[19]

Parker's accomplishments, however, illustrated the hazards of the new style of police professionalism. While it uprooted corruption and instilled the department with a sense of mission, the militaristic approach aggravated relations with some segments of the community. The majority of the public, the white middle and upper classes, were highly impressed by Parker's reforms (and he carefully cultivated their support through sophisticated public relations). The lower classes, and particularly members of the growing black and Chicano ghettos in Los Angeles, found themselves the targets of the "war on crime." The department developed the technique of aggressive preventive patrol, designed to stop, question, and frisk large numbers of suspicious persons. Minorities came to view this as systematic harassment. Los Angeles police officers, meanwhile, developed a shorthand for "suspicious" persons which inevitably emphasized young blacks as potential criminals.

Race relations in Los Angeles steadily deteriorated, and leaders in the black community voiced criticisms of the police department. Parker's "war on crime" ideology, however, had a built-in defense mechanism. The police represented the "thin blue line" between civilization and savagery—a theme Parker developed in innumerable speeches and articles. Following Hoover's example, he wrapped himself in the American flag and attacked all his critics as Communists or persons who unwittingly served the purposes of international communism. In two important respects, then, the military style of police professionalism aggravated race relations. It increased tension-filled contacts between police and minorities and at the same time provided a defense against any and all charges of misconduct. Thus, the accomplishments of police reform through the 1950s set the stage for the police–community-relations crisis of the 1960s.

The "war-on-crime" ideology also put the police in conflict with the emerging standards of due process. In the 1955 case of *People* v. *Cahan,* the California supreme court invoked the "exclusionary rule." The rule, which excluded illegally obtained evidence from use in trials, had been applied to federal proceedings in 1914 *(Weeks* v. *U.S.)* and, by the 1950s, in a number of individual states. Parker immediately attacked the *Cahan* decision, charging that "the effect . . . has been catastrophic as far as efficient law enforcement is concerned." In a publicity blitz, he displayed charts purporting to show the "skyrocketing effect" of the decision on the crime rate. Parker's argument that court decisions expanding the meaning of due process had "handcuffed" the police anticipated by several years the national controversy over the role of the U.S. Supreme court in the 1960s.[20]

California Corrections

California embarked on an aggressive program of correctional reform in the 1940s, joining the U.S. Bureau of Prisons as a leader in the field. Governor Earl Warren strongly supported reform, endorsing new legislation and appointing progressive administrators to key positions. Two new institutions, the Youth Authority (1941) and the Adult Authority (1944), were the principal instruments of a new approach to correctional treatment.[21]

The California Youth Authority, a three-member board appointed by the governor, exercised a wide range of correctional functions. The most dramatic innovation was a shift of much of the sentencing power. Upon finding an individual guilty, a judge could either grant probation or commit the offender to the Youth Authority. The staff of the authority would then determine the type of correctional institution, the length of sentence, and the eventual date of release. The authority, with a large staff to diagnose and classify those referred, established a range of different types of correctional facilities, including forestry camps for low-risk offenders. Correctional leaders hailed the California approach as a "daring break from tradition," an effort to provide the institutional mechanism for truly individualizing treatment.

The California Adult Authority was based on the same concept. The judge committed the offender to the authority, which then diagnosed the individual, determined the proper sentence, granted parole, and carried out parole supervision. The Adult Authority did not exercise as many different functions as the Youth Authority, for the administration of the prison remained under the Deparment of Corrections. Governor Warren recruited the highly respected Richard McGhee as director of corrections. McGhee then launched a construction program that yielded five new penal institutions by 1958. All were medium-security facilities, and this permitted greater specialization of function, giving the Adult

Authority a wider range of treatment forms to consider. Institutional expansion meant that the prison population also increased. The number of California prisoners rose from 5,700 in 1944 to 19,202 in 1958, an increase described by the American Correctional Association as "unprecedented in American history." The California initiatives had a disturbing effect: the "age of treatment" brought more and more persons under some form of state supervision.[22]

Other important developments took place within the California correctional system as a consequence of its commitment to individualized treatment. Group counseling became a major part of the California treatment process. In 1956 an estimated five thousand inmates were involved in group sessions. Even more important, the Department of Corrections made a firm commitment to research, establishing a Research Division in 1957. The attempt to individualize treatment demanded greater sophistication in predicting the effect of sentences (probation versus prison) and the probable success of individuals on parole. Building upon the Gluecks' prediction tables, the California researchers developed a system of "base expectancy rates" designed to predict the likelihood of future criminal behavior and thus assist in parole decision-making. The California research apparatus was truly impressive when compared with that of other states. Unfortunately, however, it came to focus almost exclusively on the problem of predicting recidivism. Not only did it exclude other correctional issues but, as later critics pointed out, it tended to produce results overly favorable to ongoing programs within the Department of Corrections.[23]

Progress in corrections throughout the rest of the country was mixed through the 1940s and 1950s. One hopeful sign was a wave of reform in the South. Southern states still occupied their traditional role as the home of the most notoriously barbaric penal systems in the country. To evoke images of frightening conditions, one only had to mention the names of the major prisons, such as Angola (Louisiana) and Parchman (Mississippi). Authorities at Tucker Prison Farm in Arkansas handed virtually the entire job of running the institution to armed inmates. In the late 1960s, Warden Tom Murton confirmed the worst rumors that had circulated for years when he discovered the graves of murdered inmates.[24]

The public still remained largely indifferent to prison conditions, and it generally required a scandal of major proportions to bring about change. Thirty-one inmates in the Louisiana prison at Angola slashed their Achilles tendons to protest conditions there in 1951. The resulting publicity, national in scope, prompted an overhaul of the state's entire corrections system and, for the first time, the hiring of professional penologists rather than political hacks to run the prisons. The Angola scandal coincided with a wave of prison riots across the country. The worst riots occured in the state penitentiaries of New Jersey (Trenton), Ohio (Columbus), and Michigan (Jackson) and provoked investigations of prison conditions. Journalist John Bartlow Martin published a popular exposé, *Break Down the Walls* (1954), while the American Prison Association established a special committee to investigate the causes of prison riots.[25]

The American Prison Association responded to the crisis of the early fifties by reaffirming its commitment to rehabilitation and individualized treatment. In 1954 the organization changed its name to the American Correctional Association and the title of its official publication from *Prison World* to the *American Journal of Correction*. These changes were part of a more general trend toward the use of euphemisms. Solitary confinement cells, which guards and inmates both called "the hole," became "adjustment centers." The rhetoric was designed to conceal the reality of power and coercion inherent in the prison system. Nevertheless, the exact nature of the penal experience began to emerge in the work of sociologists who studied the prison. Publication of Donald Clemmer's *The Prison Community* in 1940 was a landmark event that was later followed by Gresham Sykes's *The Society of Captives* (1958) and the various contributions to *Theoretical Studies in Social Organization of the Prison* (1960).[26]

The reality of the prison experience made a mockery of the lofty rhetoric of correctional professionals. In practice virtually all of the resources and energy of the prison were devoted to maintaining custody over inmates. At best treatment-oriented programs consumed no more than 5 to 10 percent of prison budgets; and even then nothing was allowed that might undermine security. Standards for correctional personnel lagged far behind those for police. A job as a guard (now a "correctional officer") was often the last resort for the person without skills. The day-to-day administration of the prison, meanwhile, was shaped by a complex network of cliques. At Stateville penitentiary in Illinois, Warden Joseph Ragen maintained a rigid authoritarian regime from 1936 to 1960. He constructed a network of subordinates who owed personal loyalty to him. The captains, in turn, built small empires of their own, extracting feudal loyalty from lieutenants, sergeants, and guards.[27]

The exercise of power in the prison community was a complex phenomenon. The warden might control his subordinates, but together they did not completely control the prison. An inmate subculture with a clearly defined power structure and differentiated roles exercised considerable power of its own. A trade-off between staff and inmates developed: the inmates accepted the general routine of prison life ("did time"), and in return the staff overlooked systematic violations of prison rules (contraband money, bootleg alcohol and drugs, pervasive homosexuality, including gang rapes, and random violence). Prison violence was frighteningly routine. Staff "goon squads" brutalized inmates, while rapes, assaults, and murders between inmates were even more common.

Under the surface, meanwhile, the prison community was undergoing profound changes in the 1950s. In the northern states prison populations shifted from predominantly white to predominantly black. At Stateville black inmates increased from 47 percent of the total in 1953 to 58 percent in 1960 and 75 percent by 1974. Authorities at Stateville, Attica (New York), and other large prisons continued to hire their guards from the nearly all-white rural communities nearby. Thus, the atmosphere in the prison community became more and more dominated by the tensions between white rural guards and black big-city inmates. Race relations behind prison walls paralleled the deteriorating situation between the police and minorities in the ghettos.

The initial tremors of prison racial conflict in the 1950s involved the Black Muslims. The Nation of Islam, increasingly dominated by the charismatic leadership of Malcolm X, had great success recruiting among black prisoners. Although the ideology of black nationalism and hatred of "white devils" frightened prison officials, it may have rehabilitated more offenders than all of the treatment programs. Even in progressive California, prison officials attempted to suppress the Muslims, denying that Islam was a valid religion, banning the Koran and other publications, and turning down requests for special diets and religious services. Fighting for their religious autonomy, the Muslims drove in the opening wedge of what eventually became a flood of prisoners'-rights litigation.

The Transformation of Earl Warren

No individual embodied the conflicting trends in criminal justice better than Earl Warren. During his career he underwent a remarkable transformation, crossing from one side of the ideological spectrum to the other. He began in the late 1930s as an advocate of vigorous crime control. By the 1960s he was both the symbol and principal author of the U.S. Supreme Court's due-process revolution, which expanded individual rights and placed limits on the authority of criminal-justice agencies.

Warren joined the Alameda County (Oakland) district attorney's office in 1920. He was elected DA in 1925 and served until 1939. From that point until his appointment to the U.S. Supreme Court in 1953, he dominated California politics. He was elected state attorney general in 1939 after winning both the Republican and Democratic primaries. Using the same bipartisan approach, he was elected governor in 1942 and reelected in 1946 and 1950. The Republican party nominated him for Vice-President in 1948, and he was a major power broker at the 1952 GOP convention. In return for this support, President Eisenhower appointed him Chief Justice of the U.S. Supreme Court in 1953.[28]

Although he stoutly maintained in his memoirs that he never changed his legal philosophy, Warren in fact experienced a total conversion. In the 1930s he regularly addressed the meetings of the California Peace Officers' Association. The chiefs welcomed his hard-hitting attacks on the problem of crime and critics of the police. His deeds matched his law-and-order rhetoric. As both DA and attorney general, he was involved in cases that haunted his later career. In the controversial "Point Lobos" case of 1936, Warren was accused of jury manipulation and other improprieties in securing murder convictions of left-wing labor leaders. In 1942 he encouraged President Roosevelt to issue the infamous Executive Order #9066 authorizing the round-up and detention of Japanese-Americans.

The man who in 1954 authored the *Brown v. Board of Education* decision against school segregation and championed the rights of the individual used racist stereotypes to support one of the worst violations of civil liberties in American history in 1942. What caused Warren's change of heart? Events such as the 1943 race riots probably helped make him aware of the extent of racism. Moreover, as he achieved higher office his perspective on issues undoubtedly changed, and he shed the prosecutor's obsession with obtaining convictions. Finally, Warren simply absorbed and reflected the currents of change within the American legal community. The growing emphasis on due process and the rights of the individual constituted a historic shift that was the work of many people.

The "due-process revolution" led by the U.S. Supreme Court under Chief Justice Earl Warren (1953–1969) did not fully reach the area of criminal justice until the early 1960s. Nonetheless, its general outlines were clearly evident in the 1950s. The civil-rights movement was unquestionably the major force for change. The demand for equality for black Americans touched virtually every sector of American life. Civil-rights litigation through the 1940s and 1950s affected voting, housing, and, most important, education. The historic *Brown v. Board of Education* decision indicated that the Supreme Court was firmly committed to racial equality.

The civil-rights movement had several important consequences. It sensitized an entire generation to the question of civil rights.

First the courts, then the White House, and finally the Congress responded to the thrust of the movement. In the process the movement precipitated a rethinking of the entire question of individual rights, including areas not directly related to racial equality. Thus, the Warren Court in the 1960s adopted a broadly libertarian posture. Finally, as the civil-rights movement grew it confronted a number of purely procedural questions. As Archibald Cox observes in his study *The Warren Court*, consideration of such questions was often "influenced by the realization that in another case they might affect the posture of a Negro in a hostile southern court."[29] In this way the civil-rights movement set the stage for the due-process revolution in criminal procedure in the 1960s.

Meanwhile, leaders of the legal profession began in the 1950s to ask new questions about the administration of criminal justice. Supreme Court Justice Robert H. Jackson issued the challenge, declaring that "no one really knows just how our criminal law system is working and what its defects really are." Legal scholarship had largely confined itself to the study of case law, but this left untouched the hidden reality of the day-to-day administration of justice. In response to Jackson's challenge, the American Bar Foundation moved into the realm of social-science research. With funding from the Ford Foundation and a research plan developed by Arthur Sherry in 1955, the ABF launched an intensive investigation of the administration of criminal justice in three selected states: Wisconsin, Kansas, and Michigan. In the words of one participant, the project was "a profound departure in point of view for the legal profession."[30]

The day-to-day administration of justice, the ABF researchers soon discovered, was far more complex than they had imagined. Consequently, they chose to focus their attention on five critical "decision points" involving the detection of crime, arrest, prosecution, adjudication, and sentencing. Each decision, they discovered, involved a broad exercise of discretion. The administration of justice, in other words, consisted of a long sequence of discretionary decision-making that was both hidden from public view and largely ungoverned by any standards or guidelines. This in turn raised serious questions about the quality of justice. Could the ideal of equal justice under the law be achieved when so many crucial decisions were left to the whims of individual police officers, prosecutors, judges, probation and parole officers, and others?[31]

The ABF project sparked a major reevaluation of the administration of justice. Concern about the effect of discretion was reflected both in further research and in the mounting number of lawsuits challenging the operations of local agencies. This attack on arbitrary and capricious decision-making was another major source of the due-process revolution. The reform of criminal justice in the 1960s and 1970s involved a major effort to bring discretionary decision-making under control.

9

CRISIS OF CRIME
AND JUSTICE, 1960–PRESENT

A DECADE OF PROTESTS

The 1960s was the most turbulent decade in American history. Never before had so many different crises engulfed society simultaneously. There was racial polarization, with protest and violence on both sides; militant protest against an unpopular war; three political assassinations; the emergence of a youth counterculture that rejected the values of established society; and the development of both radical political underground sects and a systematic pattern of illegal actions by the authorities themselves. The violence of the decade was symbolized by the assassin's gun, napalm, the clenched fist, and the burning ghetto. But violence was nothing new in American life. More serious was the pervasive sense that society no longer worked, that the basic social institutions were no longer capable of serving the needs of the American people. One historian titled his account of the decade *Coming Apart.*[1]

The crises of the 1960s were those of law, order, and justice. Civil-rights activists broke the law with sit-ins because the law sustained racial injustice. Students protested an unjust and illegal war being fought in the name of international order. Ghetto rioters directed their fury at the police officer, the most convenient symbol of a society that denied them equal justice under law. And protest begot reaction. As the challenges mounted, the established order sought to reassert its authority and impose control. The polarization over law and order brought the issues of criminal justice to the forefront of national politics. The 1968 presidential election revolved around the questions of the Vietnam war and law and order. The advent of LEAA brought the federal government directly into the administration of criminal justice, completing the nationalization of crime control.

Underlying the turmoil of the sixties was a revolution in expectations. The criminal-justice system faced unprecedented new demands. The "consumers" demanded not just more and better service, but often conflicting services. The civil-rights movement represented the demand for equal justice by black Americans. Increasing numbers of the general public, meanwhile, expected the police and courts to provide swift and efficient service. As crime rates rose, an increasingly conservative segment of the public demanded that the police, the courts, and the prisons somehow take action to reduce crime. Finally, the courts intervened in virtually every aspect of the criminal process and, in a series of decisions known collectively as the due-process revolution, demanded that agencies conform to the standards of the U.S. Constitution.

The Cops in the Ghetto

The criminal-justice crisis of the 1960s focused on the cops in the ghetto. Riots engulfed virtually every major city between 1964 and 1968, and most were sparked by a routine incident involving the police. The civil-rights movement set the stage for the riots. Beginning with the sit-ins in 1960, the tempo of the civil-rights movement escalated rapidly. As black Americans demanded full equality, their tolerance for long-standing abuses dropped accordingly. The police became the symbol of an unjust society. The entire country watched the evening news as Birmingham, Alabama, Public Safety Director "Bull" Connor set police dogs and fire hoses upon civil-rights demonstrators. Blacks in the northern ghettos increasingly saw the virtually all-white police departments as an army of occupation. Ironically, the conduct of police officers had improved substantially since the days of the

Wickersham Commission report on police brutality. But in the intervening thirty years, black expectations had far outpaced police improvements. By the mid-sixties the ghettos were a tinderbox.

The spark that ignited the riots occurred on July 16, 1964, when a white New York City police officer shot and killed a black teenager. Black leaders in the Harlem ghetto organized protests demanding disciplinary action against the officer. On July 18th, demonstrators marched on the Twenty-eighth Precinct headquarters. Police efforts to break up the crowd only aroused the seething passions. Looting and burning erupted that night and lasted for two full days. Moderate civil-rights leaders could not control the mobs. When the Harlem riot was brought under control, disorders broke out across town in the Brooklyn ghetto of Bedford Stuyvesant. When it was all over, the toll included one person dead, more than one hundred injured, almost five hundred persons arrested, and millions of dollars worth of property destroyed.[2]

Since conditions were essentially the same in all the ghettos, it was hardly surprising that rioting spread contagiously. Rochester, New York, experienced disorders the day after peace returned to New York City. In the summer of 1964, rioting also erupted in Philadelphia, Jersey City, and a few other cities. The nation braced for another "long hot summer" the next year and got even worse than it expected. A riot in the Watts ghetto of Los Angeles was one of the worst racial disturbances in American history to that date, leaving thirty-four persons dead, a thousand injured, four thousand arrested, and property damage estimated at $35 million. Even more ominous was the overt political dimension of rioting, with its cries of "burn, baby, burn" and "get whitey." Other riots took place in Chicago and San Diego that summer. The summer of 1966 was still worse, with disturbances all across the country: Los Angeles, Chicago, Cleveland, Omaha, Dayton, San Francisco, and Atlanta were among the forty-three cities affected.

But the worst was yet to come. Rioting again struck nationwide in 1967, and the violence in Newark and Detroit exceeded even that of the 1965 Watts riot. Disorders engulfed Newark for five days, leaving twenty-three dead and more than $10 million worth of property destroyed. The Detroit riot a week later lasted nearly a week and resulted in forty-three deaths. Initial accounts reported property damage as high as $500 million, but later reports lowered the total to something in the neighborhood of $40 million. The day peace returned to Detroit, President Lyndon Johnson appointed a special commission to investigate the problem of civil disorders. The National Advisory Commission on Civil Disorders (the "Kerner Commission") delivered its report in March 1968, roughly one month before rioting again swept the ghettos, this time in the wake of the assassination of Dr. Martin Luther King. Then, curiously, the outbursts disappeared. The summer of 1968 was a quiet one and, despite continuing racial tensions, no major disorders occurred in any subsequent year.

The Kerner Commission identified racism as the basic underlying cause of the riots, concluding that "our nation is moving toward two societies, one black, one white—separate and unequal." The report summarized the dreary facts of institutional racism: unemployment, discrimination in jobs and housing, inadequate social services, unequal justice at the hands of the law, and so on. The ghetto was the product of white racism: "White institutions created it, white institutions maintain it, and white society condones it." Finally, the report issued a call for a renewed commitment to end racism and expand the opportunities for black Americans.[3]

If institutional racism was the basic problem, police actions were frequently the direct cause of riots. The 1964 Harlem riot followed the shooting of a black teenager by a white police officer, as did the 1966 San Francisco and Atlanta riots and several others. The riots in Philadelphia (1964), Watts (1965), and Newark (1967) were set off by routine traffic incidents. And the 1967 Detroit riot followed a police raid on an after-hours bar in the ghetto. As the symbol of authority, the police officer functioned as a lightning rod for all the accumulated resentments.

The police became the focus of national attention. Several facts emerged from the report of the Kerner Commission and other investigations. The employment of black police officers lagged far behind the growth of the black population. Blacks represented

34 percent of the population of Cleveland but only 7 percent of the police officers; 31 percent of the city of Oakland but only 4 percent of the police; and 63 percent of the District of Columbia but only 21 percent of the police. In short, police forces were virtually all-white institutions. Moreover, police conduct still left much to be desired. Despite the improvements of the previous thirty years, police brutality and abuse of power were common enough to cause pervasive resentment. A presidential crime commission found in 1967 that only 30 percent of black respondents agreed that police officers were "almost all honest," compared with 63 percent of white respondents.[4]

Inadequate supervision, particularly in terms of the use of deadly force, was a particular problem. Many departments provided no guidelines on when to shoot, despite hours of training on how to clean, assemble, and fire handguns. In Los Angeles the police shot and killed sixty persons in the thirty months prior to the Watts riot. Blacks easily got the impression that police had a license to shoot them—and in the South that had traditionally been the case. The situation was even worse during a riot, when discipline completely collapsed and officers fired their guns indiscriminantly into the night. Much of the reported sniper fire was undoubtedly ricocheting bullets from the guns of other police officers. Accounts of the Detroit riot noted the fewer reports of sniper activity in areas controlled by the more disciplined federal troops and national guardsmen.[5]

The individual cop on the beat received the brunt of the anger of ghetto residents. Militants labeled the cops "pigs," charging that they were all fat, lazy, bigoted, and prone to violence. Even much of the educated and liberal white middle class shared this unflattering image of the police. Ironically, the stereotype of the cop as a "pig" was similar to the traditional racist image of the black American as a "nigger." The cops themselves responded by seeing all their critics as bomb-throwing militants. As a result they were unable to perceive that much of the black community, the most heavily victimized group in society, actually wanted greater police protection. The polarized atmosphere in the ghettos involved a vicious circle of mutual stereotyping.

Academicians rushed to study the police in an effort to explain the crisis. The scholars discovered William A. Westley's concept of a police subculture, which he had formulated in a 1950 study of the Gary, Indiana, police. The special circumstances of police work, particularly the constant possibility of danger and the need to assert authority in the face of often overt resistance, cultivated a distinct set of attitudes and behavior patterns. The police distrusted and feared the public and found support in group solidarity. They felt justified in either using force or lying to cover up any misconduct. Jerome Skolnick, building upon Westley's work, argued that the demands of productivity, the necessity to obtain "results" with arrests and convictions, induced officers to bend the law in obtaining confessions or evidence. The norms of police work, he concluded, were at odds with the idea of the rule of law.[6]

Studies of the police did not sustain the stereotype of the cop as pig. The typical officer was rather idealistic, motivated by a desire to serve the public and attracted to policing because it offered job security, good pay with liberal benefits, the status of a "profession," and prospects for career advancement. Although conservative on most political issues, the average officer was not necessarily more extreme in his views than the typical conservative. In other words, the cop was not a violence-prone right-wing extremist. "Are policemen prejudiced?" David Bayley and Harold Mendelsohn asked in their study of police–community relations in Denver. "The answer is yes, but only slightly more so than the community as a whole." Put another way, "police officers share the ethnic prejudices of the community as a whole." Bayley and Mendelsohn agreed with Westley and Skolnick that "factors peculiar to the police occupation" determined attitudes and behavior and that officers, regardless of background, were socialized into the subculture. Albert Reiss, for example, found that black officers were just as likely to use excessive force against black suspects as white officers. Incidents of misconduct were generally a response to an open challenge to their authority.[7]

The crisis in the ghettos revived the police–community-relations movement, which had faded into obscurity since the 1943 riots but had never quite died. Most of the ideas developed twenty years before were refurbished in the 1960s. Police–community-relations experts stressed the need for sensitivity training for police officers, the hiring of more black officers (and greater promotional opportunities for those on the force), formal liaison with leaders of the black community, and meaningful discipline of genuine police misconduct. Police administrators added a few new ideas of their own. Departments opened "storefront" offices in the ghettos (thereby reversing a sixty-year-old trend toward centralization), often under the direction of special community-relations units. Some black officers experienced rapid promotion as the police sought to put black faces in visible roles. Other innovations included such things as "ride-along" programs, competitive sports events between the police and black groups, or special summer camps for ghetto youngsters. Many of these were little more than public-relations gimmicks, public gestures with little long-term effects on the role of the police in the ghetto.

Police critics demanded more. The radical solution was "community control," decentralizing the police department and putting the police in each neighborhood under the control of elected boards of commissioners. When the concept was placed on the ballot in Berkeley, California, in 1970, voters rejected it by a 2-1 margin, with even the black community voting against it. The liberal solution called for "civilian review" of complaints against the police by an appointed panel of citizens which included at least some who were completely independent of the police department. The concept of civilian review boards fared little better than community control. Existing review boards in New York City and Philadelphia were terminated because of concerted opposition from the rank-and-file police.[8]

Crime and Crime-Fighting

The police–community-relations crisis coincided with two other important developments: a dramatic rise in serious crime, and the intervention of the federal courts into law-enforcement practices.

Although the three events were independent phenomena, they became hopelessly confounded in the polarized atmosphere of the 1960s.

The incidence of serious crimes against persons and property began to rise at an alarming rate in 1963. Over the previous twenty years crime had increased rather slowly (and homicide had actually declined since reaching a peak in the 1930s). Steady and often substantial increases occurred every year after 1963 (a small decline in 1972 was erased by an enormous rise in 1974, the largest in any single year). Between 1960 and 1974, the total volume of crime increased by 203 percent; total "index crimes" jumped from 3,363,700 to 10,192,000. When adjusted for population growth, the crime rate per 100,000 persons rose from 1.875 in 1960 to 4.821 in 1974. Even more disturbing was the prevalence of crimes of violence, which increased faster than property offenses. Robbery, for example, rose 310 percent in the period.

The growth of crime contributed to a national crisis of confidence. In the face of assassinations, riots, and political terrorism, political pundits and scholars debated whether America was inherently a violent society. Black militant H. Rap Brown voiced the thoughts of many when he declared that violence was "as American as apple pie." The increase in crime during the sixties was in part attributable to specific factors. Because of the post–World War II "baby boom," the fifteen- to twenty-four-year-old segment of the population grew by over a million persons a year in the sixties. Perhaps half of the increase in crime was due to the disproportionately large number of people in this highly "crime-prone" group. Technological unemployment left a growing underclass of poor and alienated in the slums, while the consumer goods of the affluent middle class (color TVs, stereos, expensive cameras, etc.) constituted expanded "opportunities" for crime. Finally, the spread of drug usage created a distinct drug subculture involved in illegal activity.[9]

Crime did not affect all Americans equally. Studies showed that ghetto residents were the most frequent victims of serious crime. (Thus, the black community had the worst of both worlds: harassment in the form of overly aggressive police actions, and a lack of adequate police protection against serious crime.) But the middle class screamed the loudest. Public-opinion polls indicated a steady rise in concern about crime. Frank Furstenburg's study of public attitudes revealed that the "fear of crime" among the middle class was less a fear of actual victimization and more a code word for fear of changing race relations. Public concern about crime translated into increased pressure on the police to "do something."[10]

The spread of drug usage added another dimension to the crime problem. Through the 1950s and early 1960s, the use of both marijuana and heroin was confined mainly to the ghettos. In the mid-sixties, however, marijuana usage spread rapidly among college students and white middle-class youth in general. Drugs became one of the major badges of membership in a youth counterculture, along with rock music, long hair, and sexual freedom. By the 1970s the counterculture had lost its distinct identity, but the badges entered the American mainstream. Drug usage continued to spread, reaching into the junior high schools. Meanwhile, harder drugs—heroin, amphetamines, and barbiturates—also moved out of the ghettos and into the white middle class.

The drug culture supported a growing criminal subculture of suppliers. At the same time, drugs played an important symbolic role in the polarized atmosphere of the 1960s. Within the counterculture, the illegal nature of marijuana fostered an "outlaw" self-image. The overt criminal act of dealing or possessing drugs symbolized a rejection of established values. Middle-aged and middle-class Americans reciprocated and identified drug usage with the collapse of established values. With respect to drugs, *crime* became a code word for a deeply rooted conflict over values.

The Due-Process Revolution

The U.S. Supreme Court, in a series of landmark decisions, re-examined the entire criminal-justice system in the 1960s. Under the leadership of Chief Justice Earl Warren, the Court greatly expanded the rights of individuals and placed limitations on the power of criminal-justice officials. Together these decisions constituted a "due-process revolution," the introduction of a new era of individual rights into the administration of criminal justice. In *Mapp* v. *Ohio* (1961), the Court extended the "exclusionary rule" to criminal proceedings in state courts. Evidence obtained through an unreasonable search was excluded from use in trials. Cleveland, Ohio, police officers forced their way into Ms. Mapp's home waving an alleged "search warrant" that eventually disappeared. The Court expressed "considerable doubt as to whether there ever was any warrant." Thus, the evidence against Ms. Mapp was seized illegally, and her conviction was overturned. The exclusionary rule was nothing new in 1961. The Supreme Court had applied it to federal proceedings in the 1914 *Weeks* case and several states, notably California, had adopted it in the 1950s. The significance of the *Mapp* decision and the entire due-process revolution was the use of the Fourteenth Amendment to extend constitutional protections to individuals in state proceedings. By this ruling the Court "nationalized" the Bill of Rights, holding state and local units of government accountable to a single standard.[11]

The Fourteenth Amendment guarantee that "no state shall . . . deprive any person of life, liberty, or property, without due process of law" underpinned a series of equally important and controversial decisions following *Mapp*. In the 1963 case of *Gideon* v. *Wainwright,* the Court extended the Sixth Amendment guarantee of the right to counsel to state proceedings. The Court found it "an obvious truth" that a person brought into court "cannot be assured a fair trial unless counsel is provided for him." The two most controversial decisions by the Court involved the Fifth Amendment guarantee of protection against self-incrimination. The *Escobedo* (1964) and *Miranda* (1966) decisions enraged the police. Danny Escobedo had been denied access to his attorney while in police custody. In overturning his conviction, the Court ruled that a suspect had a constitutional right to consult with an attorney when "the investigation is no longer a general inquiry into an unsolved crime, and has begun to focus on a particular suspect."

With the *Miranda* decision, the Court examined an earlier stage in the criminal process. Speaking for a deeply divided Court,

Chief Justice Warren ruled that upon arrest, an individual had a constitutional right to "be warned prior to questioning that he has a right to remain silent, that any statement he does make may be used as evidence against him, and that he has a right to the presence of an attorney, either retained or appointed." The Court noted the long history of "third-degree" tactics and cited contemporary police textbooks which advised various psychological techniques for obtaining confessions. The decision led to the now familiar "Miranda warning," advising suspects of their rights.

With the *Escobedo* and *Miranda* decisions, the Supreme Court extended its inquiry into the long-hidden realm of police arrest and interrogation tactics. The police response was predictable. In the inflamed atmosphere of the mid-sixties, the police and their supporters charged that the Court had "handcuffed" them in their effort to deal with crime. Already feeling besieged by charges of police brutality, riots, rising crime rates, and public pressure to "do something" about it, the police made the Court the scapegoat for their problems. Later studies showed that the *Mapp*, *Escobedo*, and *Miranda* decisions did little to hinder police work. Suspects commonly waived their right to remain silent and willingly talked to investigators. The exclusionary rule had its greatest impact on drug-possession and concealed-weapons cases, situations that always posed the most difficult search-and-seizure problems.[12]

The controversy over the Supreme Court's decisions on police tactics acquired political significance. In the 1968 presidential election campaign, both Richard Nixon and George Wallace charged the Court with being "soft on crime" by "handcuffing the police" and "coddling criminals." Despite the limited effect of the Court's decisions on police procedures, many people accepted the idea that it had contributed to the rise in crime. Both conservatives and liberals exaggerated the significance of the decisions. Conservatives were wrong in believing that the Court had handcuffed the police, while liberals falsely assumed that Court decisions were automatically implemented. In fact, compliance was easily avoided.

The decisions had several important consequences that were both unintended and largely overlooked in the ensuing controversy. The decisions brought police procedures into public view.

As a result public expectations about the quality of police performance reached new heights. At the same time, the decisions forced the police to improve their training and supervision. Few people realized that the Court had intervened largely because of the failure of the police to enforce standards of conduct on their own. Thus, it gave a new impetus to police professionalization.

Meanwhile, the Court probed other aspects of the administration of justice. It rejected the traditional "hands-off" doctrine regarding prison administration. Arguing instead that the Constitution followed the offender into prison, the Court opened the door for a wave of prisoners'-rights litigation. And in another landmark case, *In re Gault* (1967), the Court struck at the very heart of the juvenile court. Gerald Gault had been sentenced to several years in a juvenile institution for allegedly making an obscene phone call. Young Gault never had the benefit of counsel, was never confronted by his accusers, never given the right to cross-examine, and was found guilty on the basis of a "confession" that was never put in writing. The Court ruled that informal proceedings of this sort, which had always been central to the idea of juvenile justice, were unconstitutional. The ruling that juveniles were entitled to the same constitutional rights as adult defendants sent shock waves through the entire juvenile-justice system.

RESPONSE TO CRISIS:
THE NEW FEDERAL ROLE

The deepening crisis of law, order, and justice provoked a response by the federal government. The issue of "law and order" first surfaced in national politics during the 1964 presidential campaign. Attacks on "lawlessness" and "crime in the streets" by Republican candidate Barry Goldwater appealed to a growing white backlash against civil-rights militancy and ghetto riots. President Lyndon Johnson remained firm in his commitment to civil rights but sensed that his opponent had hit upon a potentially important issue. After his landslide victory, therefore, Johnson moved quickly to make the crime issue his own.

In early March 1965, Johnson issued a major statement entitled "Crime, Its Prevalence, and Measures of Prevention," outlining two important initiatives. First, he created a presidential crime commission, the President's Commission on Law Enforcement and Administration of Justice, the first such group since the Wickersham Commission. Second, he called for legislation to authorize federal grants-in-aid to criminal justice. This resulted in the Office of Law Enforcement Assistance (OLEA), the forerunner of LEAA. Between September 1965 and June 1968, OLEA dispensed $21 million, most of it going to support training, research, and demonstration projects. Although modest by the later standards of LEAA, OLEA's activities represented a new role for the federal government in criminal justice.[13]

The President's crime commission was a characteristic political gesture by President Lyndon Johnson. He sought to achieve consensus by appointing a panel of distinguished persons, carefully balanced to represent conservative and liberal viewpoints. Commission members included a moderate black (Whitney M. Young of the Urban League), a police chief (Thomas J. Cahill, San Francisco), a former Republican attorney general (William P. Rogers), and a liberal academic (Kingman Brewster, president of Yale). Fifteen of the nineteen commissioners were attorneys. The staff which conducted the actual work of the commission was dominated by lawyers and liberal academicians. Executive Director James Vorenberg taught at Harvard Law School, and Deputy Director Henry Roth was a former U.S. prosecutor.

After two years of work, the commission in 1967 published its final report, *The Challenge of Crime in a Free Society,* as well as nine task force reports. *The Challenge of Crime* was rather liberal in its basic thrust. It did not advocate a "get-tough" approach to crime, instead emphasizing the need for more research, higher qualifications for all criminal-justice personnel, and greater coordination of the national crime-control effort. The most significant impact of the report was its "systems" orientation, reflecting the influence of consultants drawn from the field of systems analysis. The staff produced a flow chart of the entire criminal-justice system which has since been reprinted in virtually every textbook on the subject. The commission popularized the term *criminal-*

justice system and promoted a comprehensive approach to the administration of justice. Its work brought to completion a trend that had been developing since the turn of the century: the concern with efficiency, inputs and outputs, and cost-benefit effectiveness.

Critics complained that the report failed to establish priorities. The 203 recommendations in *The Challenge of Crime in a Free Society* were presented as equally significant. On a number of important questions, the final report was muddled. It failed to take a clear position on the Supreme Court's recent decisions affecting police tactics, and it skirted the question of riots. Some of the recommendations were potentially in conflict. On one page the report recommended that all police recruits have a college degree, while on another it called for more recruitment of minorities. It ignored the fact that raising the formal educational requirement would tend to discriminate against minority applicants who suffered from inadequate educational opportunities. Local departments increasingly wrestled with this thorny dilemma.

In the area of corrections, *The Challenge of Crime* spoke with a clear voice. The report strongly endorsed the concept of diverting cases out of the system without prosecution and the development of "more extensive community programs providing special, intensive treatment as an alternative to institutionalization."[14] Diversion and "community-based" correctional programs enjoyed wide popularity as a result of the commission's endorsement. They expressed the latent anti-institutional bias in correctional thinking. Jails and prisons did not work and should be used only as last resorts. Effective correctional treatment meant maintaining and strengthening the offender's ties to the community.

One result was a dramatic decline in the number of persons in prison. In 1962 there were a total of 220,000 in the country; by 1969 the number had dropped to 188,000. The decline was especially significant considering the sharp increase in crime during the same period. In the 1970s, however, another shift occurred and prison population reached new heights. By 1975 inmates totaled 225,000, and two years later the figure was an all-time record of 283,000.

The ideology of *The Challenge of Crime in a Free Society* was consistent with the other programs of President Johnson's "Great Society." The "war on crime" proposed by the crime commission matched the "war on poverty" of the Office of Economic Opportunity (OEO). Both efforts reflected the buoyant optimism of mid-sixties liberalism, especially the belief that government programs could eliminate social ills. On the subject of juvenile delinquency, the President's crime commission and OEO subscribed to virtually identical theories: unemployment, the lack of meaningful job opportunities, and racial discrimination were the root causes of crime; a social policy that attacked poverty and discrimination would also attack crime.[15]

The President's crime commission stimulated a number of changes in American criminal justice. It set off an "information explosion" that greatly expanded knowledge about the administration of justice. The commission not only funded research projects directly but also promoted the development of criminal-justice higher education, thereby institutionalizing a continuing research effort. Several projects sponsored by the commission had lasting implications. The "victimization" survey explored for the first time the phenomenon of unreported crime, yielding a far more accurate picture of the incidence of crime. The field studies of policing sparked a reevaluation of the day-to-day reality of police work, including the first scientific studies of the effectiveness of patrol. The most important of these was the Kansas City Preventive Patrol Experiment, which challenged the crime-prevention value of routine patrol. The experiment was sponsored not by LEAA but by the Police Foundation, established in 1970 with funds from the Ford Foundation.

The Politics of Law and Order

The Challenge of Crime in a Free Society recommended that the federal government do more to assist improvements in the administration of justice. Instead of the nearly $27 million spent in the previous fiscal year ($7 million through OLEA, $20 million through other crime and delinquency programs), the commission envisioned a program "on which several hundred million dollars annually could be profitably spent over the next decade."[16] Even before the report appeared, President Johnson proposed an expanded federal role. His State of the Union address in January 1967 called for passage of a "Safe Streets and Crime Control Act." The formal budget request a month later proposed a crime-control budget of $50 million the first year and $300 million the next year, mainly to support research, planning, and demonstration projects.

Johnson's crime-control proposal was quickly engulfed by the political passions of the next year and a half. The summer of 1967 witnessed the worst rioting ever in the cities. Meanwhile, the college campuses were beset by increasingly militant protests by both white and black students. Student radicalism reached its apex in the spring of 1968 when Columbia University students seized and occupied several administration buildings. University officials eventually called in the New York City police to end the occupation. In a display of "curbside justice," the police wantonly beat students and bystanders. The year 1968 saw one major crisis after another. The Tet Offensive shattered public support for the Vietnam War and set in motion efforts to withdraw. Assassins' bullets struck down first Martin Luther King and then Senator Robert Kennedy.

The multiplying crises provoked a political backlash. Frightened by riots, militant rhetoric ("black power"), confrontation tactics, and the assault on middle-class values by the counterculture, the majority of Americans were receptive to calls for "law and order." George Wallace scored surprising successes in presidential primaries with his promise to restore order and a call to "support your local police." Republican candidate Richard Nixon directed his attacks at liberal Attorney General Ramsey Clark and the U.S. Supreme Court, claiming both had been overly protective of lawbreakers. In this context Congress found an opportunity to express its support for law and order through the Omnibus Crime Control and Safe Streets Act.[17]

The Advent of LEAA

Title I of the Omnibus Crime Control and Safe Streets Act established the Law Enforcement Assistance Administration (LEAA), which replaced the three-year-old OLEA. Created in the midst of conflict with a vague and ambiguous mandate, LEAA was embroiled in controversy throughout its history. The conservative mood of the Congress in 1967–1968 shaped the agency's structure. In an effort to prevent the accumulation of power in a Washington bureaucracy, Senators McClellan and Hruska imposed a decentralized structure upon the agency. Eighty-five percent of the "action" grant funds were to be distributed to the individual states in the form of "block grants." To receive these funds, each state had to establish a State Planning Agency (SPA) and develop a comprehensive plan for using the money. The SPAs then allocated the money for state and local criminal-justice projects. LEAA in Washington held the remaining 15 percent of the action funds for allocation through discretionary grants.[18]

Under the block-grant system, LEAA virtually abdicated responsibility for establishing priorities or monitoring the use of funds. The SPAs were controlled by state and local criminal-justice officials (despite the presence of "citizens'" representatives). The police interpreted "law-enforcement assistance" to mean that LEAA was essentially a police-oriented program. They were quick to apply for grants for various riot-control equipment and other forms of hardware. This in turn encouraged the growth of the police hardware industry; in many cases the salesmen virtually wrote the applications for grants that would purchase their own equipment. Critics immediately accused LEAA of spending too much money on law enforcement, ignoring courts and corrections, and subsidizing the purchase of exotic but useless weaponry.

In Washington, LEAA directors succumbed to the "war-on-crime" ethos and indulged in a series of highly publicized programs intended to produce quick results. With the High Impact Anti-Crime Program, LEAA granted $160 million to eight cities, promising with great fanfare to reduce serious crime by 5 percent in two years and 20 percent in five years. The National Advisory Commission on Criminal Justice Standards and Goals issued its 1973 reports with the objective of reducing "high-fear" crimes 50 percent by 1983. The promises only backfired. Crime continued to rise (except for a small decline in 1972), and critics raised more questions about the value of LEAA expenditures. The agency's budget rose even faster than the crime rate, going from $63,000 in 1969 to $268,119 the next year, and to $698,919 in 1972 and a peak of $895,000 in 1975.

LEAA's performance in supporting research, the one area where federal dollars might have been most effective, was especially disappointing. Its National Institute of Law Enforcement and Criminal Justice (NILECJ) failed to establish clear priorities or a meaningful grant-review process and squandered most of its money in ill-conceived projects. The Law Enforcement Education Program (LEEP) provided loans and grants to college students in criminal-justice programs ($40 million in 1973). LEEP transformed criminal justice into a sizable and permanent presence within higher education but in the process fostered the proliferation of innumerable college programs of dubious academic quality. The number of colleges offering bachelor's degrees in criminal justice rose from 39 in 1967 to 376 in 1977. *The Quality of Police Education*, a 1978 report sponsored by the Police Foundation, condemned the academic quality of many of the two-year law-enforcement and criminal-justice college programs.[19]

When the Carter administration took office in early 1977, the failure of LEAA was too obvious to ignore. The new President promised to reorganize the agency, but two years later LEAA still did not have either a fresh mandate or even a permanent director. Carter administration incompetence was only part of the problem. The very idea of federal assistance to criminal justice had been severely damaged by the false promises of the Johnson and Nixon administrations. Critics could agree that LEAA had failed badly, but they could not agree on an alternative approach. Some seriously proposed abolishing LEAA altogether. Curiously, the agency found few strong defenders despite the millions of dollars it had dispensed since 1969.[20]

COINTELPRO: FBI Vigilantism

Not all federal actions took place in public. As it had in the past, FBI undertook a secret campaign of illegal actions against radical political groups, moderate and liberal activists, and even their families and friends. The focus of FBI vigilantism was COIN-TELPRO (counter-*inte*lligence-*pro*gram). COINTELPRO was first established in August 1956, but its activities escalated along with political dissent in the mid-sixties. In addition to illegal wiretaps and "mail surveys" that opened the mail of private citizens, FBI agents burglarized the offices of political organizations. The 239 known "black-bag" jobs included at least 90 burglaries of offices of the Socialist Workers party.[21]

Perhaps even more insidious were FBI attempts to discredit and disrupt moderate and radical black groups. Bureau agents fomented dissension within the Black Panther party by sending forged letters in the name of members attacking other members. These tactics may have provoked at least one fatal shooting among black radicals on the West Coast. The bureau's campaign to defame moderate civil-rights leader Martin Luther King included the circulation of a tape recording allegedly proving sexual misconduct on the part of King. Hoover's paranoia had a special racist flavor, and he warned bureau agents to guard against the rise of a "black messiah."

The full extent of FBI crimes did not come to light until the Watergate scandal forced a reexamination of abuses of power by all government agencies. Hoover had skillfully kept most of the bureau activities secret from his nominal superiors, the attorney general and the President, through six presidential administrations. The FBI crimes of the 1960s were a continuation of the bureaucratized vigilantism that had begun to develop in the 1930s. The FBI and its imitators ("Red Squads" in local police departments) mobilized the awesome weight of a large bureaucracy while cloaking their actions in the name of "national security."

RECENT TRENDS IN CRIMINAL JUSTICE

New Issues in Police Administration

The failure of LEAA was particularly evident with respect to the police. The hundreds of millions of dollars channeled to police departments were largely irrelevant to the most important new developments. A quiet revolution overtook American police administration beginning in the mid-sixties. The advent of police unions altered the structure of power within police departments and forced reformers to reevaluate traditional ideas about the process of changing the police.

The riots of the mid-sixties provoked a crisis of confidence within police administration. Thoughtful observers realized that the traditional precepts of police professionalization tended to aggravate police-community relations. The Kerner Commission, echoing conclusions reached by the President's crime commission the year before, reported the disturbing fact that "many of the serious disturbances took place in cities whose police are among the best led, best organized, best trained and most professional in the country." A half century of professionalization had created police departments that were vast bureaucracies, inward-looking, isolated from the public, and defensive in the face of any criticism. Automobile patrol had further insulated the patrol officer against routine face-to-face contact with much of the public. Finally, aggressive stop-and-frisk tactics designed to suppress crime aroused resentment among the most common target population: young blacks.[22]

Professionalization had also left a legacy of problems within departments. The emphasis on managerial efficiency necessitated centralizing authority and tightening the chain of command. In the most professional departments (everyone pointed to Los Angeles), the officer carried out his duties "by the book." While this had the laudable effect of reducing discretion in some areas, it also subjected the officer to an authoritarian regime of internal discipline. Within the police subculture, rank-and-file officers held at least as many grievances against their superiors as against the public.

Employment conditions in law enforcement reached a crisis in the mid-sixties. The relative salaries of police officers steadily lost ground from the late 1940s onward, as unionization produced enormous improvements in wages and working conditions in the private sector. The President's crime commission reported in 1967 that police departments were unable to attract qualified recruits. Nationally, the police were 5 percent under their authorized strength. The commission also noted that salaries compared unfavorably with those of other professions.[23] Lagging salaries only compounded the other grievances felt by the rank and file: charges of police brutality; the *Mapp, Miranda,* and *Escobedo* decisions; the authoritarian management style of their own chiefs.

Police unionism revived with a vengeance in 1966. In some of the more important cities, proposed reforms in the area of police-community relations galvanized the rank and file into action. In the particularly bitter New York City struggle, the Patrolmen's Benevolent Association emerged as a militant force during its campaign against Mayor John Lindsay's civilian review board. The PBA sponsored a referendum which resulted in a 2–1 defeat for the review board. In Boston, Cleveland, and Detroit, the rank and file also organized in opposition to liberal mayors seeking to improve police-community relations. Unlike the two previous outbursts of police unionism, the movement swept the field in the 1960s. The courts were far more tolerant of public-employee unionism, and the police chiefs were unable to effectively resist the upsurge of rank-and-file militance. By the early 1970s, virtually every major police department was engaged in collective bargaining. No single union dominated policing. Even those that joined national federations such as the Fraternal Order of Police (FOP) or International Conference of Police Associations (ICPA) retained a local orientation. Several attempts to form national unions gained only limited success.[24]

Strikes by police officers became an increasingly common feature of city life. None of the major strikes (New York City, 1971; Baltimore, 1974; San Francisco, 1975), however, produced the kind of backlash that followed the 1919 Boston police strike. Police officers also developed such alternatives to strikes as "blue-flu" epidemics, work slowdowns, or the writing of enormous numbers of tickets. The highly publicized strikes were not the most important feature of unionism. Far more significant was the redistribution of power within the department. Police chiefs accustomed to exercising virtually unlimited power suddenly found that almost every administrative decision was subject to negotiation. For better or worse, the rank and file gained a major voice in police administration.

Reformers had difficulty thinking of new strategies to improve policing. Unions tended to oppose even long-standing ideas such as rewarding educational attainment with pay increments or extra points on promotional exams. The most creative new ideas involved a de facto accommodation to the reality of rank-and-file participation. *Team policing*, whereby a team of officers was assigned to a particular geographic area on a permanent basis, enjoyed a brief period of popularity in the early seventies. This innovation was intended both to improve police-community relations and provide a larger role for the rank-and-file officer in the making of policy, but it was not too successful in practice. Enthusiasm began to fade by the mid-seventies.[25]

More promising was the *task-force* approach to innovation. The most significant instance occurred in Kansas City under Chief Clarence Kelley. Kelley gave the rank-and-file task forces the responsiblity of developing new ideas. One of the task forces eventually proposed the preventive-patrol experiment (they sought to find if they could free officers from traditional police patrol duties for some of their other new ideas). Because it involved rank-and-file officers in a planning process, the origins of the Kansas City preventive-patrol experiment were at least as important as its findings. Meanwhile, psychologist Hans Toch devised a similar task-force approach in dealing with misconduct among Oakland, California, police officers. Both projects were based on the premise that police reform in the future would involve the direct participation of the rank and file.[26]

Recruitment became an increasingly complex issue in the 1970s. The proportion of black officers in big-city police departments continued to lag behind the proportion of blacks in the cities. Critics of LEAA charged that the agency had failed to use its clout to ensure even minimal compliance with equal-opportunity employment laws. Detroit was an exception to the general rule: black officers comprised 40 percent of the force by the late 1970s. However, a reverse-discrimination suit by white officers challenged the quota system responsible for this achievement. The recruitment policies of virtually every police department were challenged by the threat of discrimination and reverse-discrimination suits.

The changing role of women police added another dimension to the personnel picture. Women officers, who had traditionally been confined to juvenile work demanded patrol assignments and opportunities for promotion. Indianapolis broke the all-male tradition by assigning two women officers to patrol duty in 1968. Other cities gradually followed suit, replacing the designation of *policeman* with the neutral *police officer*. When the Police Foundation sponsored a study of the effectiveness of women officers on patrol in Washington, D.C., the report concluded that women were just as effective as men.[27]

The recruitment of either black or female officers threatened to become a moot issue in the late seventies, when city governments faced a severe financial crisis. Several thousand police officers were released in New York as the city teetered on the brink of bankruptcy. Even in more solvent cities, the salary demands of the unions (police and other municipal workers) consumed all available new revenues. The unions faced a serious dilemma by the late seventies. Their very successes had contributed to the growing taxpayers' revolt. The police faced a public-opinion backlash and the prospect of having to do more with fewer resources.

From Rehabilitation to Punishment

Public concern about criminal justice jumped from one crisis to another, responding largely to the latest outbreak of conflict and violence. The ghetto riots focused attention on police-community relations. But when the riots ended after 1968, attention shifted to other issues. The Attica prison riot in 1971 dramatized the question of prison reform. By the mid-1970s, however, sentencing reform became the latest fad.

The crisis in corrections involved several distinct but overlapping issues. Prisoners'-rights litigation, another aspect of the due-process revolution, reflected the growing political consciousness of prison inmates, especially blacks and Chicanos. The result was an outburst of prison riots between 1969 and 1971. The riots in turn provoked a reassessment of not just the prison but the whole process of correctional treatment. Critics challenged the effectiveness, the legality, and even the underlying assumptions of corrections. By the mid-seventies a profound retreat from rehabilitation swept through public and professional thinking. For the first time in one hundred and fifty years, both the experts and the public questioned the fundamental assumptions of American corrections.

Prisoners'-rights litigation challenged and effectively defeated the traditional "hands-off" doctrine under which the courts had refused to examine administrative practices within prisons. In its most extreme version, carried over from the nineteenth century, this doctrine held that the Constitution did not follow the prisoner into prison and, upon conviction, the offender was the "slave" of the state. The intervention of the courts began with questions relating to the freedom of religion, many of them brought by Black Muslim inmates. First Amendment guarantees of freedom of the press and religion gradually were extended beyond religious literature and religious services to include the censorship of mail and other issues. Prisoners did not gain unlimited freedoms by any means, but the courts did require a reasonable balancing of individual rights with administrative needs. In the case of *Wolf* v. *McDonnell*, for example, the Supreme Court established due-process guidelines for prison disciplinary hearings. Although the decision did not completely satisfy prisoners'-rights advocates, it did place limits on the discretionary powers of prison officials.[28]

Eighth Amendment protections against cruel and unusual punishment were even more important in the evolving body of correctional law. The courts not only required reasonable standards for the use of disciplinary measures such as solitary confinement but also established minimum standards for conditions in the prison as a whole. In *Holt* v. *Sarver* (1970), a U.S. district court ruled that "the Arkansas Penitentiary System as it exists today . . . is unconstitutional." Conditions at the Cummins and Tucker prison farms subjected inmates to constant "peril and degradation"; inmates were forced to sell their own blood to obtain food, medical care, and protection from personal attack. The American Civil Liberties Union established a prisoners'-rights project in 1970 and intensified the assault on prison conditions. In 1976 Judge Frank M. Johnson found conditions in the Alabama penitentiary unconstitutional. He ordered the state to meet forty-four specific standards (the requirement of sixty square feet per inmate forced immediate reduction in the prison population), and it was estimated that to comply would cost as much as $28 million. Suggesting that under a system of rehabilitation prisoners had a "right to treatment," he ruled that enforced inmate idleness was unconstitutional.

The rising political consciousness of black prisoners led to confrontation with officials. San Quentin penitentiary in California experienced a major racial disturbance in 1967, a general strike by inmates in 1968, and a sit-down strike by 800 of the 4,000 inmates in August 1970. The strikers issued a list of fourteen demands, including the release of all "political prisoners," the hiring of black and Mexican wardens and associate wardens, and the closing of two sections of the prison "until they are made to conform to sanitary and health standards." In the racially polarized atmosphere of the country in the late sixties, increasing numbers of black inmates viewed themselves as "political prisoners," regardless of the specific offense for which they were convicted. Prison violence escalated at an alarming rate. Stabbings of inmates by other inmates in California rose from 56 in 1969 (12 fatal) to 168 in 1972 (32 fatal). An epidemic of prison riots followed, with 39 disturbances in 1969 and 70 in 1970. The wave of riots reached a bloody climax the next year at Attica.[29]

Attica and Its Aftermath

The rebellion at the New York penitentiary at Attica in September 1971 was the single most important event in the recent history of corrections. *Attica* became a code word for the failure of the entire apparatus of corrections. More than any other incident, it accelerated the movement toward a complete reexamination of the prison, the concept of rehabilitation, and the structure of criminal sentences.

The confrontation at Attica began in the summer when inmates issued two separate lists of demands. New York Director of Corrections Russell Oswald made only a token attempt to respond. Inmates then staged an impressive silent protest in August following the shooting of George Jackson, a militant black inmate in San'Quentin. On the morning of September 9th, Attica erupted. Inmates seized 40 hostages and occupied the entire D-yard section of the prison. Politically articulate inmates quickly organized the rebels, who numbered more than three fifths of Attica's 2,243 inmates, formed a governing body, and issued a list of demands. The cooperation between black and white rebels in the racially divided prison impressed all observers.[30]

For four long, tense days the rebel inmates attempted to negotiate with officials. A group of "observers" including journalist Tom Wicker, Black Panther party leader Bobby Seale, and civil-rights lawyer William Kunstler served as a go-between. Governor Nelson Rockefeller refused all requests to appear and conduct the negotiations in person. On Monday morning, September 13th, New York state police and prison guards launched an armed assault on the rebels in D-yard. When the shooting stopped nine minutes later, thirty-nine persons lay dead (four more died later), including ten hostages. Attica was the worst tragedy in the history of the American prison.

The Attica tragedy stimulated the already growing disillusionment with the entire correctional system. Several currents of thought converged in the mid-seventies to produce a broad-based repudiation of the concept of rehabilitation. One current attacked rehabilitation from the standpoint of due process. In 1959 Francis Allen pointed out the conflict between "legal values and the rehabilitative ideal." Individualized treatment, the cornerstone of American corrections for a century and a half, rested on discretionary decision-making by judges, prison officials, and parole boards. Allen charged that "procedural laxness and irregularity" resulted in a denial of equal protection of the laws. *Struggle for Justice*, a

1971 report for the American Friends Service Committee, continued Allen's line of reasoning. Correctional treatment rested "largely on speculation or on assumptions unrelated to criminality," and decisions about offenders were routinely made in "the absence of credible scientific data on the causation or treatment of crime." This devastating critique of the fundamental bases of American corrections had special significance in light of the Quaker's historic role in prison reform.[31]

For rather different reasons, other critics focused on the ineffectiveness of correctional treatment. The exaggerated promises of President Johnson's social-reform program generated a powerful backlash. The war on poverty did not eliminate poverty, nor had the war on crime reduced criminality. In *Thinking About Crime*, James Q. Wilson spoke for an influential group of "neoconservatives," former liberals who were now deeply skeptical about the capacity of government programs to effect social reform. The neoconservatives found support for their position in Robert Martinson's study *The Effectiveness of Correctional Treatment*. The findings of his survey of 231 evaluations of correctional programs were reduced to a two-word cliché: "nothing works." This distorted his evidence somewhat but, as a slogan, it was an idea whose time had come. Martinson seemed to offer the proof to support what an increasing number of people wanted to believe.[32]

If rehabilitation did not work, then what was an acceptable rationale for the disposition of criminal offenders? A far-reaching philosophical debate suddenly emerged as criminal-justice experts weighed the relative merits of punishment, incapacitation, deterrence, and rehabilitation. *Doing Justice*, the report of the Committee for the Study of Incarceration, was indicative of the new mood of the mid-seventies. The committee began its work in the immediate aftermath of Attica. A nominally liberal group, it reached the conclusion that "the severity of the sentence should depend·on the seriousness of the defendant's crime or crimes—on what he *did* rather than on what the sentencer expects he will do if treated in a certain fashion." In a word, it endorsed the philosophic position of "desert." Rejecting one hundred and fifty years of correctional theory and returning in effect to the principles of Beccaria, the report declared that the offender should be "treated *as though he deserves* the unpleasantness that is being inflicted on him."[33]

The Politics of Flat-Time Sentencing

The concept of *flat-time* or determinate sentencing gained popularity in the mid-seventies as a possible solution to the various problems of the prison and the whole rehabilitative ideal. Flat-time attracted support from a diverse coalition of liberals and conservatives and quickly became the latest fad in criminal-justice reform. In theory flat-time was deceptively simple. The punishment would fit the crime: all offenders convicted of the same crime would receive identical sentences of a determinate or fixed length. Flat-time would strip both the sentencing judge and parole boards of most if not all their discretionary power. Some flat-time proposals called for the abolition of parole altogether.[34]

Advocates of flat-time had different and often conflicting motives. Some sought to eliminate disparities in sentencing (disparities from one judge to another, disparities in the sentences handed out by the same judge) and thereby achieve greater fairness. In his book *Criminal Sentences: Law Without Order*, Judge Marvin Frankel argued forcefully against the lack of controls over judicial sentencing.[35] Most members of this group also wished to eliminate the arbitrariness inherent in parole decision-making. A quite different group, however, saw flat-time as a means of achieving greater certainty of punishment. In their view, the central problem was that too often crime went unpunished. The deterrent effect of the criminal sanction was weakened by judicial leniency and early parole release. Many in this group thought flat-time should include mandatory minimum sentences for certain crimes.

Maine, Indiana, California, and Illinois were the first to adopt some form of determinate sentencing, while proposals were debated in nearly thirty other states. In practice, flat-time proved difficult to implement. The new Maine law, while eliminating parole, actually increased the discretion of the sentencing judge, thereby compounding the problem. The new California criminal code enacted in 1976 was the most ambitious and important reform attempt. It divided felonies into four classifications. Within each the sentencing judge had a narrow range of choice (burglary: two, three, or four years). The judge could then "enhance" the sentence for prior prison terms (one year for each "prior") or for especially aggravating circumstances. The law retained "good time," and a prisoner could reduce his sentence by as much as four months out of each year. After these deductions, release would become automatic and the offender would undergo one year of parole supervision. Parole violations could be punished by a maximum of six additional months in prison.

The California law assumed great historic importance, if only because that state had been the most heavily committed to the principle of indeterminacy. Yet, California's experience illustrated the dilemmas inherent in the flat-time idea. Clearly, discretion was not eliminated. Judges still exercised some discretion, although within greatly reduced limits. Good time also continued to lend a note of indeterminacy to sentences. In addition, California law opened up the question of sentence length. How much was enough? Law-enforcement officials attacked the new law for providing sentences that were too short. Liberals replied that flat-time sentences were still too long and would aggravate the already dangerous overcrowding of prisons. As soon as flat-time took effect numerous amendments were proposed, and the future of determinate sentencing in California remained in doubt.

The greatest weakness of all of the various flat-time proposals, however, was their failure to address the problem of plea bargaining. Whatever the "fixed" sentence provided by law, there was nothing to prevent a defendant from pleading guilty to a lesser crime, thereby earning a shorter sentence. Thus, uncontrolled plea bargaining could undermine the possibilities for either fair or certain punishment. Previous experience with mandatory minimum-sentence laws and habitual-criminal laws suggested that they were easily evaded. Plea bargaining became a subject of increased public attention in the 1970s. The bargain struck by Vice

President Spiro Agnew in 1973, which resulted in a sentence of probation, dramatized the inherent arbitrariness and unfairness of the practice.

Capital Punishment

Sentencing discretion was most critical in cases involving the death penalty. Eventually the U.S. Supreme Court intervened and in a series of decisions required states to provide judges and juries with guidelines for the imposition of the death penalty.

Long before the Court intervened, capital punishment in America underwent a subtle but profound change. Between the 1930s and the 1960s, Americans turned away from the death penalty; a majority of the public no longer viewed it as necessary punishment, and a growing minority viewed it as barbaric. Legal executions reached a peak in 1933 when 199 persons were put to death. The number dropped steadily to 82 in 1950 and only 2 in 1967. The highly publicized case of Caryl Chessman, who was finally executed in California in 1960 after years of appeals, became a focal point for revived anti–capital–punishment sentiment. After the two executions in 1967, a de facto moratorium went into effect for ten years. No one was executed in America until Gary Gilmore died before a Utah firing squad in January 1977.

The moratorium on executions was in large part due to a sustained legal assault on the death penalty led by NAACP attorneys. The interest of the NAACP was obvious: blacks in southern states were executed in disproportionate numbers. More than half of the persons executed between 1930 and 1967 (53.5 percent) were black; 60 percent of all executions occurred in seventeen southern states; blacks were executed for the crime of rape out of all proportion to the number of whites; and whites receiving the death penalty were far more likely to have the sentence commuted. Death-penalty cases were the most blatant and best-documented example of the discrimination that arose from the sequence of discretionary decisions in the criminal process.

The assault on the death penalty in the 1960s differed from those of previous eras. Instead of humanitarian arguments, the

NAACP attorneys focused on the constitutionality of death sentences. The campaign finally won a major victory in the 1972 case of *Furman* v. *Georgia*. The U.S. Supreme Court ruled that the arbitrary and capricious imposition of the death penalty was cruel and unusual under the Eighth and Fourteenth Amendments. *Furman* was not a total victory for the anti–capital-punishment forces, however. The Court was deeply divided, and all nine judges rendered opinions in the 5–4 decision. Only two justices argued that capital punishment was inherently cruel and unusual. The Court ruled that the death penalty would pass the test of constitutionality if judges and juries were given clear guidelines. A number of states hastily revised their laws, and in 1976 the Court ruled on cases from five different states. In *Gregg* v. *Georgia* and its companion cases, the Court affirmed its earlier opinion, upholding statutes that provided guided discretion and striking down those that provided no guidelines for the sentence of death.[36]

THE FUTURE OF CRIMINAL JUSTICE

The struggle over capital punishment was only one part of the larger crisis of demand affecting the administration of justice in the late 1970s. Public expectations were not simply greater; they were conflicting. The latent conflict between the crime-control and the due-process perspectives, as defined by Herbert Packer, was a daily reality. One segment of the public demanded swifter and more effective suppression of crime. Another segment demanded greater procedural regularity and equality of treatment.

As we have seen, the conflicting pressures impinged directly on the police. Vocal segments of the public demanded that the police do something to prevent crime. At the same time, increased calls for service indicated a growing demand for police help in a wide range of noncriminal matters. By the late 1970s, however, a taxpayers' revolt raised the prospect of budgetary cutbacks. Citizens were also far more conscious of the legal aspects of police work and not reluctant to bring suit or file complaints when they felt unjustly treated. Police officers, meanwhile, had demands of their own and expressed those demands with increasing effectiveness through their unions.

The correctional system felt the impact of equally strong but conflicting pressures. The disillusionment with rehabilitation brought into question fundamental correctional practices. Some citizens sought a return to punishment: mandatory minimum sentences, longer prison terms, and an end to parole as an easy way out of prison. Others were disturbed about the crimes of the prisons themselves, particularly the lack of even the most minimal standards of decency. Correctional officials also were caught between restive and politically conscious inmates, on the one hand, and prison staff who, like the police, were turning toward unionism, on the other.

The intervention of the courts in so many areas of criminal justice had a special historical significance. By examining such matters as police procedures and prisoners' rights, the courts were in effect demanding that society complete the unfinished business of the administration of justice. Historically, the administration of justice had been informal and irregular. The modern institutions of justice—the police, the prisons, the correctional programs—had been left to operate without any procedural guidelines. The demand for rules was a development of enormous long-term consequence.

By the end of the 1970s, many criminal-justice experts felt at an impasse. Never before had public awareness of criminal justice been as high. And never before had the experts themselves understood the actual processes of the administration of justice as well. The research revolution of the 1970s had produced an unprecedented outpouring of data on criminal justice. Yet, the experts were not sure what to do with all this knowledge. The experience of the previous fifteen years had left them deeply chastened. The "wars on crime" promised first by Lyndon Johnson and then by Richard Nixon had both failed to achieve their stated objectives. Moreover, the false promises had generated a potent backlash of disillusionment. The experts were inclined to promise less and, for the most part, were unwilling to venture firm predictions about the future of criminal justice.

EPILOGUE: THE MEANING OF "POPULAR JUSTICE"

At the dawn of the 1980s, the concept of a "popular justice" had as many contradictory meanings as it had throughout the history of American criminal justice. In terms of public attitudes, the administration of justice had probably never been so unpopular. Few were satisfied that justice was being done. One segment of the public was convinced that the criminal-justice system had failed to protect citizens against crime, while another believed that the system itself was the problem, that the agencies of criminal justice inflicted harm on those who fell into its clutches.

The growth of a vast criminal-justice bureaucracy, what we routinely call the criminal-justice system, had a number of important consequences. Over a period of some two hundred years, it had greatly reduced direct public participation in the administration of justice. The decline of the jury was only one of the more obvious aspects of this long-term development that included the passing of the citizen night watch and public punishments and the decline in the number of elected judges. Measured in terms of direct participation, then, the administration of justice was far less "popular" than it once had been. This was a positive development, insofar as it had helped to curb the influence of popular passions. The lynch mob and the vigilante group had long been two of the less attractive features of the American style of popular justice. But at the same time, the bureaucracies—vast, impenetrable, often self-serving— were the source of much of the public distrust and dissatisfaction with the state of criminal justice.

At the heart of the matter lay one of the fundamental dilemmas of democracy. The criminal-justice system in the second half of the twentieth century had begun—but only begun—to serve a broader segment of the public in a fairer, and more equal and decent manner. Yet, this accomplishment had been achieved through essentially elitist and undemocratic means. The courts had imposed new standards of equal treatment, while "professionalism" was also often a device to insulate an agency from community demands. The history of American criminal justice seems to suggest that what the people wanted has not always resulted in either the fairest or most effective administration of justice.

SUGGESTIONS FOR FURTHER READING

The field of criminal justice is relatively new. Professional historians have managed to ignore many important criminal-justice topics until fairly recently. As a result the existing body of literature is rather small. There are enormous gaps in our knowledge about crucial aspects of the administration of justice. The following is a short list of the most important works.

There is no published history of American criminal justice. Lawrence Friedman has sketched the outlines of a history in "The Devil is Not Dead: Exploring the History of Criminal Justice," *Georgia Law Review*, 11 (Winter 1977): 257-274. One should also consult John Conley, "Criminal Justice as a Field of Research: A Review of the Literature, 1960-1975," *Journal of Criminal Justice*, 5 (Spring 1977): 13-28, although a number of important works have been published subsequently.

Legal historians have also tended to ignore the criminal law. There is no history of the substantive criminal law in America, although Lawrence Friedman's *A History of American Law* (New York: Simon and Schuster, 1973) is extremely useful. No student should fail to look at Leon Radzinowicz's monumental *A History of English Criminal Law* (London: Stevens and Sons, 1948-).

Historical patterns of criminal behavior present a treacherous field of investigation. Two important articles are Roger Lane, "Urbanization and Criminal Violence in the 19th Century: Massachusetts as a Test Case," in Hugh Davis Graham and Ted Robert Gurr, eds., *The History of Violence in America* (New York: Bantam, 1969), and Theodore Ferdinand, "The Criminal Patterns of Boston Since 1849," *American Journal of Sociology*, 73 (July 1967): 84-99. Recent book-length treatments include Douglas Greenberg, *Crime and Law Enforcement in the Colony of New*

York, 1691-1776 (Ithaca: Cornell University Press, 1976), and the much less successful Erik Monkkonen, *The Dangerous Class: Crime and Poverty in Columbus, Ohio, 1860-1885* (Cambridge: Harvard University Press, 1975)

There is a growing body of scholarship on the police. The best complete treatment is Robert Fogelson, *Big City Police* (Cambridge: Harvard University Press, 1977). Other works include James Richardson, *The New York Police: Colonial Times to 1901* (New York: Oxford University Press, 1970); Roger Lane, *Policing the City: Boston, 1822-1885* (New York: Atheneum, 1971); Wilbur Miller, *Cops and Bobbies: Police Authority in New York and London, 1830-1870* (Chicago: University of Chicago Press, 1977); and Samuel Walker, *A Critical History of Police Reform: The Emergence of Professionalism* (Lexington: Lexington, 1977).

On the history of the courts, consult Friedman's *History of American Law* and Henry J. Abraham's *The Judicial Process*, 4th ed. (New York: Oxford University Press, 1980), which includes a comprehensive bibliography. Robert Ireland's *The County Courts in Antebellum Kentucky* (Lexington: University of Kentucky Press, 1972) explores a crucial but largely neglected subject, the administration of justice in the lower courts.

Blake McKelvey's recent *American Prisons: A History of Good Intentions* (Monclair: Patterson Smith, 1977) is the only complete history of the subject. Much has been written about the origins of the prison. No one should neglect David Rothman's *The Discovery of the Asylum* (Boston: Little, Brown, 1971), while the various works of Harry Elmer Barnes, including *The Evolution of Penology in Pennsylvania* (1927; reprint ed., Montclair: Patterson Smith, 1968), are still valuable. An extremely important treatment of recent prison history is James B. Jacobs, *Stateville: The Prison in Mass Society* (Chicago: University of Chicago Press, 1977).

Juvenile justice is the subject of several works, including Anthony M. Platt, *The Child Savers: The Invention of Delinquency* (Chicago: University of Chicago Press, 1969); Joseph Hawes, *Children in Urban Society: Juvenile Delinquency in Nineteenth Century America* (New York: Oxford University Press,

1971); and Robert Mennel, *Thorns and Thistles, Juvenile Delinquents in the United States, 1825–1940* (Hanover: University Press of New England, 1973).

There is a sizable body of literature on violence in American life. Useful starting points include various essays in Graham and Gurr, *History of Violence in America,* and the documents and introduction in Richard Hofstadter and Michael Wallace, eds., *American Violence: A Documentary History* (New York: Vintage, 1971). And most important are the essays on violence and vigilantism in Richard Maxwell Brown, *Strain of Violence* (New York: Oxford University Press, 1975).

Unfortunately, there is no history of racism in the administration of criminal justice. One should begin with the standard works on the history of blacks, Chicanos, and American Indians for relevant material.

The administration of criminal justice intersects with other aspects of American life. Although scholars have an unfortunate tendency to remain within the confines of academic disciplines, one can find important materials in works in the history of social welfare, urban government, and other topics.

Finally, we should acknowledge the contribution of several publishers who have made available many of the classic works in criminal justice in convenient reprint editions. Particularly notable are Patterson Smith, Arno Press, and AMS Press.

NOTES

CHAPTER 1

1. Massachusetts, *The Book of the General Lawes and Libertyes Concerning the Inhabitants of the Massachusetts,* facsimile edition, ed. Thomas G. Barnes, (San Marino, Calif.: Huntington Library, 1975), pp. 5-6.
2. Leon Radzinowicz, *A History of English Criminal Law* (London: Stevens, 1948-), I, 3.
3. Roscoe Pound, *Criminal Justice in America* (New York: Da Capo, 1975), ch.4.
4. Perry Miller, *Errand into the Wilderness* (Cambridge: Harvard University Press, 1956).
5. Graeme Newman, *The Punishment Response* (Philadelphia: Lippincott, 1978), pp. 61-69, 120.
6. Abbott Emerson Smith, *Colonists in Bondage: White Servitude and Convict Labor in America, 1607-1776* (Chapel Hill: University of North Carolina Press, 1947), chs. 5, 6.
7. David Rothman, *The Discovery of the Asylum* (Boston: Little, Brown, 1971).
8. Pennsylvania, Guardians of the Poor, *A Compilation of the Poor Laws of the State of Pennsylvania from the Year 1700 to 1788, Inclusive* (New York: Arno, 1971), pp. 12-13.
9. Harry Elmer Barnes, *A History of the Penal, Reformatory and Correctional Institutions of the State of New Jersey* (Trenton: Quigley, 1918), pp. 37-50.
10. Alice Morse Earle, *Curious Punishments of Bygone Days* (New York: Duffield, 1907), pp. 30-37.
11. Cited in Joseph E. Hawes, *Children in Urban Society: Juvenile Delinquency in Nineteenth Century America* (New York: Oxford University Press, 1971), p. 13.
12. A. Leon Higginbotham, Jr., *In the Matter of Color—Race and the American Legal Process: The Colonial Period* (New York: Oxford University Press, 1978), p. 81.
13. Julian P. Boyd, "The Sheriff in Colonial North Carolina," *North Carolina Historical Review,* 5 (1928): 151-181; Charles S. Sydnor, *American Revolutionaries in the Making* (New York: Free Press, 1965), ch. 6.

14. Boyd, "The Sheriff in Colonial North Carolina"; Douglas Greenberg, *Crime and Law Enforcement in the Colony of New York, 1691-1776* (Ithaca: Cornell University Press, 1976).
15. James Richardson, *The New York Police: Colonial Times to 1901* (New York: Oxford University Press, 1970), p. 16; Roger Lane, *Policing the City: Boston, 1822-1855* (New York: Atheneum, 1971), ch. 1.
16. Richardson, *New York Police*, ch. 1; Lane, *Policing the City*, ch. 1.
17. Sydnor, *American Revolutionaries*, pp. 74-86.
18. Julius Goebel and T. Raymond Naughton, *Law Enforcement in Colonial New York: A Study in Criminal Procedure, 1664-1776* (Montclair: Patterson Smith, 1970), pp. 497-507.
19. Harry Elmer Barnes and Negley Teeters, *New Horizons in Criminology*, 2nd ed. (New York: Prentice-Hall, 1951), pp. 459-464.
20. Michael Zuckerman, *Peaceable Kingdoms: New England Towns in the Eighteenth Century* (New York: Vintage, 1970), ch. 3.
21. Greenberg, *Crime and Law Enforcement*; Roger Lane, "Crime and the Industrial Revolution: British and American Views," *Journal of Social History*, 7 (Spring 1974): 287-303.
22. Greenberg, *Crime and Law Enforcement*, p. 25.
23. David H. Flaherty, "Law and the Enforcement of Morals in Early America," in *Perspectives in American History*, 5 (1971): 207-253.
24. Greenberg, *Crime and Law Enforcement*, pp. 99, 190.
25. Jerome Frank, *Courts on Trial* (Princeton: Princeton University Press, 1949), chs. 8, 9.
26. Goebel and Naughton, *Law Enforcement in Colonial New York*, *passim*.
27. Greenberg, *Crime and Law Enforcement*, p. 130. Lawrence Friedman, *A History of American Law* (New York: Simon and Schuster, 1973), pp. 61-62.
28. Kai T. Erikson, *Wayward Puritans: A Study in the Sociology of Deviance* (New York: Wiley, 1966), pp. 116-117.
29. Ibid., ch. 3.
30. Ibid., pp. 137-159.
31. Alan Reitman, ed., *The Pulse of Freedom* (New York: New American Library, 1976).
32. Richard Maxwell Brown, *The South Carolina Regulators* (Cambridge: Harvard University Press, 1963).
33. Richard Maxwell Brown, *Strain of Violence: Historical Studies of American Violence and Vigilantism* (New York: Oxford University Press, 1975), pp. 95-133.
34. Harry Elmer Barnes, *The Repression of Crime* (New York: Doran, 1926), pp. 47-54; Barnes, *The Evolution of Penology in Pennsylvania* (Montclair: Patterson Smith, 1968), pp. 23-71.

CHAPTER 2

1. Peter Gay, *The Enlightenment: An Interpretation*, 2 vols. (New York: Knopf, 1966-1969).

2. Cited in James Heath, ed., *Eighteenth Century Penal Theory* (London: Oxford University Press, 1963), a valuable collection of the major writings on criminal justice.
3. Patrick Colquhoun, *A Treatise on the Police of the Metropolis* (Montclair: Patterson Smith, 1969); Michel Foucault, *Discipline and Punish: The Birth of the Prison* (New York: Pantheon, 1978), pp. 81–82.
4. The following quotes are from Cesare Beccaria, *On Crimes and Punishments* (1764; reprint ed., Indianapolis: Bobbs-Merrill, 1963).
5. Marcello Maestro, *Cesare Beccaria and the Origins of Penal Reform* (Philadelphia: Temple University Press, 1973); Leon Radzinowicz, *A History of English Criminal Law* (London: Stevens, 1948–), I, 1–79.
6. The following quotations are from John Howard, *The State of the Prisons* (4th ed., 1792; reprint ed., Montclair: Patterson Smith, 1973).
7. John H. Langbein, "The Historical Orgins of the Sanction of Imprisonment for Serious Crime," *Journal of Legal Studies,* 5 (January 1976): 35–60.
8. Norman Johnston, *The Human Cage: A Brief History of Prison Architecture* (New York: Walker, 1973), pp. 16–21.
9. William E. Nelson, *The Americanization of the Common Law: The Impact of Legal Change on Massachusetts Society, 1760-1830* (Cambridge: Harvard University Press, 1975), p. 97.
10. Sir William Blackstone, *Commentaries on the Laws of England,* Book the Fourth, 1803 ed. (New York: Kelley, 1969); Lawrence Friedman, *A History of American Law* (New York: Simon and Schuster, 1973), pp. 88–89.
11. Friedman, *History of American Law,* pp. 256–257; William E. Nelson, *Americanization of the Common Law.*
12. Richard Maxwell Brown, *Strain of Violence: Historical Studies of American Violence and Vigilantism* (New York: Oxford University Press, 1975), pp.41–66.
13. Ibid., p. 45.
14. Ibid., pp. 95–133.
15. Harry Elmer Barnes, *The Repression of Crime* (New York: Doran, 1926), p. 192.
16. Ibid., p. 119.
17. Benjamin Rush, Essays, in Philip E. Mackey, ed., *Voices Against Death: American Opposition to Capital Punishment, 1787-1975* (New York: Franklin, 1976), pp. 1–13).
18. Blake McKelvey, *American Prisons: A History of Good Intentions* (Montclair: Patterson Smith, 1977), p. 7.

CHAPTER 3

1. Martino Beltrani Scalia, "Historical Sketch of National and International Penitentiary Congresses in Europe and America," in *Transactions of the National Congress on Penitentiary and Reformatory Discipline* [1870] (Washington: American Correctional Association, 1970), pp. 267–277.
2. Robert Wiebe, *The Search for Order* (New York: Hill and Wang, 1967).

3. Allan Silver, "The Demand for Order in Civil Society: A Review of Some Themes in the History of Urban Crime, Police, and Riot," in David J. Bordua, ed., *The Police: Six Sociological Essays* (New York: Wiley, 1967), pp. 1–24; Michel Foucault, *Discipline and Punish: The Birth of the Prison* (New York: Pantheon, 1978).

4. Daniel Boorstin, *The Americans: The Democratic Experience* (New York: Vintage, 1974), pp. 26–33.

5. Richard Maxwell Brown, *Strain of Violence: Historical Studies of American Violence and Vigilantism* (New York: Oxford University Press, 1975), pp. 3–36.

6. Milton Gordon, *Assimilation in American Life: The Role of Race, Religion, and National Origins* (New York: Oxford University Press, 1964).

7. Philip Taft and Philip Ross, "American Labor Violence: Its Causes, Character and Outcome," in Hugh Davis Graham and Ted Robert Gurr, eds., *The History of American Violence* (New York: Bantam, 1969), pp. 281–395.

8. Jane H. Pease and William H. Pease, *The Fugitive Slave Law and Anthony Burns: A Problem in Law Enforcement* (Philidelphia: Lippincott, 1975); Brown, *Strain of Violence*, pp. 251–260.

9. Roger Lane, *Policing the City: Boston, 1822–1885* (New York: Atheneum, 1971), ch. 3.

10. Robert Wintersmith, *The Police and the Black Community* (Lexington: Lexington, 1974), ch. 2.

11. T. A. Critchley, *A History of Police in England and Wales*, 2nd ed. rev. (Montclair: Patterson Smith, 1972), ch. 2.

12. Wilbur R. Miller, *Cops and Bobbies: Police Authority in New York and London, 1830–1870* (Chicago: University of Chicago Press, 1977).

13. Samuel Walker, *A Critical History of Police Reform: The Emergence of Professionalism* (Lexington: Lexington, 1977), p. 71; Robert Fogelson, *Big City Police* (Cambridge: Harvard University Press, 1977), ch. 1.

14. Leonhard Fuld, *Police Administration* (Montclair: Patterson Smith, 1971), pp. 116–126.

15. Jonathan Rubinstein, *City Police* (New York: Ballantine, 1974), pp. 3–26.

16. John J. Flinn, *History of the Chicago Police* (Chicago: Police Book Fund, 1887), p. 206.

17. Lincoln Steffens, *Autobiography* (New York: Harper, 1931), pp. 206–207.

18. Miller, *Cops and Bobbies*.

19. Mark Haller, "Historical Roots of Police Behavior: Chicago, 1890–1925," *Law and Society Review*, 10 (Winter 1976): 303–324.

20. Raymond B. Fosdick, *American Police Systems* (New York: Century, 1920), ch. 2.

21. David Rothman, *The Discovery of the Asylum* (Boston: Little, Brown, 1971), p. 180.

22. W. David Lewis, *From Newgate to Dannemora: The Rise of the Penitentiary in New York, 1796–1848* (Ithaca: Cornell University Press, 1965), ch. 6.

23. Gustave de Beaumont and Alexis de Tocqueville, *On the Penitentiary System in the United States and Its Application in France* (1833; reprint ed., Carbondale: Southern Illinois University Press, 1964).

24. Enoch C. Wines and Theodore W. Dwight, *Report on the Prisons and Re-*

formatories of the United States and Canada (1867; reprint ed., New York: AMS, 1973), p. 124.

25. Ibid., p. 114.
26. Ibid., p. 138.
27. Ibid., p. 177.
28. Ibid, pp. 175–176.
29. U.S. Commissioner of Labor, *Second Annual Report*, "Convict Labor," 1886 (Washington, 1887).
30. Wines and Dwight, *Report on the Prisons*, p. 255.
31. Ibid., p. 253.
32. Ibid., pp. 252–253.
33. *Report of the Prison Discipline Society of Boston* (1828; reprint ed., Montclair: Patterson Smith, 1972), p. 16; Mark T. Carleton, *Politics and Punishment: The History of the Louisiana State Penal System* (Baton Rouge: LSU Press, 1971), ch. 1.
34. Beaumont and Tocqueville, *On the Penitentiary System in the United States*, p. 121.
35. Wines and Dwight, *Report on the Prisons*, pp. 120–122.
36. Blake McKelvey, *American Prisons: A History of Good Intentions* (Montclair: Patterson Smith, 1977), pp. 15–17, 66–70.
37. Dorothea Lynde Dix, *On Behalf of the Insane Poor: Selected Reports* (1843; reprint ed., New York: Arno, 1971), p. 4.
38. Philip English Mackey, ed., *Voices Against Death: American Opposition to Capital Punishment, 1787–1975* (New York: Franklin, 1976), pp. xi–liii.
39. Lawrence Friedman, *A History of American Law* (New York: Simon and Schuster, 1973), p. 252.
40. Joseph Hawes, *Children in Urban Society: Juvenile Delinquency in Nineteenth-Century America* (New York: Oxford University Press, 1971), ch. 3.
41. *Annual Reports of the Children's Aid Society* (New York: Arno, 1971); Hawes, *Children in Urban Society*, ch. 6.
42. Hawes, *Children in Urban Society*, ch. 6.
43. Robert S. Mennel, *Thorns and Thistles: Juvenile Delinquents in the United States, 1825–1940* (Hanover: University Press of New England, 1973), ch. 2.
44. Wines and Dwight, *Report on the Prisons*, p. 415.
45. Ibid., p. 414.
46. Ibid., pp. 412–415; Anthony M. Platt, *The Child Savers: The Invention of Delinquency* (Chicago: University of Chicago Press, 1969), pp. 103–104.

CHAPTER 4

1. Michel Foucault, *Discipline and Punish: The Birth of the Prison* (New York: Pantheon, 1978), p. 268.
2. Enoch C. Wines and Theodore W. Dwight, *Report on the Prisons and Reformatories of the United States and Canada* (1867; reprint ed., New York: AMS, 1973), p. 62.

3. Harry Elmer Barnes and Negley Teeters, *New Horizons in Criminology*, 2nd. ed. (New York: Prentice-Hall, 1951), pp. 557–558.
4. *Transactions of the National Congress on Penitentiary and Reformatory Discipline* (1870; reprint ed., Washington: American Correctional Association, 1970), pp. 541–547.
5. Zebulon R. Brockway, "The Ideal of a True Prison System for a State," in ibid., pp. 38–65. The following quotations from Brockway are from this paper.
6. John Augustus, *John Augustus: First Probation Officer* (1852; reprint ed., Montclair: Patterson Smith, 1972), pp. x–xi.
7. United States, *Attorney General's Survey of Release Procedures*, II, *Probation* (Washington, 1939), pp. 3–24.
8. Edward H. Savage, *Police Records and Recollections* (1873; reprint ed., Montclair: Patterson Smith, 1971), pp. 168–169.
9. Wines and Dwight, *Report on the Prisons*, p. 115.
10. Ibid., p. 112; Eugenia C. Lekkerkerker, *Reformatories for Women in The United States* (Groningen: Wolters, 1931).
11. Lekkerkerker, *Reformatories for Women*, pp. 93–94, 102.
12. Blake McKelvey, *American Prisons: A History of Good Intentions* (Montclair: Patterson Smith, 1977), p. 86.
13. New York State Division of Parole, "The Origins of Parole and Conditional Pardons," in C. L. Newman, ed., *Sourcebook on Probation, Parole and Pardons*, 3rd ed. (Springfield: Thomas, 1968), pp. 17–37.
14. Wines and Dwight, *Report on the Prisons*, pp. 304–305.
15. Barry Salkin, "The Pardoning Power in Ante-Bellum Pennsylvania," *Pennsylvania Magazine of History and Biography*, 100 (October 1976): 507–520.
16. *Report of the Prison Discipline Society of Boston* (1852; reprint ed., Montclair: Patterson Smith, 1972), p. 12.
17. Board of State Charities of Massachusetts, *Third Annual Report*, 1867 (Boston, 1867), p. 100.
18. Wines and Dwight, *Report on the Prisons*, p. 342.
19. Christopher Hibbert, *The Roots of Evil: A Social History of Crime and Punishment* (n.p.: Minerva, 1968), pp. 147–149.
20. Gaylord B. Hubbell, "Reformatory Discipline as Applied to Adult Criminals," in *Transactions of the National Congress*, pp. 169–179.
21. McKelvey, *American Prisons*, pp. 83–87.
22. Edward Lindsey, "Historical Sketch of the Indeterminate Sentence and Parole System," *Journal of Criminal Law and Criminology*, 16 (May 1925): 22–23.
23. Zebulon R. Brockway, *Fifty Years of Prison Service: An Autobiography* (1912; reprint ed., Montclair: Patterson Smith, 1969), pp. 286–298.
24. Edward Lindsey, "Historical Sketch of the Indeterminate Sentence and Parole System," *Journal of Criminal Law and Criminology*, 16 (May 1925): 9–126.
25. Marvin Zalman, "The Rise and Fall of the Indeterminate Sentence." *Wayne Law Review*, 24 (November 1977): 45–94.
26. Rollei Brinkerhoff, "What to do About Recidivists?" in *Proceedings of the National Prison Association*, 1889, (n.p.), p. 190.
27. Anthony M. Platt, *The Child Savers: The Invention of Delinquency* (Chicago:

University of Chicago Press, 1969); Joseph M. Hawes, *Children in Urban Society: Juvenile Delinquency in Nineteenth Century America* (New York: Oxford University Press, 1971), ch. 10.

CHAPTER 5

1. The liberal view is implicit in most works on criminology and criminal justice; see, for example, the President's Commission on Law Enforcement and Administration of Justice, *The Challenge of Crime in a Free Society* (New York: Avon, 1968). For the Marxist view, see Richard Quinney, *Criminology Analysis and Critique of Crime in America* (Boston: Little, Brown, 1971).

2. Theodore Ferdinand, "Criminal Patterns of Boston Since 1849," *American Journal of Sociology*, 73 (July 1967): 84-99; Roger Lane, "Urbanization and Criminal Violence in the 19th Century: Massachusetts as a Test Case," in Hugh Davis Graham and Ted Robert Gurr, eds., *The History of American Violence* (New York: Bantam, 1969), pp. 468-485; Samuel B. Warner, *The Private City* (Philadelphia: University of Pennsylvania, Press, 1971), ch. 7.

3. Joseph R. Gusfield, *Symbolic Crusade* (Urbana: University of Illinois Press, 1963).

4. John Kaplan, *Marijuana—The New Prohibition* (New York: World, 1970).

5. David R. Johnson, "A Sinful Business: The Origins of Gambling Syndicates in the United States, 1840-1887," in David Bayley, ed., *Police and Society* (Beverly Hills: Sage, 1977), pp. 17-47.

6. Lawrence Friedman, *A History of American Law* (New York: Simon and Schuster, 1973), p. 258.

7. Jerome Hall, *Theft, Law and Society*, 2nd ed. (Indianapolis: Bobbs-Merrill, 1952).

8. Samuel B. Warner and Henry B. Cabot, "Changes in the Administration of Criminal Justice During the Past Fifty Years," *Harvard Law Review*, 50 (1936-1937): 583-645.

9. Roscoe Pound, *Criminal Justice in America* (New York: Da Capo, 1975), p. 161.

10. Howard N. Meyer, *The Amendment That Refused to Die* (Boston: Beacon, 1978).

11. Jerome Frank, *Courts on Trial* (Princeton: Princeton University Press, 1949), chs. 8, 9; Jack K. Williams, *Vogues in Villainy: Crime and Retribution in Ante-Bellum South Carolina* (Columbia: University of South Carolina Press, 1959), p. 86.

12. Enoch C. Wines and Theodore W. Dwight, *Report on the Prisons and Reformatories of the United States and Canada* (1867; reprint ed., New York: AMS, 1973), pp. 516-518.

13. The Cleveland Survey of Criminal Justice, *Criminal Justice in Cleveland* (Cleveland: The Cleveland Foundation, 1922), pp. 117, 159.

14. Milton Heuman, "A Note on Plea Bargaining and Case Pressure," *Law and Society Review*, 9 (Spring 1975): 515-528.

15. Wines and Dwight, *Report on the Prisons*, pp. 498-504.

16. Robert M. Ireland, *The County Courts in Antebellum Kentucky* (Lexington: University of Kentucky Press, 1972).
17. J. Willard Hurst, *The Growth of American Law: The Lawmakers* (Boston: Little, Brown, 1950).
18. Wines and Dwight, *Report on the Prisons*, pp. 465–468.
19. H. Glick and K. N. Vines, *State Court Systems* (Englewood Cliffs: Prentice-Hall, 1973), p. 41.
20. Robert Percival and Lawrence Friedman, "Criminal Justice in the Urban Melting Pot: Arrest Patterns in Oakland, California, 1872-1910," Paper, Conference on Historical Perspectives on American Criminal Justice, Omaha, Nebraska, April, 1976.
21. Ibid., pp. 50–55.
22. Ibid., p. 30.
23. James Richardson, *The New York Police: Colonial Times to 1901* (New York: Oxford University Press, 1970), p. 190.
24. Margaret Cahalan, "Trends in Incarceration in the United States Since 1880," *Crime and Delinquency*, 25 (January 1979): 9–41.
25. John Peter Altgeld, *Live Questions: Including Our Penal Machinery and its Victims* (Chicago: Donohue and Henneberry, 1890); Clarence Darrow, *Resist Not Evil* (1902; reprint ed., Montclair: Patterson Smith, 1972), pp. 153–154.
26. C. Vann Woodward, *The Strange Career of Jim Crow*, 2nd ed. (New York: Oxford University Press, 1966).
27. Wilcomb E. Washburn, *The Indian in America* (New York: Harper, 1975), pp. 17–25.
28. Richard Maxwell Brown, *Strain of Violence: Historical Studies of American Violence and Vigilantism* (New York: Oxford University Press, 1975), pp. 95–133.
29. Ibid., p. 124.

CHAPTER 6

1. Robert Wiebe, *The Search for Order* (New York: Hill and Wang, 1967).
2. Herbert L. Packer, "Two Models of the Criminal Process," in Herbert Packer, *The Limits of the Criminal Sanction* (Stanford: Stanford University Press, 1968), pp. 149-173.
3. Sheldon Glueck, ed., *Roscoe Pound and Criminal Justice* (Dobbs Ferry, N.Y.: Oceana, 1965), pp. 57-73.
4. Ibid., p. 73.
5. Blake McKelvey, *American Prison: A History of Good Intentions* (Montclair: Patterson Smith, 1977), pp. 248-269.
6. Samuel Hays, "The Politics of Municipal Reform in the Progressive Era," *Pacific Northwest Quarterly*, 55 (October 1965): 157-169.
7. Malcolm Feeley, "Two Models of the Criminal Justice System: An Organizational Perspective," *Law and Society Review*, 7 (Spring 1973): 407-425.

8. Jerold S. Auerbach, *Unequal Justice: Lawyers and Social Change in Modern America* (New York: Oxford University Press, 1976).

9. Reginald Heber Smith, *Justice and the Poor* (New York: The Carnegie Foundation, 1919).

10. Samuel Walker, *A Critical History of Police Reform: The Emergence of Professionalism* (Lexington: Lexington, 1977), ch. 3; Robert Fogelson, *Big City Police* (Cambridge: Harvard University Press, 1977), chs. 2, 3.

11. Gene E. Carte and Elaine H. Carte, *Police Reform in the United States: The Era of August Vollmer* (Berkeley: University of California Press, 1975).

12. Walker, *Critical History of Police Reform*, pp. 79–84.

13. Ibid., pp. 61–66.

14. Ibid., p. 63.

15. August Vollmer, "Predelinquency," in IACP *Proceedings*, 1919 (New York: Arno Press, 1971), pp. 77–80.

16. Chloe Owings, *Women Police* (New York: Hitchcock, 1925), pp. 99–100, 166–167.

17. Mary E. Hamilton, *The Policewoman* (New York: Stokes, 1924), pp. 4, 170.

18. Walker, *Critical History of Police Reform*, pp. 94–98.

19. Ibid., p. 96.

20. Ibid.

21. Howard B. Woolston, *Prostitution in the United States* (Montclair: Patterson Smith, 1969), ch. 4.

22. Walker, *Critical History of Police Reform*, p. 100.

23. Raymond B. Fosdick, *Chronicle of a Generation: An Autobiography* (New York: Harper, 1958), p. 147.

24. Walker, *Critical History of Police Reform*, pp. 102–103.

25. Sanford J. Ungar, *FBI* (Boston: Little, Brown, 1971), pp. 39–40; Max Lowenthal, *The Federal Bureau of Investigation* (New York: Harcourt Brace, 1950), pp. 3–10.

26. Bruce Smith, *The State Police* (New York: MacMillan, 1925), ch. 1.

27. McKelvey, *American Prisons*, pp. 237–238.

28. Thorsten Sellin, cited in Stephen Shafer, *Theories in Criminology* (New York: Random House, 1969), p. 128.

29. Joseph F. Fishman, *Crucibles of Crime: The Shocking Story of the American Jail* (New York: Cosmopolis, 1923), pp. 27–34, 69–70, 93.

30. Harvey H. Hougen, "Kate Barnard and the Kansas Penitentiary Scandal, 1908–1909," *Journal of the West*, 17 (January 1978): 9–18; Corrine Bacon, comp., *Prison Reform* (New York: AMS, 1974), pp. 49–107.

31. Bacon, *Prison Reform*, pp. 147–164.

32. Eugenia C. Lekkerkerker, *Reformatories for Women in the United States* (Groningen: Wolters, 1931), pp. 104–111.

33. Bacon, *Prison Reform*, pp. 109–145.

34. Ibid., p. 127.

35. McKelvey, *American Prisons*, pp. 249–253.

36. Bacon, *Prison Reform*, pp. 201–203.

37. Ibid., pp. 165–246.

38. McKelvey, *American Prisons*, pp. 331–332.

39. Ibid., ch. 11.

40. Fred R. Johnson, *Probation for Juveniles and Adults* (New York: Century, 1928), pp. 12-13.
41. United States, *Attorney General's Survey of Release Procedures*, II, *Probation* (Washington, 1939), pp. 1-10.
42. Robert H. Gault, "The Parole System—A Means of Protection," *Journal of Criminal Law and Criminology*, 5 (March 1915): 799-806.
43. Marvin Frankel, *Criminal Sentences: Law Without Order* (New York: Hill and Wang, 1972).
44. Philip E. Mackey, ed., *Voices Against Death: American Opposition to Capital Punishment, 1787-1975* (New York: Franklin, 1976), pp. xi-liii; Hugo Adam Bedau, ed., *The Death Penalty in America* (Garden City, N.Y.: Anchor, 1964), pp. 343-359.

CHAPTER 7

1. William Preston, *Aliens and Dissenters: Federal Suppression of the Radicals, 1903-1933* (Cambridge: Harvard University Press, 1963).
2. Charles Lam Markman, *The Noblest Cry: A History of the American Civil Liberties Union* (New York: St. Martin's, 1965), chs. 2, 3.
3. Arthur Waskow, *From Race Riot to Sit-In* (Garden City: Anchor, 1967).
4. Allan Spear, *Black Chicago* (Chicago: University of Chicago Press, 1967).
5. Anthony M. Platt, ed., *The Politics of Riot Commissions, 1917-1970* (New York: Collier, 1971).
6. Francis Russell, *A City in Terror—1919—The Boston Police Strike* (New York: Viking, 1975).
7. Sterling Spero, "The Rise and Fall and Revival of Police Unionism," in Spero, *Government as Employer* (Carbondale, Ill.: Southern Illinois University Press, 1972), pp. 252-272.
8. William A. Westley, *Violence and the Police: A Sociological Study of Law, Custom, and Morality* (Cambridge: MIT Press, 1970), ch. 4.
9. Mark Haller, "Civic Reformers and Police Leadership: Chicago, 1905-1935." in Harlan Hahn, ed., *Police in Urban Society* (Beverly Hills: Sage, 1971), pp. 39-56.
10. Cleveland Survey of Criminal Justice, *Criminal Justice in Cleveland* (Cleveland: The Cleveland Foundation, 1922).
11. Missouri Association for Criminal Justice, *Missouri Crime Survey* (1926; reprint ed., Montclair: Patterson Smith, 1968); Illinois Associated for Criminal Justice, *Illinois Crime Survey* (1929; reprint ed., Montclair: Patterson Smith, 1968).
12. Missouri Association for Criminal Justice, *Missouri Crime Survey, pp. 4-6.*
13. Ibid.
14. National Commission on Law Observance and Enforcement, *Lawlessness in Law Enforcement* (Washington, 1931), pp. 103, 121, 153.
15. National Commission on Law Observance and Enforcement, *Penal Institutions, Probation and Parole* (Washington, 1931), pp. 172-173.

16. Blake McKelvey, *American Prisons: A History of Good Intentions* (Montclair: Patterson Smith, 1977), pp. 300-306.
17. National Commission on Law Observance and Enforcement, *The Causes of Crime* (Washington, 1931).
18. Ibid., p. 58; McKelvey, *American Prisons*, pp. 268-274.
19. National Commission, *Causes of Crime*, I, p. 139.
20. Ibid., I, ch. 4.
21. Sheldon and Eleanor Glueck, *500 Criminal Careers* (New York: Knopf, 1939), p. vii.
22. Ibid., p. 506.
23. Rescue Pound in ibid., pp. 280-296.
24. Norman H. Clark, *Deliver Us From Evil: An Interpretation of American Prohibition* (New York: Norton, 1976), chs. 6, 8.
25. Humbert Nelli, *The Business of Crime* (New York: Oxford University Press, 1976), ch. 6.
26. Gerald Mast, *A Short History of the Movies* (Indianapolis: Pegasus, 1971), pp. 272-276.
27. President's Research Committee on Social Trends, *Recent Social Trends* (New York: McGraw-Hill, 1933), p. 1128.
28. Sanford Ungar, *FBI* (Boston: Little, Brown, 1971), ch. 16.
29. Arthur Millspaugh, *Crime Control by the National Government* (Washington: Brookings Institution, 1937), pp. 50-53.
30. Ungar, *FBI*, pp. 48-55.
31. Committee on Uniform Crime Records, *Uniform Crime Reporting* (New York: International Association of Chiefs of Police, 1929), pp. ix-xiii.
32. Samuel Walker, *A Critical History of Police Reform: The Emergence of Professionalism* (Lexington: Lexington, 1977), pp. 157-159.
33. Athan Theoharis, "The FBI's Stretching of Presidential Directives, 1936-1953," *Political Science Quarterly*, 91 (Winter 1976-1977): 649-672.
34. Walker, *Critical History of Police Reform*, pp. 159-166.
35. Morton Halperin, *The Lawless State* (New York: Penguin, 1976); Ungar, *FBI*, pp. 96-146.

CHAPTER 8

1. Alfred McClung Lee and Norman D. Humphrey, *Race Riot* (New York: Dryden, 1943).
2. Richard M. Dalfiume, "The 'Forgotten Years' of the Negro Revolution," *Journal of American History*, 55 (June 1968): 90-106.
3. Joseph E. Weckler and Theo Hall, *The Police and Minority Groups* (Chicago: International City Management Association, 1944); Joseph Lohman, *The Police and Minority Groups* (Chicago: Chicago Park District, 1947).
4. California, Department of Justice, *A Guide to Race Relations for Peace Officers* (Sacramento, 1946).
5. International City Management Association, *Municipal Police Administra-*

tion, 8th ed. (Washington, D.C.: ICMA, 1977); Louis A. Radelet, *The Police and the Community* (Beverly Hills: Glencoe, 1973).

6. International City Management Association, *The Municipal Yearbook* (Chicago: ICMA, 1943), pp. 440–442.

7. International Association of Chiefs of Police, Bulletin No. 4, "Police Unions" (September 1944).

8. Sterling D. Spero, "The Rise, Fall and Revival of Police Unionism," in Spero, *Government as Employer* (Carbondale: Southern Illinois University Press, 1972), pp. 288–294.

9. Eleanor Glueck, "Wartime Delinquency," *Journal of Criminal Law, Criminology and Police Science*, 33 (July-August 1942): 119–135.

10. Harrison Salisbury, *The Shook-Up Generation* (New York: Harper & Row, 1959).

11. Albert K. Cohen, *Delinquent Boys* (New York: Free Press, 1955); Walter B. Miller, "Lower Class Culture as a Generating Milieu of Gang Delinquency," *Journal of Social Issues*, 14, No. 3 (1958): 5–19.

12. Gresham Sykes and David Matza, "Techniques of Neutralization: A Theory of Delinquency," *American Journal of Sociology*, 22 (December 1957): 664–670; Edwin H. Sutherland and Donald R. Cressey, *Criminology*, 3rd ed. (Philadelphia: Lippincott, 1939).

13. Richard A. Cloward and Lloyd Ohlin, *Delinquency and Opportunity* (New York: Free Press, 1960).

14. William H. Moore, *The Kefauver Committee and the Politics of Crime* (Columbia: University of Missouri Press, 1974).

15. Sanford J. Ungar, *FBI* (Boston: Little, Brown, 1976), pp. 392–405.

16. Gene E. Carte and Elaine H. Carte, *Police Reform in the United States: The Era of August Vollmer* (Berkeley: University of California Press, 1975), pp. 26–30, 68–71.

17. William J. Bopp, *O. W. : O. W. Wilson and the Search for a Police Profession* (Port Washington, N.Y.: Kennikat, 1977), ch. 5.

18. O. W. Wilson, *Police Administration*, 2nd ed. (New York: McGraw-Hill, 1963); ICMA, *Municipal Police Administration*.

19. Paul Jacobs, *Prelude to Riot* (New York: Vintage, 1968), pp. 13–60.

20. William H. Parker, *Parker on Police* (Springfield: Thomas, 1957), pp. 113–123.

21. Blake McKelvey, *American Prisons: A History of Good Intentions* (Montclair: Patterson Smith, 1977), pp. 336–348.

22. American Correctional Association, *Manual of Standards for Correctional Institutions* (Washington: ACA, 1959), p. 15.

23. Robert Martinson, "California Research at the Crossroads," *Crime and Delinquency*, 22 (April 1976): 178–191.

24. McKelvey, *American Prisons*, pp. 322–327.

25. John Bartlow Martin, *Break Down the Walls* (New York: Ballantine, 1954).

26. Donald Clemmer, *The Prison Community* (New York: Holt, Rinehart and Winston, 1958); Gresham Sykes, *The Society of Captives* (Princeton: Princeton University Press, 1958); Richard A. Cloward, ed., *Theoretical Studies in the Social Organization of the Prison* (New York: Social Science Research Council, 1960).

27. James B. Jacobs, *Stateville* (Chicago: University of Chicago Press, 1977), ch. 2.

28. Leo Katcher, *Earl Warren: A Political Biography* (New York: McGraw-Hill, 1967).
29. Archibald Cox, *The Warren Court* (Cambridge: Harvard University Press, 1968), p. 6.
30. Donald M. McIntyre, ed., *Law Enforcement in the Metropolis* (Chicago: American Bar Foundation, 1967), pp. vii–xi.
31. Donald J. Newman, "Sociologists and the Administration of Criminal Justice," in Arthur B. Shostak, ed., *Sociology in Action* (Homewood: Dorsey, 1966), pp. 177–187.

CHAPTER 9

1. William O'Neill, *Coming Apart* (Chicago: Quadrangle, 1971).
2. *Report of the National Advisory Commission on Civil Disorders* (New York: Bantam, 1968).
3. Ibid., p. 1.
4. *Report of the National Advisory Commission on Civil Disorders;* President's Commission on Law Enforcement and Administration of Justice, *The Challenge of Crime in a Free Society* (New York: Avon, 1968), pp. 255–257.
5. Gary Marx, "Civil Disorder and the Agents of Social Control," *Journal of Social Issues,* 26, No. 1 (1970): 19–57.
6. William A. Westley, *Violence and the Police: A Sociological Study of Law, Custom, and Morality* (Cambridge: MIT Press, 1970); Jerome Skolnick, *Justice Without Trial* (New York: Wiley, 1967), ch. 11.
7. David Bayley and Harold Mendelsohn, *Minorities and the Police* (New York: Free Press, 1969), pp. 25, 144, 147; Albert Reiss, *The Police and the Public* (New Haven: Yale University Press, 1971), p. 147.
8. Ronald Kahn, "Urban Reform and Police Accountability in New York City, 1950-1974," in Robert Lineberry and Louis H. Massotti, eds., *Urban Problems and Public Policy* (Lexington: Lexington, 1975), pp. 107–127.
9. Introduction, in Richard Hofstadter and Michael Wallace, eds., *American Violence: A Documentary History* (New York: Vintage, 1971), pp. 3–43.
10. Frank Furstenburg, Jr., "Public Reaction to Crime in the Streets," *American Scholar,* 40 (Autumn 1971): 601–610.
11. Archibald Cox, *The Warren Court* (Cambridge: Harvard University Press, 1968), ch. 4.
12. Theodore L. Becker, ed., *The Impact of Supreme Court Decisions* (New York: Oxford University Press, 1973).
13. Gerald Caplan, "Reflections on the Nationalization of Crime, 1964-1968," *Law and the Social Order,* 3 (1973): 583–635.
14. President's Commission, *Challenge of Crime in a Free Society,* p. 412.
15. Samuel Walker, "Reexamining the President's Crime Commission: 'The Challenge of Crime in a Free Society' After Ten years," *Crime and Delinquency,* 24 (January 1978): 1–12.
16. Caplan, "Reflections," p. 608.
17. Richard Harris, *The Fear of Crime* (New York: Praeger, 1969).

18. Twentieth Century Fund Task Force, *Law Enforcement: The Federal Role* (New York: McGraw-Hill, 1976).

19. Lawrence W. Sherman, et al., *The Quality of Police Education* (San Francisco: Jossey-Bass, 1978).

20. Gerald Caplan, "Criminology, Criminal Justice, and the War on Crime," *Criminology*, 14 (May 1976): 3-16.

21. Nelson Blackstock, *COINTELPRO: The FBI's Secret War on Political Freedom* (New York: Vintage, 1976).

22. *Report of the National Advisory Commission on Civil Disorders*, p. 301.

23. President's Commission on Law Enforcement and Administration of Justice, Task Force Report, *Police* (Washington, 1967), pp. 134-135.

24. Hervey Juris and Peter Feuille, *Police Unionism* (Lexington: Lexington, 1973).

25. Lawrence W. Sherman et al., *Team Policing: Seven Case Studies* (Washington: The Police Foundation, 1973).

26. National League of Cities, *Changing Police Organizations: Four Readings* (Washington: National League of Cities, 1973); Hans Toch, *Agents of Change* (Cambridge, Mass.: Schenkman, 1975).

27. The Police Foundation, *Women in Policing* (Washington: The Police Foundation, 1972).

28. Sheldon Krantz, *Model Rules and Regulations on Prisoners' Rights and Responsibilities* (St. Paul: West, 1973).

29. Robert Sommer, *The End of Imprisonment* (New York: Oxford University Press, 1976), ch. 4.

30. Tom Wicker, *A Time to Die* (New York: Ballantine, 1976).

31. Frances L. Allen, *The Borderland of Criminal Justice* (Chicago: University of Chicago Press, 1964), p. 38; American Friends Service Committee, *Struggle for Justice* (New York: Hill and Wang, 1971), ch. 3.

32. James Q. Wilson, *Thinking About Crime* (New York: Basic Books, 1975); Robert Martinson, "What Works?—Questions and Answers About Prison Reform," *Public Interest*, No. 35 (Spring 1974): 22-54.

33. Andrew Von Hirsch, *Doing Justice* (New York: Hill and Wang, 1976), p. xvii.

34. Twentieth Century Fund Task Force, *Fair and Certain Punishment* (New York: McGraw-Hill, 1976); David Fogel, *"We Are the Living Proof . . .": The Justice Model for Corrections* (Cincinnati: Anderson, 1975).

35. Marvin Frankel, *Criminal Sentences: Law Without Order* (New York: Hill and Wang, 1973).

36. Michael Meltsner, *Cruel and Unusual: The Supreme Court and Capital Punishment* (New York: Random House, 1973).

INDEX